Revelation & Social Reality

Learning to Translate What Is Written into Reality

Paul Lample

Palabra Publications

ISBN 978-1-890101-70-1

Palabra Publications
7369 Westport Place
West Palm Beach, Florida 33413
U.S.A.
1-561-697-9823
1-561-697-9815 (fax)
books@palabrapublications.info
www.palabrapublications.com

Cover photograph: Ryan Lash

O thou who longest for spiritual attributes, goodly deeds, and truthful and beneficial words! The outcome of these things is an upraised heaven, an outspread earth, rising suns, gleaming moons, scintillating stars, crystal fountains, flowing rivers, subtle atmospheres, sublime palaces, lofty trees, heavenly fruits, rich harvests, warbling birds, crimson leaves, and perfumed blossoms. Thus I say: "Have mercy, have mercy O my Lord, the All-Merciful, upon my blameworthy attributes, my wicked deeds, my unseemly acts, and my deceitful and injurious words!" For the outcome of these is realized in the contingent realm as hell and hellfire, and the infernal and fetid trees, as utter malevolence, loathsome things, sicknesses, misery, pollution, and war and destruction.[1]

—BAHÁ'U'LLÁH

It is clear and evident, therefore, that the first bestowal of God is the Word, and its discoverer and recipient is the power of understanding. This Word is the foremost instructor in the school of existence and the revealer of Him Who is the Almighty. All that is seen is visible only through the light of its wisdom. All that is manifest is but a token of its knowledge. All names are but its name, and the beginning and end of all matters must needs depend upon it.[2]

—BAHÁ'U'LLÁH

Preface

WHEN A NEW REVELATION IS BROUGHT to humanity, it upsets the equilibrium of the old social order. It unites the hearts and minds of those who recognize it and thus forges a new community. From within that community must emerge a consciousness that can decipher and a capacity that can apply the new teachings in order to make the world a different place. How do we move from a world centered on materialism and self-gratification to one that is centered on the application of spiritual principle and service to humanity? How do we transcend dissension and destructive criticism to harvest the fruits of critical thought in a united search for truth? What is the nature of the process through which we understand the meaning of the Sacred Texts and put the teachings into practice so that we can contribute to the unfoldment of an ever-advancing civilization?

This book explores how, as Bahá'ís, we try to understand the Word of God as given to us in Bahá'u'lláh's Revelation and how we act on our understanding to achieve His purpose. It consists of six chapters, divided into two parts. Part I consists of four chapters. The first introduces the challenge of transforming social reality through the impetus of divine revelation. The second chapter looks at how Bahá'ís engage in a process of learning to comprehend and act on the teachings in light of the guidance provided by two authoritative centers: the Book, with its designated Interpreters, and the Universal House of Justice. Chapters 3 and 4 examine this approach to Bahá'í understanding and practice, first in relation to the expansion and consolidation of the Cause over the decade beginning with the Four Year Plan in 1996 and then in relation to the generation and application of knowledge aimed at engaging society and contributing to the advancement of civilization, with particular attention to experience in the field of social and economic development.

Part II addresses possible objections to the perspective offered in Part I that arise from contemporary—specifically postmodern—thought. Postmodern concerns are particularly sensitive to questions of knowledge and power, and the presentation in Part I on understanding and action may be dismissed by some as being naïve or coercive. Chapters 5 and 6 do not attempt to provide a comprehensive Bahá'í perspective on knowledge and power but are, instead, a response to a particular kind of criticism that might be directed toward the Faith.

Throughout the book, but especially in the last two chapters, there is an effort to correlate, to some extent, Bahá'í teachings with contemporary thought. This is because Bahá'ís do not understand and act in isolation from the world. Concepts and methods that shape the intellectual life of humanity impose themselves upon us, shape our perspectives on the Faith, and define the terms in which as a community we engage the wider society. At the same time, perspectives compatible with the Bahá'í teachings emerge in the work of contemporary thinkers who are attempting to resolve problems of knowledge and power arising from the challenge of postmodernism. Some of the authors whose works are touched upon are prominent in their fields, while others may be marginal. The purpose is not to give a thorough survey of contemporary concerns but to draw on specific insights that shed light on aspects of Bahá'í practice. Highlighting such insights, however, does not imply endorsement of the views of these thinkers; Bahá'u'lláh's teachings cannot be subsumed by or considered fully compatible with any particular school of thought.

Because the primary focus of this book is the exploration of how the Bahá'í world comes to understand Bahá'u'lláh's teachings and translate them into action, it does not explore in depth the nature of the spiritual forces released by divine revelation and how they drive the community forward. In all of the processes concerning understanding and practice discussed in this book, the inherent spiritual nature of the activity is assumed. God exercises His will for the achievement of His purpose. No one can limit or fully rationalize the mysteries of the movement of His hand. In the work of the Faith, objectives can be achieved only when spiritual disciplines such as prayer, meditation, fasting and bringing oneself to account each day are put into effect and the bounties of God are received. Nevertheless, these spiritual forces operate in a real, not a magical, way. It is attraction to God and the love of Bahá'u'lláh that gives us the strength to exercise control over our conduct, to properly apply divine principles and laws, to subdue the ego and work in harmony with others. And when we inevitably fail to meet the mark at a given stage of development, it is our love for Bahá'u'lláh that helps us forgive each other and forget the past, demonstrate tolerance and love, and pick ourselves up, heal our wounds and renew our collective efforts. Yet, as we labor in the path leading to divine civilization, we cannot hold an overly simplistic view that spiritual forces will do all the work: that we pray and our wishes are granted; that we teach and "something happens" to create social change; that an Assembly decides and, because it is a divine institution, the correct outcome is guaranteed.

Throughout the dispensation, Bahá'í thinkers will grapple with the profound concepts surrounding a "Bahá'í perspective" on Revelation, knowledge, and action to change the social order. A few words on such a fundamental subject at this stage can hardly be considered definitive. The tentative ideas put forward in this book are the limited and fallible views of one individual. They do not represent the position of any Bahá'í institution. They should not be unthinkingly adopted as truth nor pose a threat to the heartfelt strivings of any believer. They are merely a contribution to the discourse of those believers who are struggling to come to terms with problems of understanding and knowledge, of religious practice and social change, and who are attempting to correlate Bahá'í and contemporary worldviews. In this respect, I greatly appreciate and am indebted to many Bahá'ís whose ideas have catalyzed the thoughts offered here. This book is a reworking of a number of papers and presentations offered since 1995 in various settings and was largely completed by 2004. A version was included as background for a discussion about the generation of knowledge and the advancement of civilization in an Internet forum hosted by FUNDAEC in 2007; the thoughtful comments of participants led to a reorganization of the material and further revision of certain sections.

The past thirteen years marks a period of creative ferment in the Bahá'í world. In the work of expansion and consolidation and in the work of social and economic development a new culture of learning has been born and a growing number of believers are gaining first-hand experience about how to apply the teachings to the challenges facing their communities. In some places, admittedly, new ideas and approaches are applied in a rigid and dogmatic way; however regrettable, this is an unavoidable feature of learning and change. Where a healthy approach has been maintained, new capabilities have been cultivated and individuals, communities, and institutions are beginning to learn how to learn—that is, how to take the guidance found in the teachings and in the messages of the Universal House of Justice and translate it into effective action.

Bahá'í intellectual life is still in its earliest stages. Struggles, misunderstandings, and problems arise—but these are birth pangs, not a hardening of the arteries. This book offers an approach to Bahá'í thought and action that avoids the extremes of absolute certainty or skepticism while accommodating faith and critical thought. Within the limits of human capacity, we can learn, little by little, day by day, to grasp the intended meaning and aim of Bahá'u'lláh's Revelation and contribute to the transformation of social reality for the well-being and unity of all.

PART I

Revelation, Understanding and Action

1

Constructing the Kingdom

TO BE A BAHÁ'Í IS TO RECOGNIZE BAHÁ'U'LLÁH as a Manifestation of God. But recognition requires more than calling oneself by His name. As 'Abdu'l-Bahá explains: "The man who lives the life according to the Teachings of Bahá'u'lláh is already a Bahá'í," while "a man may call himself a Bahá'í for fifty years and if he does not live the life he is not a Bahá'í."[1] Thus, as Bahá'ís, we strive to understand Bahá'u'lláh's teachings and to translate them into action in the world, thereby helping to create the civilization He envisioned.

For each of us our work begins with the endeavor to put the teachings into practice in our daily lives. The more we understand the Revelation and the more we adhere to its spiritual discipline, the greater our capacity to lead a life that is pleasing to God. However, a Bahá'í life is not lived in isolation. It is forged in active engagement with the world, working with others and contributing to the advancement of society. The study and application of the teachings, therefore, implies the weaving of the personal and the social.

Collectively, we receive the gift of the Word of God, and through its application we are to raise the Kingdom of God on earth; that is, we are to gradually contribute to the building of a new social order that is shaped by the truths of the Revelation of Bahá'u'lláh. This statement appears simple; yet, implicit in it is a challenge to reflect deeply about how we are to understand and behave. Achieving Bahá'u'lláh's intended purpose for the human race requires new morals, new ways of generating knowledge, new ways of communicating, new ways of acting, and new institutions. How do we Bahá'ís, with our diverse, sometimes conflicting, understandings of Bahá'u'lláh's teachings, collaborate to bring about the society that reflects His will? How do we overcome the tension between individual freedom and social order? How do we balance the demands of science and religion? How do we ensure that it is the Revelation that shapes our reality, and not the assumptions and habits of contemporary culture? How do we firmly adhere to valid traditional practices while embracing the imperative of change? How do we overcome the tendency so common among human beings to take sides and fight? Questions like these abound. The answers will have to be found in learning, over time, to better understand the Text and translate it into efficacious action consistent with its divine intent.

Understanding and the Construction of Social Reality

When a child is born into the world, the mind is as yet undeveloped. It has predefined measures of potentiality—a capacity for language and memory, an ability to integrate the impressions of the senses, an association with the soul, and so on—but little of this is as yet manifest. From the start, the infant, through the use of the mind, forms subjective impressions of the world around it, a process that continues through childhood to adolescence and adult life. Subjective impressions—thoughts about reality—are tested in the world against objective reality, resulting in a continual change in comprehension and behavior.

This process may be illustrated by what is called "object permanence." If an object is removed from the field of vision of a young infant, attention immediately shifts. It is as if that object no longer exists. After some weeks, the infant has rearranged its "mental library" based on a new idea: that objects continue to exist even when they can no longer be seen. With this understanding it will then try to follow the path of an object, looking to the floor, for example, for a toy that a moment ago was in plain sight. Throughout life, interplay between subjective interpretation and objective reality continually shapes understanding and action. Human beings are designed to learn from encounters with reality. Science, one may say, has emerged in this way to be the knowledge system that allows for systematic exploration of and a degree of mastery over physical reality.

Bahá'ís understand that there is another dimension to these encounters. There is a spiritual reality beyond the physical one. Comprehension of this spiritual reality involves an encounter with Bahá'u'lláh's Revelation. Reading and study of the Sacred Text, moments of prayer and meditation, discussion with other Bahá'ís, interaction with the Bahá'í community, efforts to live according to the teachings, acts of service, and other similar experiences provide fresh insights into spiritual reality and fruitful patterns of spiritual and moral action. The mental structures and habits of behavior of a Bahá'í are continually tested and shaped in response to the verses of the Word of God.

We can gain insights into the nature of this encounter by reflecting on our own personal experience. When initially learning about the Faith, or at some point in our upbringing as Bahá'ís, we eagerly study a range of subjects. These are topics that are personally important, that attract us to the Faith, confirm our belief in Bahá'u'lláh and shape our basic understanding of the teachings. Too often, however, this period is short-lived—we become confirmed and the process of reorganization of our "mental library" comes to a halt. We "know" what we need to know. Our thirst is satisfied. Our questions are resolved. And, based on the new mental arrangement, the ways of a new lifestyle are set. We are, of course, aware of the immensity of the ocean of Bahá'u'lláh's Revelation, yet we are content with a familiar and comfortable beach at the ocean's shore. Except for the occasional new idea introduced in a talk, a course, or a book, the patterns of thought and action change little. We derive great joy from being Bahá'ís, but our Bahá'í life has fallen into a routine. And this continues until something awakens us: a new fact forcing itself on our consciousness, a rewarding service that reminds us of the challenges of creating a new world order, a mystical insight during prayer or study, an exposure to a new culture, a stark experience of the suffering in the world. Thus we come to realize, again and again, that there is more to the teachings than we previously thought.

In the same way that engagement with the Bahá'í teachings can settle into a familiar routine, involvement in the world can become regulated by fixed horizons of consciousness. Our lives can drift along the currents set by society while our purpose is to create a new one. The potential for progress in understanding and for establishing new arrangements in the social order is limitless, yet our patterns of behavior can impose severe restrictions on what we can accomplish. An ongoing process of study of the Revelation, a continued expansion of understanding, and a corresponding transformation of behavior are clearly needed.

'Abdu'l-Bahá states that "the reality of man is his thought."[2] What is the relationship of this reality with that true reality that may be called the "thought of God"? We find in the Bahá'í Writings that both the physical and the spiritual reality, expressed in nature and in Revelation, are expressions of the will of God. Bahá'u'lláh states:

> Say: Nature in its essence is the embodiment of My Name, the Maker, the Creator. Its manifestations are diversified by varying causes, and in this diversity there are signs for men of discernment. Nature is God's will and is its expression in and through the contingent world. It is a dispensation of Providence ordained by the Ordainer, the All-Wise. Were anyone to affirm that it is the will of God as manifested in the world of being, no one should question this assertion.[3]

And He also states:

> It behoveth thee to consecrate thyself to the will of God. Whatsoever hath been revealed in His Tablets is but a reflection of His will.[4]

God, through His will, is the creator of reality. We are inserted into this physical and spiritual reality and are shaped by it. Our personal reality, then, consists of those structures that have formed in our own mind to organize our experience of the outer world. But the process is a dynamic one. Human beings are not passive observers of reality and our personal reality, our thought, is not simply imposed upon us. In a very specific way we may consider ourselves—collectively—as co-creators of reality, for through the power of the human mind and our interactions, the world undergoes continued transformation. 'Abdu'l-Bahá explains:

> . . . He has chosen the reality of man and has honored it with intellect and wisdom, the two most luminous lights in either world. Through the agency of this great endowment, He has in every epoch cast on the mirror of creation new and wonderful configurations. If we look objectively upon the world of being, it will become apparent that from age to age, the temple of existence has continually been embellished with a fresh grace, and distinguished with an ever-varying splendor, deriving from wisdom and the power of thought. . . .
>
> Consider carefully: all these highly varied phenomena, these concepts, this knowledge, these technical procedures and philosophical systems, these sciences, arts, industries and inventions— all are emanations of the human mind.[5]

By the term "co-creator of reality" is not meant that humanity is a partner with God. It is an acknowledgment that the attributes of God the Creator, the Fashioner are reflected in human beings. Bahá'u'lláh has designed a new world order, we are the construction workers; He is the genetic engineer of the seed of a new civilization, we are the farmers who tend it.

We can understand this special role of humanity by noting that most of what we perceive to be reality—the world with which we interact every day—is not physical reality at all. It is social reality. Consider the difference between the ecological diversity of the planet—its mountains, oceans, deserts, forests—and the political boundaries separating nations. Consider the differences of phenotype among human beings and the cultural or racial discriminations to which they have given rise. Culture, language, beliefs, institutions, educational systems—all are real, all have an impact on our understanding, but are all products of the human mind. Social reality mediates our engagement with the world, physical and spiritual, and it is this reality that we have the capacity to create anew.

Some insights from the work of the philosopher John Searle in his book *The Construction of Social Reality* are useful in this context. Searle is interested in describing the nature of the shared reality that is woven from collective human agreement and which exists beyond the level of the physical, chemical, and biological structures:[6]

> In a sense, there are things that exist only because we believe them to exist. I am thinking of things like money, property, governments, and marriages. Yet many facts regarding these things are "objective" facts in the sense that they are not a matter of your or my preferences, evaluations, or moral attitudes. I am thinking of such facts as that I am a citizen of the United States, that the piece of paper in my pocket is a five dollar bill, that my younger sister got married on December 14, that I own a piece of property in Berkeley, and that the New York Giants won the 1991 Superbowl. These contrast with such facts as that Mount Everest has snow and ice near the summit or that hydrogen atoms have one electron, which are facts totally independent of any human opinions. Years ago I baptized some of the facts dependent on human agreement as "institutional facts," in contrast to noninstitutional, or "brute," facts. Institutional facts are so called because they require human institutions for their existence. In order that this piece of paper

should be a five dollar bill, for example, there has to be the human institution of money. Brute facts require no human institutions for their existence. Of course, in order to state a brute fact we require the institution of language, but the fact stated needs to be distinguished from the statement of it.[7]

Searle notes that the structure of social reality has a tremendous complexity. A simple visit to a restaurant has a reality that includes immediately visible aspects, including the social meaning of "money," "waiter," "restaurant," "chair," and invisible, underlying aspects such as the concept of employment, an economic system, an agricultural system, and government regulations. There is also a normative dimension of social reality, in that the waiter can be rude or polite, the food unsatisfying or delicious. The complex structure of social reality has layers and layers of meaning; even language itself, the vehicle for the communication of these ideas, is a social construct.

Although social reality is built from shared human understanding, it is not arbitrary or supported merely by an endless circularity of self-referential discourse. In Searle's perspective, all social reality eventually rests upon the brute facts of physical reality.[8] For example, the concept of money began when, in place of the general practice of a bartered exchange of goods or services, a concrete commodity such as gold consistently took the place of one of the traded elements. It then moved to ever more abstract representations, from coin, to paper currency, and now to pixels on a computer screen. Yet Searle observes that the entire structure of social reality is taken for granted by individuals, who are brought up in a culture that conveys social facts in the same way it presents rocks or trees.[9]

Human beings live in social reality as naturally as animals live in the physical world. It is, essentially, invisible. As Searle explains, although there may be rules that guide a particular institution, we do not live as if we are following the rules. Rather, we internalize a set of behaviors that result in our following the rules. An athlete plays a sport such as baseball without thinking of the rules, which would only be invoked by an umpire to adjudicate a rare and unusual circumstance. Most action is spontaneous and natural. If, Searle states, there were a remote island where individuals played the game as part of their culture without a written set of rules, children would absorb the proper behaviors through instruction and coaching. For example, after three strikes, the child is told to relinquish the bat to the next player. An anthropologist who comes to that island could, by observation, record a set of rules, but as far as the inhabitants of the island are concerned, behavior is regulated without the need for a list of rules. Thus participation in social reality by itself shapes what we know and do.

Social reality is an expression of human agreement.[10] Someone is the president of a country and has the powers of that office because a system of government is created and acknowledged by the inhabitants of that country. When the fundamental agreements which frame belief and behavior change, social reality will change, as in the case of the dramatic collapse of communism in countries across Europe and Asia in a matter of months around 1990, after having been a commanding presence that dominated the lives of hundreds of millions for over a half-century.

The manner of change in social reality is evident in the period following the institution of slavery in the United States. At the uppermost levels of this social reality existed the economic system in which one human being could legitimately own another as property. The slave was defined as less than human. The social structure was not reinforced by the casual beliefs of individuals alone; all of the systems of human knowing were brought to bear to justify the social order. Teachings of the Bible were invoked to affirm that the slave must obey the master and that beings of dark skin were inferior; to deny this was to deny the Word of God. Sciences were utilized to justify the superiority of the white race; if any were to object, they could be dismissed as uninformed individuals contending with empirical facts of the physical world. And how deep was the change in collective understanding after the bloody struggle in which the existing social order was overturned and slavery ended? Superficial at best. The constructed reality of slavery was legally abolished, only to be succeeded by Jim Crow laws and other forms of social oppression. The economic system of slavery was exchanged for de facto control through sharecropping. It would take another century for the civil rights movement to overthrow certain political and social inequalities. And even those substantial changes did not alter the underlying powerful substructures of social reality that supported white privilege. Institutionalized racism, for example, still leaves its mark on a significant number of African Americans through inferior educational options, oppressive social conditions, restricted opportunities to advance economically, and the demand to compromise a sense of self and culture—to "be white"—in order to advance.

Today insights from biology tell us that, physically, there can be no meaningful definition of race applied to human beings. Yet how many levels of social facts affecting collective consciousness and behavior must change in order to create a social reality that reflects the oneness of humanity? Even if we could list them all, how do we move from one social order to the next?

The significance of analyses like Searle's for our consideration of human understanding and action is that most of the reality with which human beings are concerned *is* social reality. We participate in social reality and we are shaped by it. In the earliest encounters, for example, parents engage a child through a language that, because of its structure and the way in which it carries cultural assumptions, shapes the mind and the manner in which the child approaches reality. Further, perhaps more than any other factor, the particular country of birth, with the attendant forces that mold the economic, educational, political and social environments and opportunities, plays a determinant role in defining who a person can and will be, despite any inherited potentiality. Yet, social reality is not static; it is mutable. It forms us, but because it owes its existence to common human understanding, we have the power to contribute to reshaping it.

The realization that human reality is, to a great extent, a mutable social reality opens the way for fresh insights into Bahá'u'lláh's teachings about social transformation. Revelation creates consensus around new truths so that we, the co-creators of reality, can begin to transform the existing social order. Indeed, our ultimate aim, the Kingdom of God, a new civilization born of the new world order of Bahá'u'lláh, is itself a new social reality. Human will freely aligns with the divine will, which serves as the basis for the agreements that shape society: "Thy will be done on earth as it is in heaven."[11] 'Abdu'l-Bahá states:

> Material civilization has reached an advanced plane, but now there is need of spiritual civilization. Material civilization alone will not satisfy; it cannot meet the conditions and requirements of the present age; its benefits are limited to the world of matter. There is no limitation to the spirit of man, for spirit in itself is progressive, and if the divine civilization be established, the spirit of man will advance. Every developed susceptibility will increase the effectiveness of man. Discoveries of the real will become more and more possible, and the influence of divine guidance will be

increasingly recognized. All this is conducive to the divine form of civilization. This is what is meant in the Bible by the descent of the New Jerusalem. The heavenly Jerusalem is none other than divine civilization, and it is now ready. It is to be and shall be organized, and the oneness of humankind will be a visible fact.[12]

The Obligation of Bahá'ís to Contribute to a New Social Reality

"It is incumbent upon every man of insight and understanding," Bahá'u'lláh states, "to strive to translate that which hath been written into reality and action."[13] To be a Bahá'í, to "live the life," means to comprehend the Word of God and act on it, individually and collectively. It is to make the reality of one's personal life and the pattern of society at large reflect the teachings. Bahá'u'lláh Himself affirms that "the object of every Revelation" is to "effect a transformation in the whole character of mankind, a transformation that shall manifest itself both outwardly and inwardly, that shall affect both its inner life and external conditions." Otherwise, He observes, "the futility of God's universal Manifestations would be apparent."[14]

"All men have been created to carry forward an ever-advancing civilization,"[15] Bahá'u'lláh declares. And He avers that "such means as lead to the elevation, the advancement, the education, the protection and the regeneration of the peoples of the earth have been clearly set forth by Us and are revealed in the Holy Books and Tablets."[16]

The malleability of the social order and the need to transform it in accordance with Bahá'u'lláh's teachings is a theme that appears again and again in the Bahá'í Writings. 'Abdu'l-Bahá notes that "Among the results of the manifestation of spiritual forces will be that the human world will adapt itself to a new social form, the justice of God will become manifest throughout human affairs, and human equality will be universally established."[17] "As we view the world around us," Shoghi Effendi states, "we are compelled to observe the manifold evidences of that universal fermentation which, in every continent of the globe and in every department of human life, be it religious, social, economic or political, is purging and reshaping humanity in anticipation of the Day when the wholeness of the human race will have been recognized and its unity established."[18] This fermentation, involving a twofold process

of integration and disintegration, is a result of the direct impact of
a new Revelation:

> The hollow and outworn institutions, the obsolescent doctrines
> and beliefs, the effete and discredited traditions which these
> [negative] forces represent, it should be observed, have, in certain
> instances, been undermined by virtue of their senility, the loss
> of their cohesive power, and their own inherent corruption. A
> few have been swept away by the onrushing forces which the
> Bahá'í Faith has, at the hour of its birth, so mysteriously released.
> Others, as a direct result of a vain and feeble resistance to its rise
> in the initial stages of its development, have died out and been
> utterly discredited. Still others, fearful of the pervasive influence
> of the institutions in which that same Spirit had, at a later stage,
> been embodied, had mobilized their forces and launched their
> attack, destined to sustain, in their turn, after a brief and illusory
> success, an ignominious defeat.[19]

Why, Shoghi Effendi asks, should the arrangements that
constitute the basis of the old social order not give way to new
assumptions and new structures that can better serve humanity?

> The call of Bahá'u'lláh is primarily directed against all forms of
> provincialism, all insularities and prejudices. If long-cherished
> ideals and time-honored institutions, if certain social assumptions
> and religious formulae have ceased to promote the welfare of the
> generality of mankind, if they no longer minister to the needs
> of a continually evolving humanity, let them be swept away and
> relegated to the limbo of obsolescent and forgotten doctrines.
> Why should these, in a world subject to the immutable law of
> change and decay, be exempt from the deterioration that must
> needs overtake every human institution? For legal standards,
> political and economic theories are solely designed to safeguard
> the interests of humanity as a whole, and not humanity to be
> crucified for the preservation of the integrity of any particular
> law or doctrine.[20]

Nothing short of implementation of Bahá'u'lláh's program for
humanity, he concludes, can restore the equilibrium of the social
order.

> Humanity . . . has, alas, strayed too far and suffered too great a
> decline to be redeemed through the unaided efforts of the best

among its recognized rulers and statesmen—however disinterested their motives, however concerted their action, however unsparing in their zeal and devotion to its cause. No scheme which the calculations of the highest statesmanship may yet devise; no doctrine which the most distinguished exponents of economic theory may hope to advance; no principle which the most ardent of moralists may strive to inculcate, can provide, in the last resort, adequate foundations upon which the future of a distracted world can be built.

No appeal for mutual tolerance which the worldly-wise might raise, however compelling and insistent, can calm its passions or help restore its vigor. Nor would any general scheme of mere organized international cooperation, in whatever sphere of human activity, however ingenious in conception, or extensive in scope, succeed in removing the root cause of the evil that has so rudely upset the equilibrium of present-day society. Not even, I venture to assert, would the very act of devising the machinery required for the political and economic unification of the world—a principle that has been increasingly advocated in recent times—provide in itself the antidote against the poison that is steadily undermining the vigor of organized peoples and nations. What else, might we not confidently affirm, but the unreserved acceptance of the Divine Program enunciated, with such simplicity and force as far back as sixty years ago, by Bahá'u'lláh, embodying in its essentials God's divinely appointed scheme for the unification of mankind in this age, coupled with an indomitable conviction in the unfailing efficacy of each and all of its provisions, is eventually capable of withstanding the forces of internal disintegration which, if unchecked, must needs continue to eat into the vitals of a despairing society. It is towards this goal—the goal of a new World Order, Divine in origin, all-embracing in scope, equitable in principle, challenging in its features—that a harassed humanity must strive.[21]

In this light, Shoghi Effendi continually calls for direct action on the part of the Bahá'í community to contribute to rebuilding an ailing world, as in this passage written on his behalf and directed to Bahá'í youth:

The present condition of the world—its economic instability, social dissensions, political dissatisfaction and international distrust—should awaken the youth from their slumber and make them inquire what the future is going to bring. . . . They should therefore open their eyes to the existing conditions, study the evil forces that are at play and then with a concerted effort arise and bring about the necessary reforms—reforms that shall contain within their scope the spiritual as well as social and political phases of human life.[22]

The ultimate aim is the achievement of humanity's highest aspirations:

> The Revelation of Bahá'u'lláh, whose supreme mission is none other but the achievement of this organic and spiritual unity of the whole body of nations, should, if we be faithful to its implications, be regarded as signalizing through its advent the coming of age of the entire human race. It should be viewed not merely as yet another spiritual revival in the ever-changing fortunes of mankind, not only as a further stage in a chain of progressive Revelations, nor even as the culmination of one of a series of recurrent prophetic cycles, but rather as marking the last and highest stage in the stupendous evolution of man's collective life on this planet. The emergence of a world community, the consciousness of world citizenship, the founding of a world civilization and culture . . . should, by their very nature, be regarded, as far as this planetary life is concerned, as the furthermost limits in the organization of human society, though man, as an individual, will, nay must indeed as a result of such a consummation, continue indefinitely to progress and develop.[23]

As individual believers strive to study and apply Bahá'u'lláh's teachings in daily life, in the family, in a profession or trade, and in the wider community, the Faith grows in its capacity to join with others to contribute to, and to influence, constructive change in society. However, Bahá'u'lláh has not come merely to establish yet another alternative religious congregation in pursuit of its own aims. Rather, He has renewed the wellspring of revelation in order to raise up a new "race of men," "incomparable in character," who will "cast the sleeve of holiness over all that hath been created from water and clay."[24] The existing social order suffers from self-interest, prejudice, oppression, aggression, extreme materialism, economic disparity, and a host of other ills. "Ever since the seeking of preference and distinction came into play, the world hath been laid waste," Bahá'u'lláh states. "It hath become desolate."[25] "Blessed is he who preferreth his brother before himself," is His prescription for the world's pernicious afflictions.[26] He has created a community of people who are to unite around a new set of beliefs about human nature and well-being and sacrifice their own interests to work for justice, the unification of the human race, and the common good. A letter written on behalf of Shoghi Effendi observes that "among the earliest impressions one gets from a study of the Bahá'í teachings is the overwhelming realization of the great responsibility that devolves upon every true Bahá'í. The world awaits expectantly the humble ministration of the Bahá'í worker and much depends upon the extent to which we Bahá'ís fulfill this sacred trust."[27]

The following are only a few examples of the many passages calling upon Bahá'ís to consecrate themselves to living a life of service that, in turn, will lead to the construction of a new social reality.

> Be generous in prosperity, and thankful in adversity. Be worthy of the trust of thy neighbor, and look upon him with a bright and friendly face. Be a treasure to the poor, an admonisher to the rich, an answerer to the cry of the needy, a preserver of the sanctity of thy pledge.[28]

> Strive to be shining examples unto all mankind, and true reminders of the virtues of God amidst men. . . . Let each morn be better than its eve and each morrow richer than its yesterday. Man's merit lieth in service and virtue and not in the pageantry of wealth and riches. Take heed that your words be purged from idle fancies and worldly desires and your deeds be cleansed from craftiness and suspicion. Dissipate not the wealth of your precious lives in the pursuit of evil and corrupt affection, nor let your endeavors be spent in promoting your personal interest.[29]

> Consort with all the peoples, kindreds and religions of the world with the utmost truthfulness, uprightness, faithfulness, kindliness, good-will and friendliness; that all the world of being may be filled with the holy ecstasy of the grace of Bahá, that ignorance, enmity, hate and rancor may vanish from the world and the darkness of estrangement amidst the peoples and kindreds of the world may give way to the Light of Unity. Should other peoples and nations be unfaithful to you show your fidelity unto them, should they be unjust toward you show justice towards them, should they keep aloof from you attract them to yourself, should they show their enmity be friendly towards them, should they poison your lives

sweeten their souls, should they inflict a wound upon you be a salve to their sores.[30]

Be ye loving fathers to the orphan, and a refuge to the helpless, and a treasury for the poor, and a cure for the ailing. Be ye the helpers of every victim of oppression, the patrons of the disadvantaged. Think ye at all times of rendering some service to every member of the human race. Pay ye no heed to aversion and rejection, to disdain, hostility, injustice: act ye in the opposite way. Be ye sincerely kind, not in appearance only. Let each one of God's loved ones centre his attention on this: to be the Lord's mercy to man; to be the Lord's grace. Let him do some good to every person whose path he crosseth, and be of some benefit to him. Let him improve the character of each and all, and reorient the minds of men.[31]

The Bahá'ís must be distinguished from others of humanity. But this distinction must not depend upon wealth—that they should become more affluent than other people. I do not desire for you financial distinction. It is not an ordinary distinction I desire; not scientific, commercial, industrial distinction. For you I desire spiritual distinction—that is, you must become eminent and distinguished in morals. In the love of God you must become distinguished from all else. You must become distinguished for loving humanity, for unity and accord, for love and justice. In brief, you must become distinguished in all the virtues of the human world—for faithfulness and sincerity, for justice and fidelity, for firmness and steadfastness, for philanthropic deeds and service to the human world, for love toward every human being, for unity and accord with all people, for removing prejudices and promoting international peace. Finally, you must become distinguished for heavenly illumination and for acquiring the bestowals of God.[32]

The Role of Revelation in Creating a New Social Reality

Given the limitations on human understanding and the nature of human interaction, we can try to imagine—assuming that it is at all possible—the task before the Manifestation of God. The Manifestation has an innate grasp of reality. As 'Abdu'l-Bahá explains, He knows reality just as a person knows his or her own body; it is a knowledge that does not depend upon the senses.[33] How, then, with a complete understanding of the student's capacity and the social milieu, does He fulfill the role of divine Educator? How does He bridge the wide gulf between His knowledge of reality and the human capacity to know in order to help humanity advance, individually and collectively?

Although the knowledge of the Manifestation is unlimited, the teachings conveyed to humanity are clearly circumscribed. Indeed, fundamental to the concept of progressive revelation is the understanding that all knowledge is not conveyed in a single dispensation.[34] Each Revelation offers a depiction of reality within a particular context and for an intended aim.[35] The Manifestation speaks to humanity "where we are"—confirming certain truths we know, severing us from our misconceptions and from notions that are no longer valid, and introducing us to new, often unsettling truths. Bahá'u'lláh states that at one time, the verses are "sent down in a style that conformeth to the standards of men" while at another they are conveyed in a form "transcending what the minds of men have yet conceived."[36] Revelation is adapted to the capacity of humanity to hear the message and to the particular social context of the age in which it appears. This adaptation is both a compromise with human limitations[37] and confirmation of human progress allowing for an increasing measure of Revelation in each dispensation.[38] As a message written on behalf of the Universal House of Justice explains:

> The Manifestation of God (and, to a lesser degree, 'Abdu'l-Bahá and Shoghi Effendi) has to convey tremendous concepts covering the whole field of human life and activity to people whose present knowledge and degree of understanding are far below His. He must use the limited medium of human language against the limited and often erroneous background of His audience's traditional knowledge and current understanding to raise them to a wholly new level of awareness and behavior. It is a human tendency, against which the Manifestation warns us, to measure His statements against the inaccurate standard of the acquired knowledge of mankind. We tend to take them and place them within one or other of the existing categories of human philosophy or science while, in reality, they transcend these and will, if properly understood, open new and vast horizons to our understanding.
>
> Some sayings of the Manifestation are clear and obvious. Among these are laws of behavior. Others are elucidations which

lead men from their present level of understanding to a new one. Others are pregnant allusions, the significance of which only becomes apparent as the knowledge and understanding of the reader grow. And all are integral parts of one great Revelation intended to raise mankind to a new level of its evolution.

It may well be that we shall find some statement is couched in terms familiar to the audience to which it was first addressed, but is strange now to us. For example, in answer to a question about Bahá'u'lláh's reference to the "fourth heaven" in the Kitáb-i-Íqán, the Guardian's secretary wrote on his behalf: ". . . As the Kitáb-i-Íqán was revealed for the guidance of that sect, this term was used in conformity with the concepts of its followers."

In studying such statements, however, we must have the humility to appreciate the limitations of our own knowledge and outlook, and strive always to understand the purpose of Bahá'u'lláh in making them, trying to look upon Him with His own eyes, as it were.[39]

It can be argued that social reality emerges through the vehicle of language and, at the same time, language is a component of social reality.[40] In essence, social reality is made up of words and meanings that human beings have agreed upon. It is noteworthy, then, that the Word is the instrument of the Manifestation. The Word of God rends the fabric of social order by contradicting centuries-old agreements, while providing new standards and principles that yield new understandings with which to create a new social order. The instances where the Manifestation violates the accepted rules of grammar[41] are, in this sense, highly symbolic; by contradicting the consensus on language, the Word demonstrates that a new truth and a new standard have appeared. The Word rewrites the facts of language as easily as the intersubjective facts that underlie morals, beliefs, and social relations. The essential infallibility of the Manifestation implies that His very Words are truth because His Words define the basis of social reality.[42]

Myriad passages reflect the power of the Word to reorder the human agreements that form social reality. With a new Revelation, "the heavens are cleft asunder"[43] and there appears "the new heaven and the new earth."[44] "Nothing can be effected in the world, not even conceivably, without unity and agreement," 'Abdu'l-Bahá explains, "and the perfect means for engendering fellowship and union is true religion."[45] "Naught but the celestial potency of the Word of

God, which ruleth and transcendeth the realities of all things, is capable of harmonizing the divergent thoughts, sentiments, ideas, and convictions of the children of men," He also states. "Verily, it is the penetrating power in all things, the mover of souls and the binder and regulator in the world of humanity."[46]

"The morals of humanity must undergo change," He adds. "New remedies and solutions for human problems must be adopted. Human intellects themselves must change and be subject to the universal reformation."[47] Thus the Manifestations "establish a new religion and make new creatures of men; They change the general morals, promote new customs and rules, renew the cycle and the Law."[48] In one of His talks, 'Abdu'l-Bahá explains that "In order that human souls, minds and spirits may attain advancement, tranquility and vision in broader horizons of unity and knowledge, Bahá'u'lláh proclaimed certain principles or teachings," and He concludes that through these teachings, Bahá'u'lláh has "laid the foundation of divine reality upon which material and spiritual civilization are to be founded throughout the centuries before us."[49]

The change in social reality effected by the Revelation occurs in a different way than the change designed by some segment of society itself. The effort to end slavery in the United States by legal means is a good illustration; slavery, overturned by force and a change in the law, was immediately replaced by cultural and economic forms of oppression. Rather than merely attempting to reform the social order from the outer layers of custom and common practice, the Word of God provides statements of truth that, once accepted by individuals, overturn old conceptions and form new agreements at the deepest layers of fundamental belief. Unity of thought on principle greatly reinforces the movement toward changes in behavior, social relations, and institutional arrangements. If, for example, we agree that humanity is one, then we must work out the far-reaching patterns of life and institutional arrangements that will manifest it.

A vivid explanation of how the words of the Manifestation shape social reality is found in a passage from Bahá'u'lláh.

> The question is that whereas in past Scriptures Isaac is said to have been the sacrifice; in the Qur'án this station is given to Ishmael. This is, undoubtedly, true. All, however, must fix their gaze upon the word which hath dawned from the Divine Horizon: it is incumbent upon every soul to ponder upon its sovereignty,

influence, might, and on its all-encompassing nature. There hath never been any doubt whatsoever that all these things are confirmed and corroborated only by the Word of God. It is the Word of God that transcendeth all things, creates the universe, educateth the people, guideth them who are sore athirst from separation unto the ocean of reunion, and penetrateth through the darkness of ignorance with the light of understanding. Consider: all those who believe in past Scriptures think of Isaac as the Sacrifice; likewise, the people of the Qur'án confirm this station for Ishmael. It is clear and evident to every possessor of insight and every religious person that no one was, outwardly sacrificed; all agree that an animal was sacrificed. So, ponder upon this: Why is it that a person who hath gone to the altar of sacrifice for the Beloved and yet hath come back [alive], is adorned with the raiment of 'Sacrifice of God' and accepted as such? There is no doubt that this is so because of the Word of God. Therefore, the criterion for the manifestation of all names and for confirmation and fulfillment of all stations is dependent upon the Word of God. Likewise, there is no doubt, that the Inaccessible, Unknowable [God] doth not talk as He is, and hath always been, sanctified from such conditions; rather, He speaketh through the tongue of His Manifestations. Thus the Torah issued from the tongue of Moses. The same is true of other Holy Scriptures: all were revealed by the tongues of Prophets and Messengers but, the real Speaker in all these Holy Books is the One true God. . . . It is now, therefore, established and confirmed that the station of 'Sacrifice of God' was, according to past Books, given to Isaac by Abraham and that very same station is, according to Divine Revelation, Ishmael's in the Qur'ánic Dispensation.[50]

Bahá'u'lláh's statement illustrates how the Word of God creates the human consensus that forms the basis for a new social reality. An archetype of sacrifice is created, even when no individual was actually sacrificed. This archetype is identified by the Manifestation as Isaac in the Jewish dispensation and as Ishmael in the Islamic dispensation not to catalogue objective historical fact, but to convey spiritual truth within a specific context to educate the community of believers.

This brief reflection on Revelation and its impact on social structure suggests a number of levels associated with comprehending reality from the perspective of religion. The first is reality itself, what we might consider the "mind of God." This is reality "as it is," without any point of view, far above human capacity to understand.

The second level is the revealed Word. Each Revelation is a representation of the knowledge of reality tailored by the Manifestation for a specific audience to enable them to achieve an intended purpose. According to Bahá'u'lláh, the Word of God is above any human standard or capacity to assess:

> Weigh not the Book of God with such standards and sciences as are current amongst you for the Book itself is the unerring balance established amongst men. In this most perfect balance whatsoever the peoples and kindreds of the earth possess must be weighed, while the measure of its weight should be tested according to its own standard, did ye but know it.[51]

In this perspective, the statements of Revelation may be considered as true, objective facts, comparable to the brute facts of nature that are investigated by science. Revelation gives rise to religion, a third level of the comprehension of reality, which is the body of understanding of the Book by the believers and the efforts to translate this knowledge into action, establishing new patterns of behavior and raising a new social order. If religion is in keeping with the spirit and meaning inherent in the Revelation, it is true religion; if not, as is the case during the period of the decline of a dispensation, religion becomes an empty form. It is in this light that 'Abdu'l-Bahá calls on every human being to weigh religious beliefs in the balance of science and reason since "every religion which is not in accordance with established science is superstition."[52]

LEVEL 1	**Reality** *(ontologically objective reality; reality "as it is"; the "mind of God")*
LEVEL 2	**Revelation** *(Revelation that can be known; the revealed Word of God; the Book & its authoritative interpretation)*
LEVEL 3	**Religious Belief and Practice** *(the body of religious knowledge, including methods & standards of inquiry and justification, and spiritual life and moral social practice)*

Thus, Revelation (level 2) provides us with a statement of truth about reality (level 1) that the religious community must struggle to comprehend and translate into practical action that contributes to an ever-advancing social order (level 3). The intended aim of Revelation is not achieved through a fixed procedure, a recipe, but rather, emerges from an organic process influenced by external conditions, like a tree that grows from a seed. This organic unfoldment involves a mixed collection of beliefs, including valid insight (knowledge), partial awareness, and error. Understanding changes over time—through study, dialogue and action—moving toward a fuller comprehension and expression of the meaning intended by the Author of the Revelation over time. Such effort will, however, never fully capture or exhaust all the implications of the Text.

Study, Consultation, Action and Reflection for Social Change

The Bahá'í community clearly has far to go before it reaches its lofty objectives. The social order too has to advance significantly to become the new reality that Bahá'u'lláh intends. How can such dramatic change in the individual and the society be achieved?

As noted above, the objective reality that human beings can know is the will of God as expressed in nature and in Revelation. Therefore science—the system of knowledge that guides understanding and action within the realm of nature—and religion—the system of knowledge that guides understanding and action in response to Revelation—are two means for exploring reality and for shaping social reality. These knowledge systems are complementary and overlapping in their domains. Science and religion can be likened to two "poles" that hold up the enormous tent that encompasses our view of reality. At this point in history, only one pole is raised, so vision in the tent is restricted—much of reality is obscured.

The way in which science allows us to acquire knowledge is complex and its analysis lies beyond the scope of this book; suffice it to say that scientific knowledge is fallibilistic and progressive.[53] The relationship between science and religion and the need for Bahá'ís to be involved in all fields of endeavor in order to contribute to the advancement of civilization is discussed in chapter 4.

The exploration of the will of God enshrined in Revelation calls for an ongoing study of Bahá'u'lláh's teachings. "Immerse yourselves in the ocean of My words, that ye may unravel its secrets, and discover all the pearls of wisdom that lie hid in its depths," Bahá'u'lláh exhorts.[54] And He explains that in "every age, the reading of the scriptures and holy books is for no other purpose except to enable the reader to apprehend their meaning and unravel their innermost mysteries" for "otherwise reading, without understanding, is of no abiding profit unto man."[55] Through such study of the Text, understanding and attitudes change, and the religious beliefs—of the individual and the community—evolve drawing closer and closer to the intended meanings proffered in the Revelation.

It is not sufficient, however, if one is to be a co-creator of reality, to study the Revelation but be a mere passive observer of reality. Exploration of the Writings requires more than reading and understanding. Study of the Word of God must be complemented by the effort to put the teachings into effect through a simultaneous process of action and reflection. "Live thou in accord with the teachings of Bahá'u'lláh," 'Abdu'l-Bahá urges. "Do not only read them. There is a vast difference between the soul who merely reads the words of Bahá'u'lláh and the one who tries to live them."[56] And a letter written on behalf of Shoghi Effendi explains:

> His brotherly advice to you, and to all loyal and ardent young believers like you, is that you should deepen your knowledge of the history and of the tenets of the Faith, not merely by means of careful and thorough study, but also through active, wholehearted and continued participation in all the activities, whether administrative or otherwise, of your community. The Bahá'í community life provides you with an indispensable laboratory, where you can translate into living and constructive action the principles which you imbibe from the Teachings. By becoming a real part of that living organism you can catch the real spirit which runs throughout the Bahá'í Teachings. To study the principles, and to try to live according to them, are, therefore, the two essential mediums through which you can ensure the development and progress of your inner spiritual life and of your outer existence as well.[57]

To expand the Faith, to build Bahá'í communities, to apply the teachings to address social concerns, to educate youth or children, to engage in scholarly study and research or to work in any other area for the progress of the Cause and the advancement of civilization provides opportunities for achieving a balance of study and action in which questions are raised, problems defined, and solutions attempted. The individual grows in personal knowledge and assists, through deeds, in transforming the self and the world. Personal study influences action, and action in turn influences the approach to study and understanding of the Text.

The shaping of social reality is not, however, an individual but a collective act. The Universal House of Justice explains that "a community is of course more than the sum of its membership; it is a comprehensive unit of civilization composed of individuals, families and institutions that are originators and encouragers of systems, agencies and organizations working together with a common purpose for the welfare of people both within and beyond its own borders; it is a composition of diverse, interacting participants that are achieving unity in an unremitting quest for spiritual and social progress."[58] Thus, there must be a way to coordinate the efforts of diverse believers, each engaged in their own process of study and action. Understanding reality and transforming social reality in accordance with the will of God requires unity of thought and action. This unity of thought and action is not a uniformity that delimits or homogenizes the full range of human diversity. It respects the inherent differences of thought and opinion.

To a Bahá'í, different views, rather than being a cause of dissension or conflict, should appear as a blessing of God to humanity. Individual interpretation is the fruit of our rational power and contributes to a better understanding of the teachings.[59] Diversity of opinions can be an asset to humanity if channeled productively in a search for truth. Where the teachings of the Book are not explicit, where personal interpretations differ, or where views about alternative applications of the teachings vary, consultation provides a means for the believers to unify their thoughts and actions. Consultation is not only used to reach a specific decision about a problem, but also in the search for clearer understanding. "In all things it is necessary to consult," Bahá'u'lláh states, for "it is and will always be a cause of awareness and of awakening and a source of good and well-being."[60] 'Abdu'l-Bahá explains that consultation has as its object the investigation of truth.[61] And a letter written on behalf of Shoghi Effendi states: "The principle of consultation, which constitutes one of the basic laws of the Administration, should be applied to all Bahá'í activities which affect the collective interests of the Faith, for it is through cooperation and continued exchange of thoughts and views that the Cause can best safeguard and foster its interests."[62]

Consultation is guided by a number of clearly expressed principles. Speech can exert a powerful and lasting influence for good or ill; therefore, it must be exercised with wisdom.[63] Individuals are free to put forward their views and should not be offended by the views of others.[64] Opinions are presented without passion or rancor; conflict and contention are strictly forbidden,[65] and, if they arise, discussion should cease until unity is restored.[66] The clash of differing opinions brings forth the spark of truth,[67] and all are to listen for the truth as differing opinions are shared, for reality lies where opinions coincide.[68] For this reason, to stubbornly cling to one's opinion is to ensure that the truth will remain hidden; it will inevitably lead to discord.[69] So too, "dissidence," the House of Justice explains, "is a moral and intellectual contradiction of the main objective animating the Bahá'í community, namely, the establishment of the unity of mankind."[70] Above all, the foundation of consultation is love and fellowship.[71]

When, a decision is reached through consultation by an institution, all are urged to support it. Even members of that body who voiced divergent views are to abide by the majority decision and not dispute or undermine it.[72] In this way, even if the decision is wrong, unity is preserved and the community can more quickly learn and correct its mistakes.[73]

When action must be taken but there is no clarity as to which course is best, it is sometimes desirable to allow for a diversity of actions from which lessons can be learned. Bahá'ís should be comfortable with mistakes, which are an inevitable part of the learning process. "A wide latitude for action must be allowed them, which means that a large margin for mistakes must also be allowed. . . . The Cause is not so fragile that a degree of mistakes cannot be tolerated."[74] Critical thought is welcome and necessary as a means of constructively analyzing action, so long as criticism does not undermine the authority of the institutions,[75] nor strongly stated personal opinions sow doubt into the soil of pure hearts.[76] Through reflection on action, prompted by further study and consultation, plans can be revised and more constructive strategies for action discovered.

Even after careful study, sound consultation, and united action and reflection on action, there will remain differences in the subjective viewpoints of individuals. Given the nature of reality as the "thought of God" how could it be otherwise, since human beings will ever fall short of this ultimate understanding of truth; even their grasp of Revelation is limited. Rather than taking sides and arguing about matters, the believers need to become comfortable with ambiguity, content to allow others their opinions. If these are erroneous, they will, presumably, yield to continued learning. To express a novel point of view is not, in itself, dissent, for how else can progress in human thought occur? No harm can come unless personal views are advanced in such a way as to promote division or dissension, to contend with authoritative interpretations, or to undermine the authority granted in the teachings to the institutions. Firmness in the Covenant allows for the maintenance of proper relationships of love and unity among the believers even when strong differences of opinion are held. The Guardian has explained that we should be free of any

> misunderstandings that might obscure our clear conception of the exact purpose and methods of this new world order, so challenging and complex, yet so consummate and wise. We are called upon by our beloved Master in His Will and Testament not only to adopt it unreservedly, but to unveil its merit to all the world. To attempt to estimate its full value, and grasp its exact significance after so short a time since its inception would be premature and presumptuous on our part. We must trust to time, and the guidance of God's Universal House of Justice, to obtain a clearer and fuller understanding of its provisions and implications.[77]

This statement introduces one additional factor critical for an initial grasp of how Bahá'ís enhance their understanding and act accordingly. Our work as Bahá'ís constitutes part of an organic process that unfolds over time. We have, at any given stage, a limited capacity and must act within specific circumstances; gradually capacity increases and contributes to change. The perspective of organic growth also suggests a balance between conditions that are fixed and those that are susceptible to human action, much like the kind of balance that must exist in the work of a farmer or a parent. The farmer must understand the requirements of the plant in order to ensure a bountiful harvest. The parent does not control the child, but by understanding his or her needs and nature, acts to raise a mature, self-sufficient adult. In the same way, our job as believers is to understand the purpose and organic nature of the Cause and serve it.

Shoghi Effendi repeatedly raised the concept of the Faith's organic growth, directly and indirectly. "Conscious of their high calling, confident in the society-building power which their Faith possesses, they press forward undeterred and undismayed, in their efforts to fashion and perfect the necessary instruments wherein the embryonic World Order of Bahá'u'lláh can mature and develop," he wrote.[78] A letter written on his behalf indicates: "The Bahá'í administration is only the first shaping of what in future will come to be the social life and laws of community living. . . . [W]e are learning something very difficult but very wonderful—how to live together as a community of Bahá'ís according to the glorious teachings."[79] The Guardian also describes the "Heroic, the Apostolic Age . . . in which the seed of the newborn Message had been incubating," the "Formative Period" the "Age in which the institutions, local, national and international, of the Faith of Bahá'u'lláh" are to "take shape, develop and become fully consolidated," and "the third, the last, the Golden Age" that is "destined to witness the emergence of a world-embracing Order enshrining the ultimate fruit of God's latest Revelation to mankind, a fruit whose maturity must signalize the establishment of a world civilization and the formal inauguration of the Kingdom."[80]

The nature of organic growth implies a certain tension between past and future. The Bahá'í community is, at any given moment, a mix of what we should be and what we have carried over from the old world order from which we must free ourselves. We are ever advancing toward a future that will be the fulfillment of an intended aim and purpose. At any given moment, we are trying to overcome the past and move into the future that is closer to what Bahá'u'lláh intends. We need to have the flexibility necessary for change, the patience to overcome setbacks and the creativity to make real the potentialities latent in the teachings. We need to understand that the Bahá'í community—ourselves included—encompasses a mixture of divergent views and temperaments that need to be harmonized to give added dimension and strength to our collective search for truth. At the same time, organic growth involves evolving, learning, and maturing individuals and institutions that will make mistakes and even occasionally cause harm, but that need guidance, support and space to learn. All of this adds another measure of complexity and ambiguity to the process of translating the teachings into action. Nevertheless, appreciation of organic development provides a perspective that enables each believer to work patiently and persistently for progress and productive change, with the humility necessary to acknowledge that one is bound to make mistakes and the conviction that in time the necessary transformation will appear and the Faith will not go astray.

2

Understanding and Practice in the Bahá'í Community

I N A LETTER OF NAW-RÚZ 1930, addressed to "the beloved of the Lord and the handmaids of the Merciful throughout the West," Shoghi Effendi assured the Bahá'ís of the ultimate achievement of their hopes for the well-being of humanity. "Feeble though our Faith may now appear in the eyes of men," he stated, "... this priceless gem of Divine Revelation, now still in its embryonic state, shall evolve within the shell of His law, and shall forge ahead, undivided and unimpaired, till it embraces the whole of mankind."[1] At the same time, he examined the distinctive features of the Faith designed to ensure its success, in particular "the fundamental difference existing between this world-embracing, divinely-appointed Order and the chief ecclesiastical organizations of the world."[2] "What," he asked, "can possibly be the agency that can safeguard these Bahá'í institutions, so strikingly resemblant, in some of their features, to those which have been reared by the Fathers of the Church and the Apostles of Muhammad, from witnessing the deterioration in character, the breach of unity, and the extinction of influence, which have befallen all organized religious hierarchies? Why should they not eventually suffer the self-same fate that has overtaken the institutions which the successors of Christ and Muhammad have reared?"[3]

In answer to this profound question, the Guardian points to the divinely conceived, organically developing world order of Bahá'u'lláh, which is born of and safeguarded by His inviolable Covenant. Bahá'u'lláh, he wrote,

has not only imbued mankind with a new and regenerating Spirit. He has not merely enunciated certain universal principles, or propounded a particular philosophy, however potent, sound and universal these may be. In addition to these He, as well as

29

'Abdu'l-Bahá after Him, has, unlike the Dispensations of the past, clearly and specifically laid down a set of Laws, established definite institutions, and provided for the essentials of a Divine Economy. These are destined to be a pattern for future society, a supreme instrument for the establishment of the Most Great Peace, and the one agency for the unification of the world, and the proclamation of the reign of righteousness and justice upon the earth. Not only have they revealed all the directions required for the practical realization of those ideals which the Prophets of God have visualized, and which from time immemorial have inflamed the imagination of seers and poets in every age. They have also, in unequivocal and emphatic language, appointed those twin institutions of the House of Justice and of the Guardianship as their chosen Successors, destined to apply the principles, promulgate the laws, protect the institutions, adapt loyally and intelligently the Faith to the requirements of progressive society, and consummate the incorruptible inheritance which the Founders of the Faith have bequeathed to the world.[4]

The Covenant, 'Abdu'l-Bahá explains, "is the fortified fortress of the Cause of God and the firm pillar of the religion of God." He adds:

Today no power can conserve the oneness of the Bahá'í world save the Covenant of God; otherwise differences like unto a most great tempest will encompass the Bahá'í world. It is evident that the axis of the oneness of the world of humanity is the power of the Covenant and nothing else. Had the Covenant not come to pass, had it not been revealed from the Supreme Pen and had not the Book of the Covenant, like unto the ray of the Sun of Reality, illuminated the world, the forces of the Cause of God would have been utterly scattered and certain souls who were the prisoners of their own passions and lusts would have taken into their hands an axe, cutting the root of this Blessed Tree. Every person would have pushed forward his own desire and every individual aired his own opinion![5]

Shoghi Effendi states that Bahá'u'lláh's Covenant is "unique in the spiritual annals of mankind."[6] We must be cautious, therefore, not to readily conflate the methods and concepts of Bahá'í practice with the standards current in other disciplines, whether religious or scientific, lest we merely pour new wine into old wineskins. Rather, any effort to grasp the workings of how we, as Bahá'ís, understand the teachings and translate them over time into action to contribute to transforming the social order through study, consultation, action and reflection, must include a consideration of how such understanding and practice is inseparably entwined with the two authoritative centers to which the believers must turn: "the Book with its Interpreter" and "the Universal House of Justice guided by God to decide on whatever is not explicitly revealed in the Book."[7]

Authoritative Interpretation and the Understanding of the Believers

The challenge of engagement with the Book is first, to determine to the extent possible Bahá'u'lláh's intended meaning and second, to reshape personal understandings by striving to move them into correspondence with His teachings. Some contemporary thinkers have proposed that there is no independent meaning of a text conveyed by an author; instead, each reader who comes to it invents or constructs a meaning based on personal perspective.[8] This, obviously, is not the Bahá'í view in relation to the Word of God. As previously mentioned, Bahá'u'lláh indicates that "Whatsoever hath been revealed in His Tablets is but a reflection of His Will."[9] And He states: ". . . We made plain Our meaning and set forth Our verses, that perchance men may reflect upon the signs and tokens of their Lord."[10] Once we are convinced that we are dealing with the Word of God, we can neither use conscience nor common sense to dissect and pass judgment upon it; rather, the Word weighs and reshapes conscience.[11] Bahá'u'lláh's meaning is to become our meaning. "Abandon the things current amongst you," Bahá'u'lláh exhorts, "and adopt that which the faithful Counselor biddeth you."[12] He also warns individuals against the "corruption of the text" which is "the interpretation of God's holy Book in accordance with their idle imaginings and vain desires."[13]

Because of our limited capacity we are, of course, always faced with the danger of diverging from the meaning and purpose of the Author. This is unavoidable, because human limitations make it impossible to fully grasp the intent of the Manifestation. Humility, obedience, and a learning attitude mitigate the danger. However, the problem is exacerbated when we raise a personal understanding of the Text to the level of immutable truth, or when we corrupt the Word's purity by adding foreign elements from personal beliefs.

Bahá'u'lláh has protected His Faith from the potential harm caused by personal interpretations through the establishment of His Covenant. He appointed an authorized Interpreter to expound the meaning of His Writings and established the Universal House to resolve disagreements, clarify questions that are obscure, and decide what must be done when the Text is not explicit.

Authoritative interpretation and individual interpretation are sometimes discussed in the same context, suggesting that they are different aspects of a single process. This is misleading; they are distinct in nature. Authoritative interpretation[14] conveys the true meaning of the Revelation, while individual interpretation is a function of human knowledge and subject to its limitations.

The authoritative interpretation of 'Abdu'l-Bahá and Shoghi Effendi is "a divinely-guided statement of what the Word of God means."[15] It is not merely the opinion or point of view of the Interpreter. It represents "the true intent inherent in the Sacred Texts."[16] The authorized Interpreter is an extension of the Book[17] and authoritative interpretation is as binding as the Word itself. Since all statements in the Revelation and the authorized interpretation are true, there can be no essential contradiction among them. Any apparent contradiction in meaning can be resolved by accepting the teachings as a balanced whole and seeking the perspective that reconciles apparent inconsistencies.[18]

Authoritative interpretation is a "statement of truth which cannot be varied."[19] 'Abdu'l-Bahá and Shoghi Effendi did not "change their minds" about their own interpretations. Any perceived revision in an authoritative interpretation, therefore, is attributable to some other reason. It is an elaboration or elucidation of a previous statement, an abrogation of a temporary measure, the illusion of contradiction resulting from a partial perspective, or the progressive unfoldment of the meaning of the Text.

Perhaps the most significant feature of authorized interpretation is that it allows for the progressive revelation of the meaning of the Text within the dispensation.[20] If Bahá'u'lláh had been obliged to convey the entire body of authoritative meaning of His Revelation within His lifetime, its scope would have been greatly reduced because of the limited capacity of His hearers. Clarifications could not be made for centuries until the coming of a new Manifestation. Having a channel of authoritative interpretation, however, allows the implications of the Creative Word to become evident gradually. Thus, Bahá'u'lláh veils certain meanings or leaves gaps[21] in the Book that are addressed by the authorized Interpreter in full accordance with His will and purpose. In this way, authoritative expression of the meaning of the Book was extended over a century, reaching beyond the first generation of believers, to guide the Faith's worldwide establishment.

Authoritative interpretation does not add to the Revelation; rather, it clarifies and makes apparent veiled or potential implications of the Revelation that are not explicit. The statements of authorized interpretation "throw further light upon and amplify various features"[22] of certain themes; "affirm . . . the true meaning, the real significance, the innermost secret of these verses;"[23] "reveal the purport and disclose the implications of the utterances of Bahá'u'lláh;"[24] and "state what the Book means."[25] In some cases this hidden intent is vast; in other cases, no implications lie beyond a passage in the Revealed Word, and thus, although additional meaning or insight may have been available to the Manifestation, it is not accessible to the authorized Interpreter. Consider, for example, Shoghi Effendi's extensive insights into the apparently simple phrase "new world order" from the Kitáb-i-Aqdas in contrast to his observation about the "knowledge" which when "taught from childhood" and "applied" would "largely, though not wholly, eliminate fear."

> We have no way of knowing what science Bahá'u'lláh meant when He said it would largely eliminate fear; as no further mention of it was ever made in the teachings, the Guardian cannot identify anything with this statement. To do so would depart from his function as interpreter of the teachings; he cannot reveal anything apart from the given teachings.[26]

Authorized interpretation does not, however, exhaust the meaning of the Sacred Text. Verses from the Revelation often contain multiple meanings and "the existence of authoritative interpretations in no way precludes the individual from engaging in his own study of the teachings and thereby arriving at his own interpretation or understanding."[27] Unlike the interpretations of the clergy in past dispensations, the authorized interpretations of 'Abdu'l-Bahá and Shoghi Effendi do not lead to a significant narrowing in the scope available for individual interpretation.

> They are not a progressive fossilization of the Revelation, they are for the most part expositions which throw a clear light upon

passages which may have been considered obscure, they point up the intimate interrelationship between the various teachings, they expand the implications of scriptural allusions, and they educate the Baháʼís in the tremendous significances of the Words of Baháʼuʼlláh. Rather than in any way supplanting the Words of the Manifestation, they lead us back to them time and again.[28]

At the heart of the Cause is the freedom of individuals to study the teachings, to strive for deeper understanding, and to express their views with candor. As the Universal House of Justice explains, "Individual interpretations based on a person's understanding of the teachings constitute the fruit of man's rational power and may well contribute to a more complete understanding of the Faith."[29] Yet, Shoghi Effendi makes it clear that we cannot fully comprehend the meaning of the Revelation, but can only struggle for "more adequate" insights.

> To strive to obtain a more adequate understanding of the significance of Baháʼuʼlláh's stupendous Revelation must, it is my unalterable conviction, remain the first obligation and the object of the constant endeavor of each one of its loyal adherents. An exact and thorough comprehension of so vast a system, so sublime a revelation, so sacred a trust, is for obvious reasons beyond the reach and ken of our finite minds. We can, however, and it is our bounden duty to seek to derive fresh inspiration and added sustenance as we labor for the propagation of His Faith through a clearer apprehension of the truths it enshrines and the principles on which it is based.[30]

Like all other forms of human comprehension, therefore, individual interpretation of the Sacred Text is a limited capacity, and the knowledge derived is mutable. A Baháʼí is bound by the explicit meaning of the Text and likewise must accept authorized interpretations and not deny or contend with them.[31] Nevertheless, freedom of conscience of the individual is upheld in the Faith, for "no one may be compelled to become a Baháʼí, or to remain a Baháʼí if he conscientiously wishes to leave the Faith."[32]

Understanding the meaning of the Revealed Word is not simply a rational exercise but depends upon spiritual conditions. "When a true seeker determines to take the step of search in the path leading unto the knowledge of the Ancient of Days, he must, before all else, cleanse and purify his heart, which is the seat of the revelation of the inner mysteries of God, from the obscuring dust of all acquired knowledge, and the allusions of the embodiments of satanic fancy," begins Bahá'u'lláh's admonition to those who long for spiritual knowledge and certitude.[33] And He states: "The understanding of His words and the comprehension of the utterances of the Birds of Heaven are in no wise dependent upon human learning. They depend solely upon purity of heart, chastity of soul, and freedom of spirit."[34]

At the time of enrollment, the institutions need to ensure that an individual holds a basic level of understanding to qualify for membership. A new believer, "need not know all the proofs, history, laws, and principles of the Faith,"[35] yet, should be nurtured "patiently, tactfully, and yet determinedly, into full maturity" in order to "aid him to proclaim his unqualified acceptance of whatever has been ordained by Bahá'u'lláh."[36]

Individual interpretations "continually change as one grows in comprehension of the teachings." "So, although individual insights can be enlightening and helpful, they can also be misleading."[37] Incomplete understandings are, therefore, part of the natural and healthy process of learning about the Faith over time, and no one can be said to be fully free of misperceptions. Learning continues throughout one's life as a Bahá'í and erroneous notions are naturally discarded as comprehension grows and evolves.

Individual interpretation rarely remains wholly personal. One studies the teachings and derives insights, but inevitably, these views are shared with others in a dialogical process that guides the collective quest for intersubjective agreement upon which action rests. This consultative process is to be conducted in a manner that preserves unity while striving to achieve Bahá'u'lláh's purpose for humanity. In such a dialogue, individual opinions "lack authority," and a person is to "offer his own idea as a contribution to knowledge, making it clear that his views are merely his own."[38] While "every believer is fully entitled to voice" personal views, these ideas "can never be upheld as a standard for others to accept, nor should disputes ever be permitted to arise over differences in such opinions."[39] Such views are to be expressed without pressing them on fellow believers.[40] And it is then incumbent upon the listener not to suppress the views of others, which would be a restriction of individual freedom, but to respond in a tolerant, dispassionate and courteous way. The Universal House of Justice encourages the friends to "learn to listen to the views of others without being over-awed or allowing their faith to be shaken."[41]

In general, "the institutions do not busy themselves with what individual believers think."[42] A problem arises, however, if thought becomes "expressed in actions which are inimical to the basic principles and vital interests of the Faith."[43] When someone stubbornly persists in such deleterious actions, it may be necessary for the institutions to respond. Language is the brick and mortar for construction of civilization; certain standards for its use are necessary, therefore, to ensure that the edifice does not collapse. These standards are an explicit part of Bahá'u'lláh's teachings. The Covenant protects the dialogical process and prevents harm from being caused by individuals who insist on imposing their personal opinions while contradicting explicit, authoritative statements in the Book. A letter written on behalf of the Universal House of Justice explains:

> Beyond contention, moreover, is the condition in which a person is so immovably attached to one erroneous viewpoint that his insistence upon it amounts to an effort to change the essential character of the Faith. This kind of behavior, if permitted to continue unchecked, could produce disruption in the Bahá'í community, giving birth to countless sects as it has done in previous Dispensations. The Covenant of Bahá'u'lláh prevents this. The Faith defines elements of a code of conduct, and it is ultimately the responsibility of the Universal House of Justice, in watching over the security of the Cause and upholding the integrity of its Teachings, to require the friends to adhere to standards thus defined.[44]

Hermeneutical Principles in the Bahá'í Teachings

It is evident that Bahá'ís are encouraged to use their rational powers to explore and better understand the Revelation while, at the same time, because of the limitations of these powers, they are urged to guard the integrity and purity of the teachings by not imposing personal views on others. To assist in the challenging process of acquiring understanding, many hermeneutical principles—that is, principles pertaining to interpreting or discerning the meaning of the Sacred Text—are presented in the Bahá'í Writings to guide the seeker of truth.[45] Some of these principles have already been mentioned or will be discussed in more detail in other parts of the book; they are summarized here for convenience.

The Book has an intended meaning. Bahá'u'lláh urges us to "Meditate upon that which hath streamed forth from the heaven of the Will of thy Lord" so that we may "grasp the intended meaning which is enshrined in the sacred depths of the Holy Writings."[46] Shoghi Effendi indicates that the believers should "read the writings . . . so thoroughly" as to be able to present the Faith "in its pure form" rather than to hold "some superficial idea of what the Cause stands for" and to "present it together with all sorts of ideas that are their own."[47] We cannot, therefore, simply read into the Text any meaning we wish or use quotations out of context to justify personal opinions. Our views may be right or they may be wrong, or they may reflect a partial understanding, depending on the measure of their correspondence to Bahá'u'lláh's intention. Of course, the challenge of unraveling the intended meaning is not always easy. Comprehension occurs by degree, is influenced by culture and context, and there is always some ambiguity. But this is a fundamentally different perspective from one that suggests that we can add to the Sacred Text or derive from it support for any notion that we hold.

Judgments about meaning should be made from the perspective of the Revelation. Bahá'u'lláh states that "If it be your wish, O people, to know God and to discover the greatness of His might, look, then, upon Me with Mine own eyes, and not with the eyes of any one besides Me. Ye will, otherwise, be never capable of recognizing Me, though ye ponder My Cause as long as My Kingdom endureth. . . ."[48] As previously mentioned, He indicates that we should not weigh the Book of God with human standards and sciences, since "the Book itself is the unerring balance established amongst men;" instead, "the measure of its weight should be tested according to its own standard," while "in this most perfect balance whatsoever the peoples and kindreds of the earth possess must be weighed."[49] Therefore, the more we develop a body of understanding that reflects Bahá'u'lláh's intended meaning and the more we can bring that understanding to bear when making personal interpretations of specific passages, the more likely our insights are to be valid.

There is no contradiction between authoritative passages. It may appear that certain statements in the Book contradict one another. But a difference in context or emphasis or the exploration of a single reality from different perspectives should not be misconstrued as contradiction. Letters written on behalf of Shoghi Effendi indicate that we should "always conceive of the teachings as one great whole with many facets."[50] "We must take the teachings as a great, balanced whole, not seek out and oppose to each other two strong statements that have different meanings; somewhere in between, there are links uniting the two."[51] This suggests that we should generally seek the meaning of the verses in such a way as to resolve apparent inconsistencies rather than to magnify them. It also implies that if a personal interpretation of a passage contradicts the Text or its authoritative interpretation, that individual interpretation is erroneous. As the Universal House of Justice explains, "In attempting to understand the Writings, therefore, one must first realize that there is and can be no real contradiction in them, and in the light of this we can confidently seek the unity of meaning which they contain."[52] This unity of meaning also pertains to the relationship between the Word of God and its authoritative interpretation. For, "It is the words of 'Abdu'l-Bahá and the Guardian which elucidate this vast revelation and make clear the manner in which different statements relate to one another and what is implied by the Revealed Word."[53]

— *Meaning is sometimes explicit and sometimes veiled.* Bahá'u'lláh explains that the Manifestation of God speaks a "twofold language." "One language, the outward language, is devoid of allusions, is unconcealed and unveiled; that it may be a guiding lamp and a beaconing light whereby wayfarers may attain the heights of holiness, and seekers may advance into the realm of eternal reunion. . . . The other language is veiled and concealed, so that whatever lieth hidden in the heart of the malevolent may be made manifest and their innermost being be disclosed."[54] Thus, at times we are dealing with explicit meanings and an esoteric interpretation would be inappropriate and incorrect. An example is Bahá'u'lláh's statement that the next Manifestation would not appear before one thousand years.[55] In this regard, it is also important to note that the explicit meaning is not the same as the literal meaning, as in the case of using a metaphor; Bahá'u'lláh warns in the Íqán about the error of literalism. At other times a verse has deeper meanings, and trying to hold to the outward understanding can lead to rigidity or confusion. A clear example is the meaning of the "return" of the Prophets. As Bahá'u'lláh summarizes this principle:

> Blessed those who have distinguished both the outward and the inward meaning: these, verily, are servants who have believed in the All-Embracing Word.
>
> Know, then, that whosoever adhereth to the outward meaning while oblivious of the inward meaning is of the ignorant; that whosoever adhereth to the inward meaning while oblivious of the outward meaning is of the heedless; and that whosoever understandeth the inward meaning in the light of the outward meaning is of the truly learned.[56]

The meaning of the Book cannot be exhausted. "Know assuredly," Bahá'u'lláh states, "that just as thou firmly believest that the Word of God, exalted be His glory, endureth for ever, thou must, likewise, believe with undoubting faith that its meaning can never be exhausted."[57] This opens the Text to a range of individual interpretations, including instances in which an authoritative interpretation has been made. For example, after presenting an interpretation of the meaning of the story of Adam and Eve, 'Abdu'l-Bahá explains: "This is one of the meanings of the biblical story of Adam. Reflect until you discover the others."[58] However, this concept does not imply relativism; personal interpretations are not all equally valid and some are erroneous. Rather, meaning continually emerges through study and application throughout one's lifetime and over the entire course of the dispensation in a changing historical context. The freedom of interpretation left to the individual cannot be used to justify and impose personal opinions on others or to contend with the center of authority in the Faith. In addition to His statement that the meaning of the Word is inexhaustible, Bahá'u'lláh warns:

> They who are its appointed interpreters, they whose hearts are the repositories of its secrets, are, however, the only ones who can comprehend its manifold wisdom. Whoso, while reading the Sacred Scriptures, is tempted to choose therefrom whatever may suit him with which to challenge the authority of the Representative of God among men, is, indeed, as one dead, though to outward seeming he may walk and converse with his neighbors, and share with them their food and their drink.[59]

Truth unfolds progressively within the dispensation. The meaning of the Revelation is intentionally disclosed in a gradual manner over time. "Consider the sun," Bahá'u'lláh explains. "How gradually its warmth and potency increase as it approacheth its zenith. . . . [I]f the Sun of Truth were suddenly to reveal, at the earliest stages of its manifestation, the full measure of the potencies which the providence of the Almighty hath bestowed upon it, the earth of human understanding would waste away and be consumed."[60] Again He states:

> How manifold are the truths which must remain unuttered until the appointed time is come! Even as it hath been said: "Not everything that a man knoweth can be disclosed, nor can everything that he can disclose be regarded as timely, nor can every timely utterance be considered as suited to the capacity of those who hear it."
>
> Of these truths some can be disclosed only to the extent of the capacity of the repositories of the light of Our knowledge, and the recipients of Our hidden grace.[61]

A definitive illustration of this principle is Bahá'u'lláh's injunction in the Aqdas not to marry more than two wives combined with an appeal to be content with a single partner.[62] Some early statements of 'Abdu'l-Bahá granted certain believers permission to have two wives; but He encouraged marriage to only a single wife to such an extent that some went so far as to accuse Him of abrogating Bahá'u'lláh's law.[63] Eventually, 'Abdu'l-Bahá unambiguously interpreted the passage in the Aqdas to mean that Bahá'u'lláh prescribed monogamy.[64] This was reaffirmed by Shoghi Effendi[65] who further averred that polygamy has been "rigidly suppressed by the Pen of Bahá'u'lláh."[66] The purpose of clarifying and applying the law in a gradual manner was to assist the believers to make the transition from Islamic law and cultural practice to monogamy.

In attempting to understand the Bahá'í teachings, especially in cases where passages appear incomplete or contradictory or where it appears that the Central Figures change their views, it is necessary to seek the meaning of statements in the Writings as an integrated and progressively unfolding whole. An unbiased reader who earnestly seeks a proper understanding of a Text can hardly ignore the Author's explicit counsel that meaning is sometimes intentionally veiled and gradually revealed over time in order to guard against fanatical opposition, to preserve unity, and to foster acceptance of challenging or complex truths.

Understanding is influenced by the stages of the Faith's organic development. The Bahá'í community evolves organically over time and certain passages may pertain to specific stages in this developmental process. Furthermore, each stage of the community's organic development influences the manner in which it approaches the Book and the questions it asks. The Universal House of Justice explains that a

> fundamental principle which enables us to understand the pattern towards which Bahá'u'lláh wishes human society to evolve is the principle of organic growth which requires that detailed developments, and the understanding of detailed developments, become available only with the passage of time and with the help of the guidance given by that Central Authority in the Cause to whom all must turn. In this regard one can use the simile of a tree. If a farmer plants a tree, he cannot state at that moment what its exact height will be, the number of its branches or the exact time of its blossoming. He can, however, give a general impression of its size and pattern of growth and can state with confidence which fruit it will bear. The same is true of the evolution of the World Order of Bahá'u'lláh.[67]

Allowing the Faith to unfold without imposing personal views requires "honesty and humility." In past dispensations errors arose because the believers "were overanxious to encompass the Divine Message within the framework of their limited understanding, to define doctrines where definition was beyond their power, to explain mysteries which only the wisdom and experience of a later age would make comprehensible, to argue that something was true because it appeared desirable and necessary." Bahá'ís are therefore discouraged from trying to force the Faith "into ways that we wish it to go regardless of the clear texts and our own limitations."[68]

Personal interpretations of the meaning of the Text should be weighed in the light of science and reason. Scientific knowledge and reason make an essential contribution to a sound understanding of the Bahá'í Writings. They serve as a means to weigh personal interpretations and religious beliefs,[69] as 'Abdu'l-Bahá illustrates with the example of the interpretation of "stars" falling upon the "earth." A literal meaning is impossible since "modern mathematicians have established and proved scientifically . . . each of the fixed stars to be a thousand times larger than the sun," and therefore, "If these stars were to fall upon the surface of the earth, how could they find their place there?"[70] In a talk, He further states: "If religious beliefs and opinions are found contrary to the standards of science, they are mere superstitions and imaginations. . . . If a question be found contrary to reason, faith and belief in it are impossible, and there is no outcome but wavering and vacillation."[71] Yet, while scientific understanding and reason assist in unlocking the meaning of the Sacred Text, care also must be exerted to avoid going to the extreme of distorting religious truth "almost forcibly at times, to make it conform to understandings and perceptions current in the scientific world."[72]

While Bahá'ís are called upon to weigh religious beliefs in the light of science, they should not commit the error of weighing scientific knowledge in the light of personal religious beliefs. 'Abdu'l-Bahá explains that it is possible for a Revelation to include statements about the physical world that are scientifically accurate and which transcend contemporary scientific understanding.[73] This is unsurprising given the capacity of the Manifestation of God to know reality. And, in general, "the principle of faith is to accept anything the Manifestation of God says, once you have accepted Him as being the Manifestation."[74] However, it is vital to appreciate that in certain cases, rather than intending to convey a scientific truth, a passage in the Text uses scientific concepts according to the understanding of the people as a way of illustrating a spiritual theme.[75] Further, Bahá'u'lláh sometimes uses terminology that pertains to a particular school of thought that is not in accord with contemporary scientific views, as in the Tablet to a Physician.[76] Thus, a personal interpretation of the Text is not a sufficient justification for drawing scientific conclusions or for rejecting or contending with scientific theories or methods. While study of the Bahá'í teachings may provide certain insights or a philosophical or moral framework for scientific investigation and technological applications, scripture is not scientific evidence. Science has its own body of knowledge, methods of inquiry, and system of justification and advances according to its own criteria.

History and context have implications for understanding the meaning of the Text. Understanding the historical or specific context of a portion of the Book helps to shed light on its meaning. For example, Shoghi Effendi "emphasized the study of Islam and Qur'án so that the friends would have a background against which to study the Bahá'í Writings."[77] To be aware of where, why, and to whom a Tablet was revealed, to have insight into the intellectual and cultural currents that form the background for certain statements made by the Central Figures, or to place passages in the context of Bahá'í or world history all surely contribute to a greater depth of understanding of the teachings. This does not imply, of course, that meaning of scripture is circumscribed by its particular context and that no general insights or principles can be drawn from it and applied universally. Bahá'u'lláh, as a Manifestation of God, intended His Writings for an audience that would span centuries, not just for the immediate recipient. Hermeneutical practice in the Bahá'í community must be concerned, therefore, with both the particular and universal implications of the Writings of Bahá'u'lláh and the statements of 'Abdu'l-Bahá and Shoghi Effendi. It is necessary to distinguish, for example, between instances when the Guardian was referring to a temporary measure and when he was establishing a general principle or immutable feature of the administrative order.

Determining the implications of context and history to enrich understanding of the meaning of the Text must be carried out in association with other hermeneutical principles in order to protect against two extremes that lead to a distortion of the teachings. One extreme is to insist that statements in the Writings of Bahá'u'lláh or 'Abdu'l-Bahá can only be understood in light of contemporary understanding derived from academic disciplines, such as history or philosophy, and their methods, such as various forms of historical or literary criticism. While acknowledging that methodologies from academic disciplines have value in providing insights into the meaning of texts, the House of Justice points out that there is a possibility of problems arising from the imposition "on the Bahá'í community's own study of the Revelation" of "methodologies and attitudes antithetical to its very nature."[78] The Faith simultaneously "enjoins upon its followers the primary duty of an unfettered search after truth"[79] and asserts that "there can be no question of any requirement to distort history in the so-called 'interests' of the Faith," while recognizing that historical researchers should not fall into the error of positivism, since "historical evidence . . . is always fragmentary, and may also be accidentally erroneous or even intentionally fabricated."[80] Conclusions drawn on the basis of the interpretation of historical evidence are not definitive, and must be assessed in the light of other important factors when attempting to understand the meaning of the Text.

The other extreme is to assume that, beyond whatever larger meaning is intended, statements in the Writings always present accurate facts of history and context. The situation, however, is similar to that which arises with respect to the question of scientific accuracy: sometimes a statement contains a fact, and at other times, a statement conforms to a particular understanding of the audience being addressed. For example, in one instance a letter written on behalf of Shoghi Effendi encourages acceptance of the truth of a historical statement made by 'Abdu'l-Bahá, and in another encourages gathering the known facts.[81] As another example, a Bahá'í asked 'Abdu'l-Bahá a question about Emmanuel Swedenborg and the Guardian later explained that, despite the context of the question and the believer's personal views about the reply, 'Abdu'l-Bahá's answer referred not to Swedenborg but to the Báb, the true "Emmanuel."[82] Thus, while 'Abdu'l-Bahá did possess "superhuman knowledge,"[83] a particular statement of His cannot simply be accepted as a literal truth or objective fact without further consideration. The Guardian warned that "We must not take many of 'Abdu'l-Bahá's statements as dogmatic finalities, for there are other points which when added to them round out the picture."[84]

These are only a summary of some hermeneutical principles found in the teachings; there may well be others, and perhaps, they may be described differently. In a given situation, in an effort to understand the meaning of a passage, all relevant factors must be considered and weighed in the light of the various hermeneutical principles. Often, different conclusions can be held by different individuals, and clarification of any ambiguities or contradictions must await further evidence or discussion. This is especially a challenge in applying the last two principles, when questions of scientific and historical knowledge must be reconciled with the interpretation of the Text. In response to a question as to whether statements (propositions) found in the Writings need to be taken as fact unless there is an explicit reference to a particular statement being conditioned on other information, the Universal House of Justice conveyed the following perspective:

> . . . there are some cases where passages from the Writings affirm specific facts and other cases where passages conform to the beliefs of particular peoples. It is, therefore, necessary for

the reader to determine the meaning of statements that are not explicit by applying sound hermeneutical principles found in the Teachings. While there is often room for a range of personal interpretations on such matters, and a degree of ambiguity will invariably exist in some cases, usually a common understanding is formed, which will change over time should additional evidence come to light. Differences of personal opinion about the meaning of the Text should not be allowed to create discord or wrangling among the friends.[85]

The application of the hermeneutical principles presented here and any others that may be drawn from the Bahá'í Writings cannot be reduced to a specific formula or set of rules, and caution must be exercised to avoid the extremes of absolute certainty or relativism. We can never be certain that our personal interpretations are identical with Bahá'u'lláh's intended meaning. Therefore, absolutism should be avoided whether imposed as a literal religious orthodoxy or as scientific or historical certainty. That such certainty eludes us, however, does not mean that we should raise the banner of relativism, asserting that all opinions are equally valid, that personal conscience becomes the measure of the Faith, that statements from the center of the Cause can be set aside on the basis of any individual's rationalization, or that specific aspects of the teachings can be discarded because they conflict with personal conclusions about general principles. The quest for sound understanding, instead, involves a community engaged in consultation, where differing views are welcome, unity is maintained, each individual exercises self-discipline, and varying perspectives are tested through action and reflection in a collective search for meaning that operates within the boundaries marked by the Covenant. A letter written on behalf of the Universal House of Justice states that "Bahá'í communities will need to develop greater tolerance toward ideas that may not coincide with their current understanding, and remain open to new insights."[86] Suppressing thoughtful and fairly crafted new ideas is no less harmful than unbridled criticism that masks self-serving ends. We have to struggle, therefore, to avoid certain pitfalls even as we cultivate other qualities that enhance the capacity to understand.

Among those pitfalls that impede understanding are the tendencies to overanalyze a Text, to ignore the obvious meaning in the quest for exotic interpretations, to neglect or overemphasize the social and historical context, or to interpret passages out of context or in isolation from the body of the Writings.[87] Other potential pitfalls include clinging to preconceived ideas, using a selection from the Text to contradict the whole or to contend with the center of authority in the Faith, overemphasizing individual interpretations (intellectual pride), and treating the Words of God like the words of human beings.[88]

Among those qualities that enhance our capacity to understand are effort and eagerness of search.[89] In addition, the House of Justice observes that

> other important components in this process include an attitude of prayerful humility, acceptance of the statements of the Manifestation, confidence in the knowledge that understanding of their meaning will emerge with meditation, study of the texts and the passage of time, willingness to acknowledge that one's views may be erroneous, and, courage to follow in the direction defined by the authentic sacred texts.[90]

We must learn to put forward our "views and conclusions with moderation and due humility"[91] so that our diverse perspectives can contribute to the collective effort to achieve a better understanding of Bahá'u'lláh's Revelation.

With the passing of Shoghi Effendi, the source of authoritative interpretation in the Faith came to a close, although the body of statements of 'Abdu'l-Bahá and Shoghi Effendi still stand along with the Writings of Bahá'u'lláh as part of the authoritative Text. The complexities of individual interpretation will remain with us throughout the course of the dispensation. The investigator of truth, when examining the Book, must struggle to determine when Bahá'u'lláh and His Interpreters are explicit and when metaphorical; when concepts current among the people were used and when new concepts were introduced; when scientific perspectives of the time were cited to illustrate a spiritual principle and when a statement reflects a truth about the physical reality; when historical context sheds light and when it obscures; when an authoritative interpretation is a statement that cannot be altered and when the Interpreter, as the head of the Faith, was introducing a temporary enactment. We can be neither too rigid nor too lax. On a certain point, divergent viewpoints and ambiguity may be all we can achieve at any given moment; resolution will depend on maintaining unity and acting over time under the guidance of the Universal House of Justice.

The Universal House of Justice and Bahá'í Practice

As Bahá'ís study and discuss the meaning of the Text while applying a set of hermeneutical principles, greater insight and unity of thought will emerge. The purpose of religion, however, is not simply to describe reality but to change human conduct and create a new social reality. Interpretation does not stand on its own. To test the soundness of our understanding we have to strive to apply it in action. As in science, where theory is tested by experimentation, spiritual insights must be tested by their expression in the world. The aim is to give effective material form to spiritual truth. Interpretation creates meaning. But meaning is tested in action, and action shapes reality.

To illustrate this point, consider two of the greatest mysteries of religion: the nature of God and life after death. The Bahá'í Writings indicate that both are unknowable owing to the limitations of language and of the human mind.[92] Why, then, do the Central Figures of the Faith expound upon these subjects? It is obviously not to describe the indescribable. It is to help us to have a proper understanding of our own nature and how we should behave.

Within the Revelation is a prescription for what individuals should do to enable humanity to move toward the Manifestation's intended aim. Progress is not achieved through a recipe for action, in which one step follows another with exact measures in a predetermined manner. Rather, the Revelation contains principles, methods, values, insights, and a description of forces that shape an unfolding organic process. The more we understand the nature of this organic process, the better we can serve it through our actions. Bahá'í practice, then, is concerned with translating the teachings of Bahá'u'lláh into action for individual and collective transformation within the framework of authoritative guidance. The goal is the establishment of a social order of unity, justice and peace, the Kingdom of God on earth. In essence, such practice implies living the Bahá'í life and thereby contributing to an ever-advancing civilization. A statement written on behalf of Shoghi Effendi on Bahá'í economics offers some insight into this process:

> There are practically no technical teachings on economics in the Cause, such as banking, the price system, and others. The Cause is not an economic system, nor can its Founders be considered as having been technical economists. The contribution

of the Faith to this subject is essentially indirect, as it consists in the application of spiritual principles to our present-day economic system. Bahá'u'lláh has given us a few basic principles which should guide future Bahá'í economists in establishing such institutions which will adjust the economic relationships of the world.[93]

What is true of this one aspect of the Faith is true for the aims of the Revelation as a whole. Generation after generation of believers will strive to translate the teachings into a new social reality. As emphasized in the previous chapter, this occurs through participation in all fields of human learning; it is not a project in which Bahá'ís engage apart from the rest of humanity.

Just as principles of hermeneutics found in the Text guide individual interpretation, so, too, perhaps it is possible to identify what might be regarded as principles of Bahá'í practice that guide our actions in achieving Bahá'u'lláh's purpose for humanity. Among these are firmness in the Covenant, which informs our relationship to the center of authority in the Faith, but also, between the individual and institutions and among the believers; obedience to the laws and ordinances, and effort to understand the wisdom of every injunction; the duty to teach the Faith individually and collectively through the systematic execution of the Divine Plan; consultation, which governs the collective search for truth that includes critical thought, resulting in unity of thought and action; universal participation in the work of the Faith; the administrative principles that guide collective action, including the requirement of following, in unity, the decision of an Assembly; and learning through action and reflection. These and other Bahá'í teachings influence behavior as we strive to cultivate patterns of life—spiritual, social, administrative, educational, material, and civil—that are to be distinctive features of the Bahá'í community.

The Universal House of Justice is the agency of the Bahá'í Covenant that prescribes proper action within the framework of the teachings according to the exigencies of the time. The powers and functions of the Universal House of Justice correlate with the human capacity to investigate reality and transform the social order. This body is constituted to act in a world in which human knowledge is mutable and progressive. Bahá'u'lláh states: "Inasmuch as for each day there is a new problem and for every problem an expedient solution, such affairs should be referred to the Ministers of the House of Justice that they may act according to the needs and requirements of the time."[94]

As the community learns how to translate the teachings into action, the Universal House of Justice guides the organic unfoldment of the Faith, determining, broadly, what to do and when to do it.[95] The Supreme Body is to "administer its affairs, coordinate its activities, promote its interests, execute its laws and defend its subsidiary institutions."[96] It establishes the Plans that are stages in the unfoldment of the Divine Plan, thereby unifying the efforts of National Assemblies.[97] It directs the evolution of Bahá'í administration, modifying or adding new elements. It gradually implements the laws of the Kitáb-i-Aqdas. It promotes learning for social and economic development and will, in future, initiate great humanitarian projects.

Guiding the progress of the Faith should not be confused with narrowly dictating a fixed set of doctrines or directing a highly centralized process. In general, the House of Justice does not guide action through mechanical formulas or rigid instructions. It opens an arena for action, encourages a diversity of responses worldwide, promotes learning to determine the most effective patterns of action, and unites the global community behind proven practices. The House of Justice is not omniscient, yet its decisions are binding.[98]

The authority of the Universal House of Justice, within its well-defined sphere of action, is indisputable and clearly established. Bahá'u'lláh states: "It is incumbent upon all to be obedient unto them."[99] 'Abdu'l-Bahá explains that "Whatsoever they decide is of God," and that "whoso contendeth with them hath contended with God."[100] And He states: "Whatsoever they decide has the same effect as the Text itself."[101] 'Abdu'l-Bahá also offers an emphatic guarantee to Bahá'ís that the decisions of the Universal House of Justice are reliable despite any objections or claims to authority by others:

> My purpose is this, that ere the expiration of a thousand years, no one has the right to utter a single word, even to claim the station of Guardianship. . . . Beware, beware lest anyone create a rift or stir up sedition. Should there be differences of opinion, the Supreme House of Justice would immediately resolve the problems. Whatever will be its decision, by majority vote, shall be the real truth, inasmuch as that House is under the protection, unerring guidance and care of the one true Lord. He shall guard it from error and will protect it under the wing of His sanctity and

infallibility. He who opposes it is cast out and will eventually be of the defeated.[102]

The scope of the jurisdiction of the House of Justice is broad. "Unto this body all things must be referred,"[103] 'Abdu'l-Bahá states. And He adds: "It is incumbent upon these members (of the Universal House of Justice) to gather in a certain place and deliberate upon all problems which have caused difference, questions that are obscure and matters that are not expressly recorded in the Book."[104] "Its pronouncements, which are susceptible of amendment or abrogation by the House of Justice itself, serve to supplement and apply the Law of God."[105] It is to "guide, organize, and unify the affairs of the Movement throughout the world"[106] along the course of its organic development. It "shares with the Guardian the responsibility for the application of the Revealed Word, the protection of the Faith, as well as the duty 'to insure the continuity of that divinely-appointed authority which flows from the Source of our Faith, to safeguard the unity of its followers, and to maintain the integrity and flexibility of its teachings.'"[107] And it is "destined to apply the principles, promulgate the laws, protect the institutions, adapt loyally and intelligently the Faith to the requirements of progressive society, and consummate the incorruptible inheritance which the Founders of the Faith have bequeathed to the world."[108]

Among the many responsibilities of the Universal House of Justice is legislation. Its "exclusive right and prerogative is to pronounce upon and deliver the final judgment on such laws and ordinances as Bahá'u'lláh has not expressly revealed."[109] And "inasmuch as the House of Justice hath power to enact laws that are not expressly recorded in the Book and bear upon daily transactions," 'Abdu'l-Bahá has determined, "so also it hath power to repeal the same. . . . This it can do because these laws form no part of the divine explicit text."[110]

Closely related to legislation is the responsibility for elucidation. Shoghi Effendi stated that various matters "have to be explained and elucidated by the Universal House of Justice, to which, according to the Master's explicit instructions, all important fundamental questions must be referred."[111] Elucidation is not authoritative interpretation; thus, the House of Justice does not make immutable statements about what the Sacred Text means.[112] But neither is elucidation merely the individual interpretation or opinions of the members of the House of Justice.[113] Elucidation stems from the legislative function of the House of Justice and it may, therefore, like legislation, change as time and context change.[114] Elucidation is not dependent on omniscience; it is associated with the capacity to continually make the practical judgments necessary according to the circumstances of the time in order to guide the Bahá'í world along its intended evolutionary path.

Another responsibility of the Universal House of Justice is to protect the Faith. This includes preserving proper relations of power. Postmodern philosophers have generally challenged concepts of truth, rationality and morality because they see them as formulations of language designed to maintain and exercise power over others; they therefore advocate the use of criticism to reallocate power. The Bahá'í teachings are highly sensitive to the question of language and power. But a dynamic unity, not perpetual criticism and contention, is sought. Individual initiative and the exchange of personal views—including critical thought—are essential for progress. But these must be balanced with measures that safeguard the welfare of society and preserve the healthy relationships that constitute the social order.

As noted above, if someone oversteps the bounds of individual interpretation, attempting to impose personal views on the community or to force its action along a path of personal preference, then the matter is no longer a hermeneutical question of permitting a range of opinions, but a question of behavior. The Universal House of Justice may, in such extreme cases, have to act.[115] This is not an attempt to impose dogma, but to prevent the imposition of dogma; it is not the means of quashing a dialogical process of learning, but the means of protecting it. As 'Abdu'l-Bahá explains:

> Today this process of deduction is the right of the body of the House of Justice, and the deductions and conclusions of individual learned men have no authority, unless they are endorsed by the House of Justice. The difference is precisely this, that from the conclusions and endorsements of the body of the House of Justice whose members are elected by and known to the worldwide Bahá'í community, no differences will arise; whereas the conclusion of individual divines and scholars would definitely lead to differences, and result in schism, division and dispersion. The oneness of the Word would be destroyed, the unity of the Faith would disappear, and the edifice of the Faith of God would be shaken.[116]

Conferred Infallibility and a Learning Community

In striving to acquire a better appreciation of how Bahá'ís understand the teachings and translate them into action, the question arises as to how the practice of a community that develops in a learning mode can be reconciled with the concept of conferred infallibility presented in the Bahá'í Writings. Does infallibility preclude critical thought and the search for truth? Does it imply an ability to make true statements about reality? How are Bahá'ís to understand the meaning of conferred infallibility as it operates in the unfoldment of the Faith?

The existence of an infallible religious authority is a highly suspect notion in contemporary society—secular or religious. Indeed, in many cases the infallibility of a Manifestation is not accepted by His own followers, and, for some religious people, even the infallibility of God is called into question. Infallibility, as a spiritual concept, lies beyond the capacity of any individual to fully comprehend. The Universal House of Justice has acknowledged the importance of striving to understand its functioning, but has warned the believers of the dangers of prolonged and fruitless discussions that could lead to discord.[117] Therefore, such a topic must be approached in a cautious manner. The comments here are not intended to be definitive, but are offered to clarify that there is no contradiction between the Bahá'í concept of infallibility and the ideas presented about an evolving understanding and practice in the Bahá'í community. An effort is made to preserve latitude for personal understandings about the topic.[118] At the same time, exploring a rational approach to the Bahá'í concept of infallibility should in no way detract from the spiritual bond linking the heart of the faithful believer to the Supreme Institution of Bahá'u'lláh's Cause.

The Bahá'í concept of the infallibility of the Universal House of Justice rests upon passages such as these:[119]

> It is incumbent upon the Trustees of the House of Justice to take counsel together regarding those things which have not outwardly been revealed in the Book, and to enforce that which is agreeable to them. God will verily inspire them with whatsoever He willeth, and He, verily, is the Provider, the Omniscient.[120]

> . . . essential infallibility belongs especially to the supreme Manifestations, and acquired infallibility is granted to every holy soul. For instance, the Universal House of Justice, if it be

established under the necessary conditions—with members elected from all the people—that House of Justice will be under the protection and the unerring guidance of God. If that House of Justice shall decide unanimously, or by a majority, upon any question not mentioned in the Book, that decision and command will be guarded from mistake. Now the members of the House of Justice have not, individually, essential infallibility; but the body of the House of Justice is under the protection and unerring guidance of God: this is called conferred infallibility.[121]

Unto the Most Holy Book every one must turn and all that is not expressly recorded therein must be referred to the Universal House of Justice. That which this body, whether unanimously or by a majority doth carry, that is verily the Truth and the Purpose of God Himself. Whoso doth deviate therefrom is verily of them that love discord, hath shown forth malice, and turned away from the Lord of the Covenant.[122]

Let it not be imagined that the House of Justice will take any decision according to its own concepts and opinions. God forbid! The Supreme House of Justice will take decisions and establish laws through the inspiration and confirmation of the Holy Spirit, because it is in the safekeeping and under the shelter and protection of the Ancient Beauty, and obedience to its decisions is a bounden and essential duty and an absolute obligation, and there is no escape for anyone.

Say, O People: Verily the Supreme House of Justice is under the wings of your Lord, the Compassionate, the All-Merciful, that is under His protection, His care, and His shelter; for He has commanded the firm believers to obey that blessed, sanctified, and all-subduing body, whose sovereignty is divinely ordained and of the Kingdom of Heaven and whose laws are inspired and spiritual.[123]

To begin to understand these passages about conferred infallibility, it is first necessary to recall the meaning of the essential infallibility of the Manifestation, which is summarized in the verse, "He doeth whatsoever He willeth." Although the knowledge of the Manifestation encompasses reality, it is not His purpose to describe the world factually but to convey God's will and purpose. Essential infallibility means, therefore, that the very words of the Manifestation are the will and purpose of God Himself. His words are new truths and new laws that rend asunder the existing social reality and create the basis of human agreement upon which a new social reality is to be raised. These words cannot be tested, measured, or judged by any human criteria. As ʻAbduʼl-Bahá explains:

> Briefly, it is said that the "Dayspring of Revelation" is the manifestation of these words, "He doeth whatsoever He willeth"; this condition is peculiar to that Holy Being, and others have no share of this essential perfection. That is to say, that as the supreme Manifestations certainly possess essential infallibility, therefore whatever emanates from Them is identical with the truth, and conformable to reality. They are not under the shadow of the former laws. Whatever They say is the word of God, and whatever They perform is an upright action. No believer has any right to criticize; his condition must be one of absolute submission, for the Manifestation arises with perfect wisdom—so that whatever the supreme Manifestation says and does is absolute wisdom, and is in accordance with reality. . . .
>
> In short, the meaning of "He doeth whatsoever He willeth" is that if the Manifestation says something, or gives a command, or performs an action, and believers do not understand its wisdom, they still ought not to oppose it by a single thought, seeking to know why He spoke so, or why He did such a thing. The other souls who are under the shadow of the supreme Manifestations are submissive to the commandments of the Law of God, and are not to deviate as much as a hairsbreadth from it; they must conform their acts and words to the Law of God. If they do deviate from it, they will be held responsible and reproved in the presence of God. It is certain that they have no share in the permission "He doeth whatsoever He willeth," for this condition is peculiar to the supreme Manifestations.[124]

In this light, conferred infallibility—of ʻAbduʼl-Bahá, Shoghi Effendi, and the Universal House of Justice—may also be understood as an association with the divine will and purpose. This is not a capacity to describe the world as it is, or to possess unfailing knowledge about reality, which pertain to omniscience—a condition impossible for human beings.[125] Omniscience and infallibility are distinct concepts. The Guardian was not omniscient; so, too, the Universal House of Justice "is not omniscient; like the Guardian, it wants to be provided with facts when called upon to render a decision, and like him it may well change its decision when new facts emerge."[126] Rather, conferred infallibility is an assurance that a statement or decision arising from within the designated domain of responsibility is in accordance with the will and purpose of God.

The phrase "freed from all error"[127] can be understood in the same way. 'Abdu'l-Bahá explains that "Error is the want of guidance."[128] Infallibility is freedom from error because the infallible authority does not act outside of the boundaries of God's guidance. Thus, the interpretations of the authorized Interpreter cannot vary from the intended meaning of the Word of God. Similarly, the guidance of the Universal House of Justice that directs the understanding and actions of the believers does not depart from God's will as expressed in the Text or veer from the path that leads to the achievement of His purpose for humanity in this dispensation.

In response to questions from the believers, Shoghi Effendi explained that "the infallibility of the Guardian is confined to matters which are related strictly to the Cause and interpretation of the teachings; he is not an infallible authority on other subjects, such as economics, science, etc."[129] His infallibility "covers interpretation of the Revealed Word and its application. Likewise . . . he is infallible in the protection of the Faith."[130] It is reasonable to conclude, then, that the sphere of infallibility of the House of Justice also does not extend beyond its authorized responsibilities pertaining to the Faith.[131] These include legislation on matters not expressly addressed in the Book, elucidations concerning problems that have caused difference and questions that are obscure,[132] and those duties shared with the Guardian to apply the Revealed Word, to protect the Faith, to preserve the unity of the believers, and to ensure the integrity and flexibility of the teachings.[133] Indeed, the House of Justice indicates that its infallibility extends beyond legislation, even to administering the Cause.

> The Universal House of Justice, beyond its function as the enactor of legislation, has been invested with the more general functions of protecting and administering the Cause, solving obscure questions and deciding upon matters that have caused difference. Nowhere is it stated that the infallibility of the Universal House of Justice is by virtue of the Guardian's membership or presence on that body. Indeed, 'Abdu'l-Bahá in His Will and Shoghi Effendi in his Dispensation of Bahá'u'lláh have both explicitly stated that the elected members of the Universal House of Justice in consultation are recipients of unfailing Divine Guidance.[134]

In the same way, Shoghi Effendi, when emphasizing that it is the "members of the Universal House of Justice," and "not the body of those who either directly or indirectly elect them," that have "been made the recipients of the divine guidance which is at once the life-blood and ultimate safeguard of this Revelation," associates such guidance not just with "the enactment of the legislation necessary to supplement the laws of the Kitáb-i-Aqdas," but also with "the conduct of the administrative affairs of the Faith."[135]

While there appears to be no reason to limit conferred infallibility to less than the full range of designated responsibilities of the House of Justice, there is also, most certainly, no reason to extend it further. A letter written on behalf of the Universal House of Justice states:

> Shoghi Effendi was asked several times during his ministry to define the sphere of his operation and his infallibility. The replies he gave and which were written on his behalf are most illuminating. He explains that he is not an infallible authority on subjects such as economics and science, nor does he go into technical matters since his infallibility is confined to "matters which are related strictly to the Cause." He further points out that "he is not, like the Prophet, omniscient at will," that his "infallibility covers interpretation of the Revealed Word and its application," and that he is also "infallible in the protection of the Faith."[136]

The Baháʼí concept of infallibility, therefore, should not be raised in the context of areas that clearly have nothing to do with the designated responsibilities of the House of Justice. It should not be confused with a power to possess absolute knowledge of reality, to control the conscience of individuals, or to predict future events; to do so opens the door to irrationalism, fundamentalism, or superstition. "When exchanging views about the Universal House of Justice—the body to which all things must be referred—the friends should exercise care lest they go to extremes, by either diminishing its station or assigning to it exaggerated attributes," a message written on behalf of the House of Justice explains.[137] Further, "Baháʼí institutions are bound by the teachings of the Faith to uphold freedom of expression and to safeguard the personal rights and initiative of the individual."[138] And the House of Justice states: "The provenance, the authority, the duties, the sphere of action of the Universal House of Justice all derive from the revealed Word of Baháʼuʼlláh which, together with the interpretations and expositions of the Centre of the Covenant and of the Guardian of the Cause—who, after 'Abdu'l-Bahá, is the sole authority in the interpretation of Bahá'í Scripture—constitute the binding terms of reference of the Universal House of Justice and are its bedrock foundation."[139]

The House of Justice does not issue inflexible prescriptions that are to be executed without thought by a submissive community. Rather, it guides a community engaged in a dialogical process of learning to translate the teachings into action over time to create a new social order manifested in the lives of individual believers, the creation of a distinctive Bahá'í community, and the advancement of civilization.

In one of his early letters to the believers, Shoghi Effendi warned the community to "keep the most vigilant eye on the manner and character" of the growth of the Faith, "lest extreme orthodoxy on one hand, and irresponsible freedom on the other, cause it to deviate from that Straight Path which alone can lead it to success."[140] The House of Justice is an instrument established by Bahá'u'lláh and guaranteed divine inspiration and protection by Him so that it can reliably guide the progress of the believers toward the fulfillment of God's purpose for humanity while guarding against extremes that produce sectarianism and a distortion of the teachings or practice of the Faith.

It also should be noted that nothing in the Bahá'í concept of infallibility implies that all outcomes will be painless or free of difficulties. For example, one of Bahá'u'lláh's own sons was the arch-breaker of His Covenant. In a world in which mortality is the rule, even an infallible physician will have patients die. Thus, because both chance and free will exist, infallibility—essential or conferred—cannot be associated with ideal results. Even with divine guidance, human beings have to struggle, suffer, and persevere. They have to attempt to comprehend, however imprecisely, what is written and then to translate it, incrementally, into practice until the social reality is reconstructed bit by bit to reflect the divine guidance. Infallibility offers no relief from this process. But because conferred infallibility is extended throughout Bahá'u'lláh's dispensation, Bahá'ís are assured that there will be the guidance necessary to lead to the promised spiritual civilization.

It is clear, then, that there is no contradiction between an infallible source of guidance and the functioning of a community in a learning mode. The promises of divine assistance given by Bahá'u'lláh and 'Abdu'l-Bahá enable the believers to unhesitatingly place their trust and confidence in the Universal House of Justice and faithfully follow its lead. They do their best to translate the guidance into action, and the mechanisms are in place so that the fruits of their experience can flow to the Bahá'í World Centre and to all parts of the world. Their response draws additional measures of guidance. No one can comprehend the workings of the divine forces involved, or how God acts to direct the House of Justice. It is "under the care and protection of the Abhá Beauty, under the shelter and unerring guidance of His Holiness, the Exalted One."[141] It is "the last refuge of a tottering civilization."[142] It is "the source of all good."[143] "God will verily inspire them with whatsoever He willeth, and He, verily, is the Provider, the Omniscient."[144] Our challenge, as believers, is to learn how to do our part in the light of such guidance to achieve Bahá'u'lláh's purpose for humanity.

Learning and Bahá'í Practice

The practice of the Faith within the framework of the Bahá'í teachings by the individual believer includes elements such as spiritual disciplines, deepening in the Writings, contributing to the progress of the Cause, and living the Bahá'í life. 'Abdu'l-Bahá is the perfect exemplar toward which we aspire. To "live the life" is "to have our lives so saturated with the divine teaching and the Bahá'í spirit that people cannot fail to see a joy, a power, a love, a purity, a radiance, an efficiency in our character and work that will distinguish us" and "make people wonder what is the secret of this new life in us."[145] Shoghi Effendi states that "Not until we live ourselves the life of a true Bahá'í can we hope to demonstrate the creative and transforming potency of the Faith we profess."[146]

Living a Bahá'í life involves the twofold purpose of individual and social transformation. The vital interplay between them is explained in a letter written on behalf of the Guardian:

> We cannot segregate the human heart from the environment outside us and say that once one of these is reformed everything will be improved. Man is organic with the world. His inner life molds the environment and is itself also deeply affected by it. The one acts upon the other and every abiding change in the life of man is the result of these mutual reactions.
>
> No movement in the world directs its attention upon both these aspects of human life and has full measures for their improvement, save the teachings of Bahá'u'lláh. And this is its

distinctive feature. If we desire therefore the good of the world we should strive to spread those teachings and also practice them in our own life. Through them will the human heart be changed, and also our social environment provides the atmosphere in which we can grow spiritually and reflect in full the light of God shining through the revelation of Bahá'u'lláh.[147]

In the effort to translate Bahá'u'lláh's teachings into reality, Bahá'ís collectively contribute to the building of a new civilization. This process begins within the community itself as it grows and develops and gains capacity to administer it own affairs; it gradually extends to service to the wider society. "Until the public sees in the Bahá'í community a true pattern, in action, of something better than it already has," Shoghi Effendi indicates, "it will not respond to the Faith in large numbers."[148] In describing the believer's responsibility toward society, 'Abdu'l-Bahá states, "The Bahá'ís are commanded to establish the oneness of mankind."[149] He also urges:

> Act in accordance with the counsels of the Lord: that is, rise up in such wise, and with such qualities, as to endow the body of this world with a living soul, and to bring this young child, humanity, to the stage of adulthood. . . . Perchance such ways and words from you will make this darksome world turn bright at last; will make this dusty earth turn heavenly, this devilish prison place become a royal palace of the Lord—so that war and strife will pass and be no more, and love and trust will pitch their tents on the summits of the world.[150]

In the effort to put the teachings of the Faith into practice, Bahá'ís face the previously discussed dangers of relativism, or "irresponsible freedom," where we stray from the intended meaning of Bahá'u'lláh's teachings, perhaps ignoring or inadequately responding to His laws or principles. There is also the danger of absolute self-certainty, or "extreme orthodoxy," where we cling too strictly to our own limited understandings of the teachings, presuming they are identical with Bahá'u'lláh's own intended meaning; in this respect, the practice of the Faith is reduced to a list of dos and don'ts and the institutions are reduced to the role of enforcer.[151] Practice is also affected by a tension between past and future, between the patterns of life we have developed at any given point in time that are affected by the baneful characteristics of a disintegrating society and the patterns of life we will develop that are increasingly in accord with Bahá'u'lláh's will and purpose.

The course of our personal lives, as well as the course of the development of the Faith over the entire dispensation, may be likened to walking the "Straight Path" where we advance by learning to be more effective in translating Bahá'u'lláh's teachings into reality. At any given point, we may be uncertain or in error about some aspect of our understanding of the Faith or about what we are to do. But over time, through learning and the guidance of the Universal House of Justice, we make progress.

Learning—study of the Bahá'í Writings, consultation, action and reflection on action in light of divine guidance—over the course of our lives and over the course of the dispensation is the means by which we find our way forward toward Bahá'u'lláh's intended purpose for humanity. To speak of the need for learning is an acknowledgement that we are not perfect, we make mistakes, and we must learn to do things better over time. It is also an acknowledgement that the Faith is organic, our responsibilities will evolve and capacities will develop over time, and we will act at ever higher levels of complexity and achieve greater results in the future. Without learning, our thoughts and actions are trapped in an endless circularity.

In the Four Year Plan, the Universal House of Justice particularly focused attention on consciously cultivating a capacity for learning in the Bahá'í world, and by the year 2000, observed that it had taken root.

> The culture of the Bahá'í community experienced a change. This change is noticeable in the expanded capability, the methodical pattern of functioning and the consequent depth of confidence of the three constituent participants in the Plan—the individual, the institutions and the local community. That is so because the friends concerned themselves more consistently with deepening their knowledge of the divine Teachings and learned much—and this more systematically than before—about how to apply them to promulgating the Cause, to managing their individual and collective activities, and to working with their neighbors. In a word, they entered into a learning mode from which purposeful action was pursued.[152]

The culture of learning that is emerging is characterized by dialogue rather than debate, by constructive experience at the grassroots rather than elaborate planning from the top, by systematization rather than freneticism, by reflective refinement rather than derogatory criticism. In such a culture "fear of failure finds no place."[153] The search for a simplistic formula for success is ended but so too is the justification that anything goes, that any effort is as equally effective as any other. When we do not know what to do to resolve a particular challenge, trying out a diversity of actions, close observation, and revision become the dominant characteristics of our approach. Once we find an effective solution to a challenge, energies then shift to unified action, focus, perseverance, and intensive campaigns to significantly multiply the proven course of action. All have a part to play in finding the proper balance between thought and action, between theory and practice, that results in the systematization and sustainability of effort.

Consider, for example, the range of possible relationships that exist between theory and practice. Anyone who has struggled with the growth and development of the Bahá'í community will recognize various types of response to challenges shaped by the interaction of theory and practice. The first relationship exists when our conceptual understanding of what we are doing is limited and our understanding of what kind of activity actually works in the real world is lacking (low theory, low practice). As a result, we find ourselves constantly scrambling for an appropriate response to whatever circumstances arise. Action is frenetic and ineffective. In the second relationship, some effective actions may emerge in a particular locality, but without understanding why or how they work (low theory, high practice). An example is when teaching efforts bear fruit in many new enrollments in a particular locality for a period of time. In such instances, we cannot expand on the effort or transfer this success to other places or situations. Indeed, we may not even be able to repeat the result in the same setting. A third relationship between theory and practice arises when our efforts are driven by elaborate plans, grounded in a set of theoretical ideas and supported with the full weight of the institutions, but without the practical experience that demonstrates that the plan will actually work (high theory, low practice). Under these circumstances, the community usually moves from one elaborate strategy to another, each failing to produce sustainable results. The fourth type of relationship involves thoughtful analysis complemented by practical approaches tested and proven through experience (high theory, high practice). When a Bahá'í community is able to consciously establish an effective pattern of action and understand why it works, it is able to sustain the activities over an extended period of time, constantly adjusting to evolving circumstances, while developing ever more complex and effective methods and structures. The learning that emerges is useful in, and adaptable to, a variety of communities and settings. For example, pioneering emerged as an effective approach to spreading the Faith that has been successfully replicated and adapted to the needs of the Cause on the homefront and internationally over many decades.

Beginning in 1996, the Universal House of Justice established the Four Year Plan, whose single aim was to advance the process of entry by troops. It later outlined a series of Plans through the year 2021 that would also focus on the same aim. This established a period of a quarter century in which learning would be directed toward resolving the question of how to reach out to large numbers of people, teach them, consolidate, and sustain the process over time. The experience, to date, is discussed in the next chapter. The work of Bahá'í social and economic development has also been guided by a systematic process of learning over a number of years, as described in chapter 4.

Continually asking and seeking out how to translate the teachings into action more effectively in all aspects of the Faith—teaching, administration, worship, development and others—is the nature of the culture of learning to which Bahá'ís are called. Learning involves study to understand the appropriate texts and action to see how the guidance can be translated into effective action. The aim is not to make the Bahá'í community what we want it to be, but to achieve, over time, Bahá'u'lláh's intended purpose.

The learning that generates new knowledge must be subsequently incorporated into educational efforts. Education and training, therefore, continually evolve as practice evolves. While education conveys what is known, the aim is not indoctrination, but raising up individuals capable of playing a role in the continual generation and application of new knowledge—equal participants contributing to the progress of the Faith and contributing to the building of a new civilization. To do this effectively, educational programs cannot merely present concepts from the Writings; they must be linked with the experience gained from practice. The most effective curricula will initiate an apprenticeship in Bahá'í practice, endowing the learner with the capacity to retrace the steps of those who have carried out effective service.

As we seek to establish a culture of learning, we may find it difficult to escape the pull of the old culture. Fledgling methods need patience, support and care. The impulse to harshly criticize and reject what is new or to arbitrarily maintain previous ways of doing things need to be resisted. So, too, we cannot succumb to simple formulas for action; yet, in acquiring new skills, we must go through a series of stages, the earliest of which may, indeed, give the appearance of such a mechanical approach.

Researchers Hubert and Stuart Dreyfus have suggested that individuals pass through five distinct stages from novice to expert when acquiring skills. This holds true whether the skill is technical, such as building a house, or intellectual, such as analyzing a text.[154] Each stage represents a distinct set of behaviors that are distinguishable in qualitative and recognizable ways from the other levels of performance. Without endorsing this theory, it may be useful to consider the characteristics of these stages and how an individual passes from one stage to the next in order to obtain a better understanding of the relationship between learning and experience.

At the novice stage an effort is initially made to present the student with a collection of specific elements, including facts, rules, procedures, and circumstances in which the skill is applied. Consider the example of learning how to drive a car with a manual transmission. The novice is given a number of facts and rules of behavior: a description of the pattern of shifting the gears to various levels; an explanation of when to shift gears as the engine reaches a particular level of performance; a demonstration of how to move the hands and feet to coordinate the interaction of the gear shift and clutch. In the first attempts to shift gears in a car, the novice consciously juggles the various aspects of the information learned while trying to coordinate different movements. It is not uncommon for the car to lurch violently or stall. Again and again the novice repeats the pattern, evaluating a performance based on whether the facts and rules are appropriately recalled and applied. At first, there is simply too much new information to remember and process for a satisfactory result to be achieved. Performance is awkward and mechanical. But with each experience, there is a better understanding of the information and rules presented, and the driver passes through the stages of learning by discriminating and getting the "feel" for effective action. Concepts initially ignored or misunderstood become clear. After continual practice and accumulation of experience, knowledge and action become integrated into a coordinated pattern without the need to remember context-independent facts and rules. At an expert level, the driver seamlessly integrates shifting gears into other aspects of driving practice, and can even simultaneously juggle other tasks like eating or talking on a cell phone.

Learning skills in Bahá'í practice follows similar stages. Therefore it may appear, at the beginning of a new endeavor, that the process is fairly mechanical. We cling to the guidance as if applying a formula. But this rigid and inflexible behavior, which is a natural part of learning something new, gradually becomes more sophisticated and adaptive with the accumulation of more and more experience.

Consider the establishment of the institute process in the Bahá'í world at the start of the Four Year Plan in 1996. Some countries struggled for years to have their institute become fully operational and to integrate training with systematic growth. The initial implementation of the sequence of courses and the translation of new skills into action was often wooden and awkward. Out of a desire to apply the guidance "correctly," there was a tendency in isolated cases to go to extremes. Either the institute was to provide all of the educational needs of a country through a wide range of classes, or all other activity was to be stopped so that all could take institute courses. Either everyone was to become a tutor, or a restrictive process for tutor recognition was imposed. Occasionally, individuals who taught children's classes for years were told they could no longer teach them unless they studied an institute course on child education. Firesides were abandoned in place of study circles. In some places, individuals were moved quickly through the courses without attention to the practice of skills, resulting in problems when growth did not "magically" appear.

Understandably, when new capabilities and new practices are being acquired mistakes will be made and performance will begin poorly. Attempts to follow so much new guidance without error may initially result in strict rules and rigid applications. However, through perseverance and growing experience, understanding and effectiveness gradually appear. Over time, individuals and institutions become active participants in their own learning. In country after country, the training institute has become a center of learning about how the process of entry by troops can unfold in the region it serves.

One additional aspect of learning and progress concerns the opportunity available to individuals who possess knowledge and capacity to advance the process. This place in the Faith is not reserved only for members of institutions or for a narrow intellectual class, but for all who strive to understand and act. The role of such individuals, however, is not to continually criticize efforts, to impose personal views and programs, or to undermine or cast doubt on the institutions. Their role is to act according to the teachings to the best of their ability and understanding, to foster unity of thought and action, and to accompany others as they enter the field of service, thereby contributing to the incremental progress of the Faith over time.

Applying knowledge for constructive change in the Bahá'í community does not involve self-certainty or self-interest, but self-sacrifice. It involves doing what is right, not becoming self-righteous. It sometimes requires suffering, which is an inevitable aspect of trying to champion justice. It involves absorbing the pain and anger of others and returning love and compassion in an effort to build unity. It involves demonstrating patience when understanding is lacking or capacity is undeveloped. It involves exercising power to shape and release human capacity for the advancement of the Cause and the well-being of humanity. It requires intellectual capacity to generate new knowledge, but wisdom to convey that knowledge—which can sometimes be challenging and disconcerting in the face of generally accepted belief and practice—in a manner appropriate to context. It involves proceeding with humility and flexibility to continue to grow and learn and to foster learning in others. As a letter written on behalf of Shoghi Effendi explains:

> One soul can be the cause of the spiritual illumination of a continent. Now that you have seen, and remedied, a great fault in your own life, now that you see more clearly what is lacking in your own community, there is nothing to prevent you from arising and showing such an example, such a love and spirit of service, as to enkindle the hearts of your fellow Bahá'ís. He urges you to study deeply the teachings, teach others, study with those Bahá'ís who are anxious to do so, the deeper teachings of our Faith, and through example, effort and prayer, bring about a change.[155]

3
Learning and Growth

HAVING GAINED DEEPER INSIGHT into the nature of understanding and action associated with learning to translate Bahá'u'lláh's teachings into reality, we can now explore their expression in specific contexts, beginning with the expansion and consolidation of the worldwide community. Before any extensive consideration of the subject, however, it is important to recall that, far from a narrow concern with increasing membership, the purpose of teaching others about the Faith is "to attract human beings to the divine Message and so imbue them with its spirit that they will dedicate themselves to its service, and this world will become another world and its people another people."[1] Teaching is one of the primary obligations of a believer, to be carried out as a detached act of devotion, and only with the consent of a receptive soul. How to respond is a matter for the hearer's conscience. Teaching, the act of spreading spiritual illumination, is an inherent attribute of the enkindled soul. As 'Abdu'l-Bahá states:

> God says in the glorious Qur'án, "The soil was black and dried. Then we caused the rain to descend upon it and immediately it became green, verdant, and every kind of plant sprouted up luxuriantly." In other words, he says the earth is black, but when the spring showers descend upon it that black soil is quickened, and variegated flowers are pushed forth. This means the souls of humanity belonging to the world of nature are black like unto the soil. But when the heavenly outpourings descend and the radiant effulgences appear, the hearts are resuscitated, are liberated from the darkness of nature and the flowers of divine mysteries grow and become luxuriant. Consequently man must become the cause of the illumination of the world of humanity and propagate the holy teachings revealed in the sacred books through divine inspiration.[2]

At the start of his ministry, Shoghi Effendi recognized that one of his major areas of responsibility would be to guide the believers to execute, in a more systematic manner, the Divine Plan whose provisions for the worldwide propagation of the Faith were outlined in 'Abdu'l-Bahá's Tablets to the Bahá'ís in North America. Initially, however, the means for prosecuting this Plan collectively was absent, and therefore, "It was held in abeyance for well-nigh twenty years while the fabric of an indispensable Administrative Order, designed as a divinely appointed agency for the operation of that Plan, was being constructed."[3] This first stage in the development of the administration involved a learning process that included education of the believers and the refinement of various procedures and practices pertaining to Local and National Assemblies, National Convention, elections, and the like.[4] Once the prerequisite institutional capacity was in place, Shoghi Effendi called upon national communities to adopt formal teaching plans. "The new hour has struck in [the] history of our beloved Cause," he proclaimed in 1935, "calling for nation-wide, systematic, sustained efforts in [the] teaching field."[5]

An attitude of learning was evident in the earliest efforts to formulate effective approaches to teaching. For example, Shoghi Effendi described meetings to promote world unity as "an experiment to test the efficacy of the indirect method of teaching."[6] At one point he called for a "highly salutary and spiritually beneficent experiment of encouraging a more active participation by these newly won supporters of the Faith in Latin America" to be "developed, systematized and placed on a sure and unassailable foundation."[7] Over time, certain approaches—such as firesides[8] and pioneering—proved through experience to be more effective than others, all communities were encouraged to adopt them, and they became mainstays of propagation. A letter written on behalf of the Guardian to the National Assembly of India and Burma illustrates this learning process:

> Those believers who have the means, and also the capacity to teach, should be encouraged, no matter how great the sacrifice involved, to settle in these virgin territories, until such time as a local assembly has been constituted, or at least a group of firm believers formed that can safely and gradually evolve into a firmly-organized and properly-functioning local assembly. This policy of teaching by settlement which the Guardian has also advised and

indeed urged the American believers to adopt has been proved by experience to be the most effective way of establishing the Faith in new territories, and he therefore confidently recommends it for adoption by your Assembly.[9]

Institutions and methods evolved through experience under the direction of the Guardian. Because of the careful education and loving guidance of Shoghi Effendi over the course of his ministry, the Bahá'í world was able to launch the first global Plan in 1953, the Ten Year Crusade, which linked the efforts of the twelve existing National Assemblies. As a result of their accumulated experience and capacity, the Bahá'ís were able to accomplish more in that single decade than was achieved in the previous century. More than 100 countries and territories were opened to the Faith in the first year of that Plan. By the end of the decade, more than 40 new National Assemblies were established, thousands of Local Assemblies were formed, and tens of thousands of new believers were enlisted in all parts of the world.

Shoghi Effendi explained that the growth of the Faith would involve three stages, beginning with a "steady flow" of fresh recruits that would be followed by entry by troops and mass conversion.

> This flow, moreover, will presage and hasten the advent of the day which, as prophesied by 'Abdu'l-Bahá, will witness the entry by troops of peoples of divers nations and races into the Bahá'í world—a day which, viewed in its proper perspective, will be the prelude to that long-awaited hour when a mass conversion on the part of these same nations and races, and as a direct result of a chain of events, momentous and possibly catastrophic in nature, and which cannot as yet be even dimly visualized, will suddenly revolutionize the fortunes of the Faith, derange the equilibrium of the world, and reinforce a thousandfold the numerical strength as well as the material power and the spiritual authority of the Faith of Bahá'u'lláh.[10]

Signs of the start of the second stage, marked by the entry of large numbers of new believers, were already evident in various countries in Africa, in the Pacific, and in the Mentawai Islands of Indonesia during the lifetime of the Guardian.[11] Starting in the 1950s, and accelerating over the next three decades, campaigns of rapid enrollment unfolded whereby hundreds, thousands, and even tens of thousands entered the Faith quickly in country after country.

Membership in several countries surpassed 100,000 believers, while in India, the number of believers surpassed two million.[12] Despite the success in obtaining new enrollments, however, no national community was able to achieve the appropriate balance between expansion and consolidation necessary to sustain the process of entry by troops. Chapter 9 of *Century of Light*, which analyzes growth over three decades from the mid-1960s, explains:

> The burst of enrollments brought with it, however, equally great problems. At the immediate level, the resources of Bahá'í communities engaged in the work were soon overwhelmed by the task of providing the sustained deepening the masses of new believers needed and the consolidation of the resulting communities and Spiritual Assemblies. Beyond that, cultural challenges like those encountered by the early Persian believers who had first sought to introduce the Faith in Western lands now replicated themselves throughout the world.[13]

In response to the challenges introduced by the new teaching methods, the House of Justice affirmed the validity of the process of large scale growth while encouraging all the believers with differing viewpoints to come together and achieve greater effectiveness through consultation and by refining emerging methods in practice. For example, the Amercian Bahá'í community grew from some 20,000 to over 60,000 members over a few years in late 1960s and early 1970s. When enrollments declined precipitously in 1972 from more than 20,000 the previous year, the following advice was provided:

> We note that the new teaching methods you have developed, in reaching the waiting masses, have substantially influenced the winning of your goals, and we urge the American Bahá'ís, one and all, newly enrolled and believers of long standing, to arise, put their reliance in Bahá'u'lláh and armed with that supreme power, continue unabated their efforts to reach the waiting souls, while simultaneously consolidating the hard-won victories. New methods inevitably bring with them criticism and challenges no matter how successful they may ultimately prove to be. The influx of so many new believers is, in itself, a call to the veteran believers to join the ranks of those in this field of service and to give wholeheartedly of their knowledge and experience. Far from standing aloof, the American believers are called upon now, as

never before, to grasp this golden opportunity which has been presented to them, to consult together prayerfully and widen the scope of their endeavors.[14]

The exhortation to consult and find solutions was reinforced by additional guidance calling for a balance between the processes of expansion and consolidation, a need to revise and improve teaching efforts through experience, an integration of complementary activities, and a systematization of approach. The following statements to the Bahá'í world were typical of that period:

> Teaching the Faith embraces many diverse activities, all of which are vital to success, and each of which reinforces the other. Time and again the beloved Guardian emphasized that expansion and consolidation are twin and inseparable aspects of teaching that must proceed simultaneously, yet one still hears believers discussing the virtues of one against the other.[15]

> At this stage in the development of the Faith there are many new experiments taking place in the teaching field and also in the work of consolidation. It is obvious that not all these experiments will meet with success. Many have great merit while others may have little or none. However, in the present period of transition and rapid growth of the Cause we must seek diligently for the merit of every method devised to teach and deepen the masses.[16]

> The periodic re-evaluation of the effectiveness of the teaching work is an essential factor in promoting the growth of every community. Through this process a community would re-assess its teaching program with a view to introducing improvements where necessary.[17]

> Armed with the strength of action and the co-operation of the individual believers composing it, the community as a whole should endeavor to establish greater stability in the patterns of its development, locally and nationally, through sound, systematic planning and execution of its work—and this in striking contrast to the short-lived enthusiasms and frenetic superficialities so characteristic of present-day . . . life. A Bahá'í community which is consistent in its fundamental life-giving, life-sustaining activities will at its heart be serene and confident; it will resonate with spiritual dynamism, will exert irresistible influence, will set a

new course in social evolution, enabling it to win the respect and eventually the allegiance of admirers and critics alike.[18]

> ... the community must become more adept at accommodating a wide range of actions without losing concentration on the primary objectives of teaching, namely, expansion and consolidation. A unity in diversity of actions is called for, a condition in which different individuals will concentrate on different activities, appreciating the salutary effect of the aggregate on the growth and development of the Faith, because each person cannot do everything and all persons cannot do the same thing. This understanding is important to the maturity which, by the many demands being made upon it, the community is being forced to attain.[19]

Unfortunately, despite such guidance, the potential to sustain sizable growth was not realized. Without effective consolidation to complement rapid enrollment, new believers could not be deepened, communities were not organized, and the children—the next generation of believers—were not educated. Quickly won gains evaporated because the large number of new believers could not be confirmed in active service. This is not to deny the spiritual receptivity or the genuine expressions of faith of those who embraced the Cause during this time. It is, however, an acknowledgement that, often, belief did not crystallize into new patterns of Bahá'í life. "A sustained entry by troops," the Universal House of Justice has subsequently observed, "cannot be achieved by a mere series of spasmodic, uncoordinated exertions, no matter how enthusiastic."[20]

Rather than achieving a balance between expansion and consolidation, or a unity of thought and action that would facilitate learning about large-scale expansion, efforts to bring about growth were generally formulated in most countries according to two competing perspectives. One stressed expansion, and the other, consolidation; each supported its position with carefully selected quotations and anecdotal evidence. Yet, no matter which position became dominant in a given community, the result was the same— growth could not be sustained. Rapid enrollments without effective follow-up produced large communities and many newly formed Assemblies but few deepened, capable believers or institutions that could function without consistent outside help. Overemphasis on consolidation produced an inward, congregational focus and administrative efficiency that prized order but eclipsed the initiative necessary to grow. Dedicated believers and communities were trapped in an enervating paradox. When they aspired to achieve great victories in teaching, they committed their all to activities that increased numbers which were difficult to consolidate; when they worried about the tentative nature of their gains, they retreated to an educational and administrative agenda that stifled expansion.

The last great surge of expansion during this period occurred in the middle of the Six Year Plan. In the period of two years from 1988 to 1990, the worldwide community grew by some one million[21] to over five million believers; once again, however, consolidation of these gains proved to be a formidable obstacle.

A Turning Point of Epochal Magnitude

From the start of the global Plans formulated under the direction of the House of Justice which aimed at large scale expansion, it took over 30 years before a body of experience could be generated that pointed to new, more effective, and more systematic endeavors. As mentioned in *Century of Light*:

> The significance of these three decades of struggle, learning and sacrifice became apparent when the moment arrived to devise a global Plan that would capitalize on the insights gained and the resources that had been developed. The Bahá'í community that set out on the Four Year Plan in 1996 was a very different one from the eager, but new and still inexperienced body of believers who, in 1964, had ventured out on the first of such undertakings that were no longer sustained by the guiding hand of Shoghi Effendi. By 1996, it had become possible to see all of the distinct strands of the enterprise as integral parts of one coherent whole. . . .
>
> Although the struggles of these decades were relatively modest—at least when set against the standard of the Heroic Age—they provide the present generation of Bahá'ís with a window on what Shoghi Effendi describes as the cyclical nature of the Faith's history: "a series of internal and external crises, of varying severity, devastating in their immediate effects, but each mysteriously releasing a corresponding measure of divine power, lending thereby a fresh impulse to its unfoldment." These words put into perspective the succession of efforts, experiments, heartbreaks and victories that characterized the beginning of large-scale teaching, and prepared the Bahá'í community for the much greater challenges ahead.[22]

The Four Year Plan in 1996 marked a "turning point of epochal magnitude."[23] From the experience and struggles of the previous period, it was now possible to set the global community on a new course of action. "Entry by troops," the House of Justice wrote, "is not merely a stage of the progress of the Cause destined to occur in its own good time, dependent on the receptivity of the population as a whole—it is a phenomenon which the Bahá'í communities, by their own activities, can prepare for and help to bring about. It is also a process which, once started, can be sustained."[24] As the House of Justice subsequently explained at Riḍván 1996:

> The phrase "advance in the process of entry by troops" accommodates the concept that current circumstances demand and existing opportunities allow for a sustained growth of the Bahá'í world community on a large scale; that this upsurge is necessary in the face of world conditions; that the three constituent participants in the upbuilding of the Order of Bahá'u'lláh—the individual, the institutions, and the community—can foster such growth first by spiritually and mentally accepting the possibility of it, and then by working towards embracing masses of new believers, setting in motion the means for effecting their spiritual and administrative training and development, thereby multiplying the number of knowledgeable, active teachers and administrators whose involvement in the work of the Cause will ensure a constant influx of new adherents, an uninterrupted evolution of Bahá'í Assemblies, and a steady consolidation of the community.
>
> Moreover, to advance the process implies that that process is already in progress and that local and national communities are at different stages of it. All communities are now tasked to take steps and sustain efforts to achieve a level of expansion and consolidation commensurate with their possibilities. The individual and the institutions, while operating in distinctive spheres, are summoned to arise to meet the requirements of this crucial time in the life of our community and in the fortunes of all humankind.[25]

This statement by the Universal House of Justice offered a crucial clarification around which unity of thought on entry by troops could be established. After so many years of confusion about large-scale growth, every national community could recognize that it was engaged in a single process of expansion and consolidation. While some were a bit ahead, and others a bit behind, all could advance. And to advance is to act in a systematic manner within the limits of existing resources and opportunities, not to implausibly leap from inaction to achieve barely imaginable results. "All should recognize," the House of Justice stated, "that entry by troops is an inevitable stage in the development of the Cause."[26] It was a process that would advance in all parts of the world, even those that appeared to be unreceptive to the Faith.

Furthermore, the House of Justice was able to pinpoint for the Bahá'í world the central obstacle to sustaining entry by troops: the inability to develop human resources at a rate necessary for carrying out the multitude tasks involved in accelerated growth. The central concern of the new Plan was to confront this challenge.

> With the growth in the number of enrollments, it has become apparent that such occasional courses of instruction and the informal activities of community life, though important, are not sufficient as a means of human resource development, for they have resulted in only a relatively small band of active supporters of the Cause. These believers, no matter how dedicated, no matter how willing to make sacrifices, cannot attend to the needs of hundreds, much less thousands, of fledgling local communities. Systematic attention has to be given by Bahá'í institutions to training a significant number of believers and assisting them in serving the Cause according to their God-given talents and capacities.
>
> The development of human resources on a large scale requires that the establishment of institutes be viewed in a new light. In many regions, it has become imperative to create institutes as organizational structures dedicated to systematic training.[27]

In addition to calling for a new approach to the development of human resources, the Four Year Plan provided an extraordinary wealth of guidance necessary for understanding the task at hand. Indeed, the Plan was grounded in eleven messages, including eight messages directed to various regions made up of groups of countries.[28] Among the topics discussed in detail were the role of the individual, the institutions, and the local community in advancing the process of entry by troops; the development of plans at the national, regional, and local levels; the evolution of the pattern of community life through stages of increasing complexity; and the responsibilities of the Counsellors and the Auxiliary Board members. In short, the Plan addressed the integration of all elements necessary to initiate and sustain the process of entry by troops.

The Four Year Plan resulted in a change in the Bahá'í community. A new state of mind, a new culture, systematization, and learning became the watchwords of a transition in Bahá'í practice related to growth and development. In November 1999, as the Four Year Plan was drawing to a close, the Universal House of Justice extended the period during which the worldwide community would continue to focus on advancing the process of entry by troops through the year 2021.

> The two stages in the unfoldment of the Divine Plan lying immediately ahead will last one year and five years respectively. At Riḍván 2000 the Bahá'í world will be asked to embark on the first of these two stages, a twelve-month effort aimed at concentrating the forces, the capacities and the insights that have so strongly emerged. The Five Year Plan that follows will initiate a series of worldwide enterprises that will carry the Bahá'í community through the final twenty years in the first century of the Faith's Formative Age. These global Plans will continue to focus on advancing the process of entry by troops and on its systematic acceleration.[29]

The Four Year Plan, the Twelve Month Plan, the Five Year Plans beginning in 2001 and 2006, and the subsequent Plans that will unfold until the year 2021 are a series of progressive steps of action and reflection on action in which the Bahá'í world is learning how to advance the process of entry by troops. During this period, the community will transform its understandings, its patterns of life, and many aspects of its institutional arrangements. The change of Bahá'í culture is the fruit of a change in the Bahá'í approach to understanding and practice—how we understand what is written and translate it into reality and action—as it pertains to the growth of the Faith.

The Experience of Colombia and the Ruhi Institute

Early in the Four Year Plan, a number of national communities attempted to develop training materials for their new institutes based on the criteria outlined by the Universal House of Justice, which called for a "well-defined sequence of courses"[30] and "well-organized, formal programs consisting of courses that follow appropriately designed curricula."[31] "The purpose of such training," the House of Justice explained "is to endow ever-growing contingents of believers with the spiritual insights, the knowledge, and the skills needed to carry out the many tasks of accelerated expansion and consolidation, including the teaching and deepening of a large number of people—adults, youth and children."[32] National communities were encouraged not to waste time on abstract theoretical concerns, nor to divert energy by offering a diverse catalog of courses. Rather, attention was to be given to a basic sequence of a few courses, preferably existing ones of proven effectiveness, that would rapidly confirm a significant number of believers and prepare them to contribute to the process of entry by troops. Training was intended as a means, not as an end in itself. As it turned out, diverse attempts by communities to create materials for a sequence of institute courses did not produce the desired result. Over time, more and more national communities adopted materials developed years earlier by the Ruhi Institute in Colombia, which enabled them to greatly accelerate their training process. The efficacy of these materials proved themselves through experience worldwide; so pronounced were the results that the materials were eventually promoted directly by the International Teaching Centre in 2000:

> The Ruhi Institute curriculum had been tested and adapted over many years. It has enabled the friends in different countries to get the institute system up and running in a short time. Rather than having the participants be passive listeners to a wide array of unconnected talks, the Ruhi Institute materials seek to engage the friends fully in the process of learning. Bahá'ís with diverse cultural and educational backgrounds have found the curriculum's deceptively simple approach, based heavily on connecting the believers to the Creative Word, both appealing and empowering.[33]

And at Riḍván 2004, the Universal House of Justice wrote:

> As foreseen, the training institute is proving to be an engine of growth. On assessing the opportunities and needs of their respective communities, the great majority of National Spiritual Assemblies have chosen to adopt the course materials devised by the Ruhi Institute, finding them most responsive to the Plan's needs. This has had the collateral benefit that the same materials have been translated into many languages and, wherever Bahá'ís travel, they find other friends following the same path and familiar with the same books and methods.[34]

Finally, a decade after the start of the Four Year Plan the House of Justice concluded:

When in our message dated 26 December 1995 we underscored the need for a formal program of training, we were aware that certain elements of a curriculum meeting the necessary requirements existed in the materials of the Ruhi Institute. It was our conviction, however, that the accumulated experience at that point did not justify our recommending a specific set of materials to be used by training institutes throughout the world. Therefore, the messages written by us and on our behalf in the early part of the Four Year Plan encouraged National Spiritual Assemblies and the Counsellors to open the way for training institutes to follow whatever curriculum they deemed appropriate. Yet, conscious of the inherent difficulty in creating comprehensive programs, we repeatedly expressed the view that the execution of plans should not await protracted decisions on the question of curriculum and that materials readily available should be used. The availability of such materials was limited worldwide, and National Spiritual Assemblies and institute boards began to adopt the books of the Ruhi Institute as they became aware of them, often through the Counsellors. By the time the Four Year Plan came to a close, it was all too apparent that national communities which had vigorously set out to implement the sequence of courses designed by the Ruhi Institute were far ahead of those who had attempted to develop their own program.

It was the Five Year Plan, however, that served to convince Counsellors, National Assemblies and boards everywhere of the merits of the Ruhi Institute curriculum. The introduction of the seventh book in the Institute's main sequence at the start of the Plan enabled many to appreciate more the intimate connection between the flow of individuals through a sequence of courses and the movement of clusters from one stage of growth to the next. Indeed, as progress was achieved in hundreds of clusters, it became clear to institutions at all levels that the content and order of the main sequence prepared the friends to carry out those acts of service required by the pattern of growth being established in a cluster. We have, in fact, described the dynamics of this relationship in our message of 27 December 2005.

We have now familiarized ourselves with the Ruhi Institute's present plans for curriculum development, which increasingly draw on experience worldwide in sustaining large-scale expansion and consolidation . . . With these thoughts in mind, we have reached the conclusion that the books of the Ruhi Institute should constitute the main sequence of courses for institutes everywhere, at least through the final years of the first century of the Formative Age when the Bahá'í community will be focused on advancing the process of entry by troops within the framework for action set forth in our 27 December message.

To select one curriculum to be used by training institutes worldwide for a certain period of time is not to ignore the variety of needs and interests of the friends as they endeavor to better equip themselves to understand and apply the teachings of Bahá'u'lláh. Nor does it in any way diminish the value of the efforts made to develop courses and materials to respond to these needs. It is not intended to suggest, either, that one curriculum should necessarily appeal to everyone. What this decision does imply, however, is that the present demands of the growth of the Faith are such that, for some years to come, training institutes should not attempt to meet all of the needs and interests of the friends.

The institutions of the Faith will continue to respect the wishes of those who, for whatever reason, do not feel inclined to participate in the study of the books of the Ruhi Institute. . . . What we ask of such friends, as we have in the past, is that they not allow their personal preferences to hamper in any way the unfoldment of an educational process that has shown the potential to embrace millions of souls from divers backgrounds.[35]

The educational approach of the Ruhi Institute was developed over more than two decades as part of a wider process of learning about large-scale expansion that took the Colombian community from a few hundred individuals in 1970 to more than 50,000 by 1990.[36] That community's struggle to find effective methods for expansion and consolidation was the same struggle taking place simultaneously in many other countries. Rather than succumbing to the tendency to split into competing viewpoints that often paralyzed progress elsewhere, however, the Bahá'ís in Colombia were able to maintain their unity, eventually establishing a culture of learning based on action and reflection. Their experience is recounted in the book, *Learning About Growth: The Story of the Ruhi Institute and Large-Scale Expansion of the Bahá'í Faith in Colombia.*

With a well-established unity of purpose to teach the masses and a newly achieved unity of thought on the nature of expansion and consolidation, the Colombian friends once again turned their attention to the practical path that would lead them to their cherished goal of large-scale expansion. At first, much of the consultation was directed to the search for a prescription that would bring about rapid success, but it soon became clear that such a quest was in vain and that the path to mass conversion would have to be pursued with constancy and discovered step by step. "What method to use" was not a simple matter to be determined though the clash of differing opinions; it would have to be the object of a long learning process and approached systematically and with perseverance.

. . . Plans and methods could not be perfect from the beginning, but had to evolve and increasingly reflect the principles of the Faith. These principles, themselves, would progressively come to be understood with greater clarity as everyone pursued diligently the goals that were set for each stage of the teaching process. The teachers and administrators of the Faith had to understand that many of their tasks were straightforward, even simple; they would have to resist the temptation to exaggerate the importance and complexity of their own roles and contributions. The most they could expect from themselves was to engage wholeheartedly in an intensive plan of action and an accompanying process of reflection and consultation. This reflection and consultation had to be carried out in unshakable unity and with a spirit of utmost humility. The main thrust of consultation had to be the objective analysis of possible courses of action and the evaluation of methods and results, all carried out in light of the Writings of the Faith. The purpose of joint reflection was to seek in the unfathomable depths of the ocean of Revelation the answers to questions, challenges, and problems and to discover the next steps in a path that, if trodden with absolute faith, would lead to unprecedented expansion. There was little more that could be done by the friends; success would be a gift from Bahá'u'lláh, in some way related to the intensity of their efforts and the spiritual quality of their endeavors.[37]

Of course, the community's commitment to a process of learning did not mean that problems would not arise or that the friends would not occasionally be confused or uncertain when evaluating results or trying to determine what to do next. But one idea became increasingly clear. It was imperative to pay attention to educating the new believers and training them to become active participants in the work of the Faith. The pattern of action and reflection that guided the search for effective methods of expansion and consolidation was now applied to the development of materials for training the new believers to become effective participants in service to the Cause. The Ruhi Institute emerged. Through a painstaking, yet joyous process of research, training and action, the Bahá'ís in Colombia gradually learned how to help new believers become confirmed and active. Their efforts gave rise to a specific approach to the creation of educational materials.

The approach to curriculum development can be summarized simply, in the following terms. Once an educational need is identified, a small group of people, working at the grass roots, consult among themselves, develop a set of ideas for educational activities, and put them into practice. The results of this practice are reviewed, evaluated and consulted upon; in light of this consultation, a modified set of educational activities is put into practice, and subjected to reflection that leads to further modification and revision. At no time in this process of curriculum development does action await the final preparation and evaluation of educational materials. At every stage, educational activities proceed with the best materials at hand, in the conviction that it is only through practice and reflection, both pursued in light of the Revelation of Bahá'u'lláh, that more appropriate curricula can gradually evolve. Yet, this is not a setting in which a few individuals are developing materials for their own use, and it does become necessary at some point to finalize the structure and content of each unit so that it may be used with confidence by others. The decision to release a final version of the materials for a given course is made simply when it is noticed that modifications are becoming negligible. It is important to note that the various aspects of this process of consultation, action and reflection are carried out parallel with one another, and not performed in a linear sequence which would be inherently artificial.[38]

This educational approach is not patterned after a specific educational theory, nor does it claim to present a "Bahá'í theory" of education.[39] At its heart is the study of the Bahá'í Writings. A specific effort is made to help the believers draw upon the Writings as a guide for action, while avoiding both an inflexible literalism intent upon "finding the one right answer" and an unfocused subjectivism that indulges in a prolonged exchange of personal views on "what the quotation means to me."[40] The tutor acts to foster the learning of the group in a participatory manner. Again a middle way is sought between the extremes of dispensing knowledge through lectures and of passively facilitating an experience driven entirely by the learners themselves with no intended goal. The responsibility for learning rests on the participants "who are constantly thinking, analyzing, formulating ideas and answering questions."[41] Memorization is part of the pedagogy, but not as rote learning. Rather, memorization of the Creative Word of God has a profound influence on stirring and galvanizing a soul. "Every word that proceedeth out of the mouth of God," Bahá'u'lláh states, "is endowed with such potency as can instill new life into every human frame."[42] This also fulfills His injunction that the believers "memorize phrases and passages bearing on various instances, so that in the course of their speech they may recite divine verses whenever the occasion demandeth it."[43] The passages come easily to mind when opportunities for teaching or proclamation arise, and their ensuing impact on hearts and minds amply demonstrates His divine promise that "so potent is their influence that the hearer will have no cause for vacillation."[44] Study is complemented by practice, whether conducted simultaneously during the gradual progression of a study circle or by participation in activities following the close of an intensive course. Indeed, the entire curriculum is organized around the concept of service through acts related to expansion and consolidation. Among the capacities cultivated are those pertaining to hosting devotional meetings, offering deepenings, educating children, teaching the Faith, and acting as a tutor of a study circle. An ever-expanding body of experience is essential for integrating the course content into new patterns of behavior, and for making sense of the material presented in courses later in the sequence.

The training program is not centered on conveying a fixed body of knowledge or on carrying out specifically defined functions, but on helping individuals to walk "paths of service."

> From among various possibilities, the Ruhi Institute has chosen "service to the Cause" as the organizing principle of its educational activities. The programs of the institute do, of course, address the importance of knowledge, the development of human potential, the need for personal transformation, and the appropriate

functioning of Bahá'í communities, just as Bahá'í courses f[
on any of the other concepts ... would also address "[
Nevertheless, the choice of an organizing principle is no[
one, for the resulting educational activities, the attitudes they
foster towards learning, and indeed the sum of all that emerges
from the educational process, will be strongly influenced by that
choice.

A believer's possibilities for service to the Cause of God are
enhanced by the development of certain capabilities, such as the
capability to teach on an individual basis, to participate in teaching campaigns organized by the community, to study the Writings
in progressively more meaningful ways, to participate effectively
in consultation, to help deepen new believers, and to educate
children and help youth channel their energies.[45]

Perhaps the most important capacity that the Ruhi materials
are designed to cultivate is the ability to participate in learning how
to advance the process of entry by troops. The focus is on raising
up thoughtful, creative protagonists of the progress of the Faith, not
mere technicians implementing a fixed methodology or formula for
expansion.[46] In an area where a sizable number of such individuals
are trained, study of the guidance, consultation, action, and reflection on action is part of the habitual practice, resulting in a culture
of learning and real progress for the Bahá'í community. Those who
serve as tutors are consciously engaged in the process of developing
these capable workers. As Book 7, *Walking Together on a Path of
Service*, emphasizes: "The purpose of our courses is to empower
the friends spiritually and morally to serve the Faith," and that
among the attributes to be cultivated are "a posture of learning,"
"dedication to the application of the Teachings," "an undeviating
sense of purpose and the will to accomplish things," and "a sense of
responsibility for one's personal growth and for the progress of the
Bahá'í community."[47]

The Bahá'ís of Colombia were attempting to sustain large-scale
expansion. From their own experiences they created training
materials to assist others to walk a path of service. The courses are
a record of the journey.

> ... a small group of people who were personally engaged in
> large-scale expansion and consolidation entered into a process of
> consultation about their successes and failures of their efforts. By
> reflecting on their own service and growth, they hoped to gain

new insights into the dynamics of the spiritual movement of entire populations. As this nucleus of people began to advance in their own paths of service and to discover certain spiritual requirements of these paths, they became engaged in an educational process that would prepare an increasing number of individuals to similarly dedicate themselves to the spiritual movement of their own people. Naturally, the courses and educational materials took shape through the same process of consultation/action/reflection that had evolved as the group's method of learning and service. Such an approach to curriculum development is clearly rooted in action.[48]

The purpose of this brief description is not to romanticize the experience of the Ruhi Institute or the Bahá'ís in Colombia. The Faith in Colombia has had, and continues to have, many trials and setbacks along with its achievements. Despite the development of the effective sequence of courses, for example, the community had not, by the start of the Four Year Plan, guided a significant percentage of its community members through the sequence of courses. Only by the end of the Five Year Plan in 2006 had a few clusters initiated intensive programs of growth. The balance between human resource development, expansion, and consolidation that can sustain the process of entry by troops remains a goal toward which Colombia, like all other countries, continues to strive. Nevertheless, the experience of the Ruhi Institute is a constructive example for the steadily evolving network of national and regional training institutes worldwide whose purpose is not simply to deliver a set of courses, but to become centers of learning capable of serving as engines of growth and development. As more and more institutes achieve this capacity for action and reflection in the light of the guidance of the Universal House of Justice, the effective programs that they create will be disseminated and adopted by other institutes thereby stimulating a global process of learning about growth that will greatly accelerate the progress of the Bahá'í world.

The materials developed by the Ruhi Institute do not constitute a Bahá'í catechism. They do not represent a body of fixed knowledge to be assimilated by every believer. The gradual adoption of these materials by Bahá'í training institutes worldwide since the Four Year Plan began was not an indication that these were the only courses that could have been used. They do not provide a formula for growth that is to be inflexibly followed; indeed, using the materials without the capacity for learning how to apply them in context, for integrating them with the many other elements necessary to sustain entry by troops, and for taking on new challenges that emerge, will not produce results. Rather, the Ruhi materials were the most practical and effective tool available at the time and proved, in action, their value as a training program designed to raise human resources that contribute to growth. They provided a basis for supporting and developing other aspects of the work, such as core activities, home visits, and intensive programs of growth. In the future, the materials will undoubtedly evolve, and will be supplemented by other courses. Such an evolution, however, can only be driven by the experience of those intimately involved in the ongoing efforts for expansion and consolidation.

A Decade of Progress

A decade of experience from 1996 to 2006, spanning the unfoldment of the Four Year, the Twelve Month, and the first Five Year Plan, illustrates how a dialogical learning process, operating under the guidance of the Universal House of Justice, contributes to the systematic progress of the Faith. As summarized above, the direction provided in the messages of the Four Year Plan emerged from an analysis of the results and experiences of previous work for entry by troops over several decades. Many national communities had a proven capacity to enlist thousands or even tens of thousands of new believers in a relatively short period of time, but were unable to complement the process through an equally effective process of consolidation; other countries, though strong administratively, had an inward focus and little growth. If there were not a change in the pattern of action followed over several decades, the Bahá'í world would not be capable of sustaining significant growth.

The Four Year Plan, the House of Justice explained in 1995, would have the single aim of advancing the process of entry by troops. This was to be achieved by "marked progress in the activity and development of the individual believer, of the institutions, and of the local community." "The next four years must witness a dramatic upsurge in effective teaching activities undertaken at the initiative of the individual," the House of Justice stated. "Thousands upon thousands of believers will need to be aided to express the vitality of their faith through constancy in teaching the Cause and by supporting the plans of their institutions and the endeavors of their communities."[49]

Some believers, surely, already had the necessary capacity to shoulder their responsibilities, yet this was not sufficient. The House of Justice observed that the effort to develop human resources endowed with the knowledge, skills and spiritual insights that would enable them to participate effectively in the process of entry by troops had to become more systematic and widespread, and, therefore, the central focus of the Plan became the establishment of a worldwide network of training institutes.

Creating in each country a system for effective training proved to be a formidable challenge. Some countries continued to struggle beyond the Plan's conclusion. Yet, the chief outcome of the Four Year Plan was the establishment of some 300 national and regional training institutes, whose courses reached over 100,000 individuals. Communities were revitalized by a host of confirmed and capable believers. This did not mean that the challenge of sustaining entry by troops was instantly resolved—quite the contrary. Progress in some areas only shed light on other problems and even greater challenges. But there was evidence everywhere that a fresh capacity was breathed into the Bahá'í world. As a result of the emergence of a new culture of learning involving study, consultation, action, and refection, Bahá'í communities were increasingly capable of identifying their challenges and making consistent progress.

Learning new patterns of effective, systematic action was extended in subsequent Plans. The Twelve Month Plan was designed to build directly on the work of the Four Year Plan. Institutes were to become fully operational in every country. Efforts were to include the development of a sequential program for child education. This reflected the reality that, first, up to the year 2000 child education in most countries was sporadic and the curriculum disjointed and, second, an advance in the process of entry by troops could be secured only if the next generation of children received a Bahá'í education. Another element of this brief Plan was the establishment of some 25 area growth programs that were carried out in selected countries to explore how systematic training could be linked with carefully organized teaching efforts to achieve sustainable growth.

By the start of the Five Year Plan in 2001, the House of Justice was able to speak of "the wealth of the experience now accumulated" and observe that "elements of a system that can meet the training needs of large numbers of believers have already been tested worldwide and have proven themselves."[50] The Plan concentrated on "two essential movements" described by the House of Justice:

> The first is the steady flow of believers through the sequence of courses offered by its training institute, for the purpose of developing the human resources of the Cause. The second, which receives its impetus from the first, is the movement of geographic clusters from one stage of growth to the next.[51]

In the Four Year Plan, most effort was directed toward establishing the structure of the institute: training tutors and creating the means to offer courses at a distance or in a central location. In many countries training centered largely on Books 1 and 2 of the Ruhi Institute. With this foundation in place, efforts in the Five Year Plan concentrated on accelerating training and initiating higher-level courses. In the period between Riḍván 1996 and February 2003, about ten thousand people completed Book 3 on teaching children's classes. By the midpoint of the Five Year Plan this figure reached 19,000—the accomplishment of seven years was nearly matched in seven months. The number completing Book 6 on teaching increased from about 3700 in February 2003 to more than 8000 in September of that year. By the end of the Plan, over a quarter of a million people had completed at least one course, and more than 35,000 had completed Book 7 which enabled them to act as tutors.

The Five Year Plan began with the effort to define specific geographic regions within a country—clusters—according to social patterns of the general population. Bahá'í communities then began to learn how to focus and organize their activities in order to reach out to the inhabitants of each cluster and to gradually create the conditions in which ever-increasing numbers would enter the Faith and assume responsibility for its progress. What the believers were learning through the institute courses had to be translated into practical patterns of action for teaching and community building. Three core activities devised principally to benefit the believers themselves—study circles, children's classes, and devotional meetings—emerged as portals for entry by troops. The following is one account of how the introduction of the institute process gradually gave rise to new activities and a growing number of enthusiastic participants:

A believer in Taiwan took the first step along the path of service and divine assistance followed. Living in . . . an area with almost no active believers, she took the initiative to begin a Bahá'í-inspired moral education class in a public elementary school. One parent was so impressed by the content of her child's class that she wished to know more. The Bahá'í teacher happened to be a trained tutor so she invited the mother to study Ruhi Institute Book 1. Not only did the mother agree, she asked five of her friends to join her!

This first study circle in the cluster, which began in March 2003, was held weekly and was supplemented by occasional deepenings on Bahá'í topics. By the time they started Book 2, all six mothers had embraced the Faith. As their faith deepened and their skills were enhanced by what they were learning through the institute process, these new believers began to hold devotional meetings and children's classes on their own. Three of these ladies in particular reached out to their friends, co-workers, and relatives, introducing them to Book 1 as well.

By December 2004, the original six participants in the first study circle had completed the entire sequence of courses. They were carrying out seven Book 1 study circles that included 24 non-Bahá'í participants in addition to four study circles for the higher courses of the sequence. They had established five children's classes for 28 mostly non-Bahá'í children, and were running a daily devotional meeting, which was attracting about 30 people. They even formed a group for junior youth after they observed the positive effect the Bahá'í Teachings had on their younger children. In total, there were 78 people regularly participating in their activities. All of the adults were mothers of preschool or school-aged children.

. . . In a neighborhood steeped in materialism and pastimes such as gambling and gossiping, these friends are inspired as they transform their lives, and in turn motivate others, by walking a spiritual path.[52]

When opened to the wider community, core activities provided opportunities for receptive individuals to intimately associate with Bahá'ís, feel the spirit of the Faith, draw inspiration and direction from the Creative Word, and participate in a social environment that promotes unity and service. Those who became Bahá'ís could immediately embark on a path of service and take their place in the forefront of activity in the cluster.

Over the course of the Plan, as the initiatives of individuals multiplied and attracted ever-wider participation, the Bahá'ís in almost 300 clusters learned how to establish intensive programs of growth, in which a gradualist approach to teaching gave way to more dynamic patterns that could incorporate large numbers of people. In certain of these clusters, year after year, hundreds of new believers could be enlisted and deepened, and a significant portion would arise to serve the Cause in some fashion. In those countries where teaching was more difficult, some clusters that had experienced little or sporadic growth before enlisted as many as 20-40 new believers in a year. The House of Justice described both these patterns:

> The pattern of expansion that unfolds, however, varies from cluster to cluster. Where the population has traditionally shown a high degree of receptivity to the Faith, a rapid influx of new believers is to be expected. In one cluster of this kind, for example, the goal of enrolling fifty souls over a three-week period in a locality was surpassed by the second day, and the team wisely decided to end the expansion phase in anticipation of activities related to consolidation. One of the primary objectives of this next phase is to bring a percentage of the new believers into the institute process so that an adequate pool of human resources will be available in future cycles to sustain growth. Those not participating in study circles are nurtured through a series of home visits, and all are invited to devotional meetings, to the celebration of the Nineteen Day Feast and to Holy Day observances and are gradually introduced to the patterns of community life. Not infrequently, the consolidation phase gives rise to further enrollments as the family members and friends of new declarants accept the Faith.
>
> In other clusters, enrollments during the expansion phase may not be high, especially in the first few cycles, and the goal is to augment the number of those willing to participate in core activities. This, then, defines the nature of the consolidation phase, which largely involves nurturing the interest of seekers and accompanying them in their spiritual search until they are confirmed in their faith. To the extent that these measures are vigorously followed, this phase can generate a considerable number of enrollments. It should be noted, however, that as learning

advances and experience is gained, the ability not only to teach responsive souls, but also to identify segments of the general population with heightened receptivity, develops, and the totality of new believers increases from cycle to cycle.[53]

The experience of the Murun cluster in Mongolia, one of the first to establish an intensive program of growth, demonstrates the unfoldment of the program across successive cycles. As described by the International Teaching Centre:

> An example of an intensive program of growth is the rural Murun cluster in Mongolia. By the end of the third year of the Plan, 46 individuals in the cluster had completed the entire sequence of courses. Steady teaching activities had resulted in 228 enrollments that year, which raised the Bahá'í population to some 500. An intensive program of growth to achieve a sizable increase in enrollments was initiated in June 2004. The first year of the program was envisioned as having four three-month cycles. An analysis of the human resources determined that more tutors might be required, so the first cycle began with a two-week intensive course on Ruhi Institute Books 6 and 7, which brought the number of believers completing the sequence to 71. This preparatory phase was followed by a two-week teaching project. Nineteen teaching teams of three to five members each were mobilized, which made contact with 780 individuals resulting in 200 new declarations, including 60 junior youth. A consolidation phase of two months immediately followed and reached the new believers and receptive individuals with home visits and core activities. Within a few weeks about 30 of these individuals had completed the first three books of the sequence and 137 children were participating in children's classes. In early November, once a majority of the new Bahá'ís were involved in the institute process and core activities, the friends in the Murun cluster felt ready to proceed with the second cycle of the growth program. Within a week the intensive teaching project had resulted in 73 new believers and an additional 10 regular devotional meetings, 32 deepening visits, 13 study circles, and one junior youth group.[54]

Subsequent cycles of the growth program in the Murun cluster showed continued progress. At the end of the third cycle there were 37 teaching teams, over 2000 in total had been contacted, and there were over six hundred new Bahá'ís.[55] Near Riḍván 2006, after eight cycles of activity, the number of Bahá'ís in the cluster surpassed 1900. The number of individuals that moved through the sequence of courses continually increased; study circles, children's classes and devotional meetings multiplied; the believers were transformed and community life enriched; the first activities for social and economic development emerged; and the friends had learned from cycle to cycle how to improve their efforts.

In 1996, Bahá'í communities were, for the most part, small and inwardly directed. In some countries this was the result of the lack of effective teaching, and, in other countries, of the lack of success in deepening the new believers who were enlisted in successive waves of teaching activity. The 26 December 1995 message of the Universal House of Justice that introduced the Four Year Plan "focused the Bahá'í world on a path of intense learning about the sustained, rapid growth of the Faith," but could only describe "in general terms the nature of the work that would have to be undertaken in meeting the challenges ahead."[56] By 2006, after a decade of learning, the House of Justice was able to describe a new pattern of action involving a coherent integration of activities for expansion, consolidation, and spiritual upliftment that were mutually reinforcing and which could be readily replicated in other areas. "The elements required for a concerted effort to infuse the diverse regions of the world with the spirit of Bahá'u'lláh's Revelation," it stated, "have crystallized into a framework for action that now needs only to be exploited."[57] "The way forward is clear, and at Riḍván 2006 we will call upon the believers to steel their resolve and to proceed with the full force of their energies on the course that has been so decidedly set."[58] The problem of sustaining large-scale expansion that stymied the Bahá'í world for almost four decades found a resolution in less than ten years.

Characteristics and Achievements of a Learning Mode

The achievements of the Four Year Plan were attributed by the Universal House of Justice to a change in the culture of the Bahá'í community that resulted from a new capacity for learning. Learning drove progress across the entire decade, from the first efforts to establish training institutes at Riḍván 1996 to the emergence of intensive programs of growth in certain clusters by Riḍván 2006. What was the nature of this learning process? What were some of the specific lessons learned?

At the start of each Plan, and at Riḍván and other strategic points during the decade, the Universal House of Justice provided guidance to the Baháʾí world based on its current level of development, summarizing what had been learned and accomplished, and outlining new directions and challenges. The Counsellors gathered several times in the Holy Land to receive guidance on the Plans and to consult on its various aspects. They returned to participate with National Assemblies in consultations on how to implement the guidance. The believers, accompanied by the Counsellors and their Auxiliary Board members, engaged in action carried out in a learning mode. Reflection meetings, intended for participatory discussions to assess experience, generate enthusiasm and improve practice, became a part of the pattern of local action.

A steady stream of questions flowed to the Baháʾí World Centre, to which the Universal House of Justice would respond with clarifications or additional elucidation. For example, study circles, initially intended as a means to provide institute courses to individuals in their communities proved to be attractive to those who were not Baháʾís but were interested in studying the teachings. As many of these individuals accepted the Faith, often after studying one or two books, it was realized that study circles could be tools of teaching as well as training. Some mistakenly concluded, however, that Baháʾís were being told to abandon firesides or other teaching methods and replace them by study circles. To a query on this matter a letter written on behalf of the House of Justice responded:

> To call upon the Baháʾí world to focus its energies on a certain set of activities at a particular stage in the unfoldment of the Divine Plan does not in any way diminish the importance of other endeavors. . . . While it is highly desirable to include seekers in study circles wherever possible, the individual believer retains the inescapable duty to teach the Faith on his or her own initiative.[59]

Another point of confusion arose when some understood that the new Four Year Plan obliged everyone to participate in institute courses. Individuals who expressed this concern received the following clarification:

> It is natural that any given educational program would not appeal to everyone, and clearly participating in the courses of an institute is not a requirement to be fulfilled by all believers. In no way, then, should those who do not wish to take part feel that they

As clusters advanced, the nature of the reflection gathering evolved from an occasion for the promotion of initiative among a small group of interested individuals to a mechanism for the integration of activities and for directing the energies of an increasing number of capable workers in intensive programs of growth organized by the institutions serving the cluster. When an intensive program of growth was established, reflection meetings became a feature of a more elaborate phase of learning and planning that included both individuals and institutions.[64]

> Key to the progress of an intensive program of growth is the phase dedicated to reflection, in which the lessons learned in action are articulated and incorporated into plans for the next cycle of activity. Its principal feature is the reflection meeting—as much a time of joyous celebration as it is of serious consultation. Careful analysis of experience, through participatory discussions rather than overly complex and elaborate presentations, serves to maintain unity of vision, sharpen clarity of thought and heighten enthusiasm. Central to such an analysis is the review of vital statistics that suggest the next set of goals to be adopted. Plans are made that take into account increased capacity in terms of the human resources available at the end of the cycle to perform various tasks, on the one hand, and accumulated knowledge about the receptivity of the population and the dynamics of teaching, on the other.[65]

Within a cluster, it was the daily struggle of individuals to grasp the Plan and act on it that drove progress. This was true not only of new believers, but also of long-time members of the community who were used to seeing others carry the responsibility for the work of teaching and deepening. So many of these believers had to overcome their fears and perceptions of inadequacy, and the courses of the training institute were particularly helpful to them as they tried to face new realities. "Discussions that revolve around the Creative Word, in the serious and uplifting atmosphere of a study circle, raise the level of consciousness about one's duties to the Cause and create an awareness of the joy one derives from teaching the Faith and serving its interests," the Universal House of Justice explained. "Confidence is patiently built as the friends engage in progressively more complex and demanding acts of service." "Seeing the possibilities and opportunities before them with new eyes," the House of Justice adds, "they witness first hand the power of Divine assistance, as they strive to put into practice what they are learning and achieve results far exceeding their expectations." Stories from across the world illustrated how "believers who enter the teaching field with trepidation" found themselves "bolstered by confirmations on all sides."[66] As one believer reported:

> At the Book 6 refresher on Saturday morning, . . . I worked on memorizing the first section of Anna's presentation. We tried to get the presentation down as closely to the text as possible, and practiced presenting it to each other over and over. I was a bit worried going into the home visit that my presentation might be a bit too rehearsed or mechanical, but it ended up turning out just fine. . . . Within our first few breaths we were sharing that the Bahá'í Faith is a world religion whose purpose is to unite humanity in one universal cause and one common faith, that Bahá'ís believe that Bahá'u'lláh is the Promised One of all ages, and that He is the Great Personage whose teachings will create a new world! I have never before shared the Faith with someone in such a forthright manner, and it felt exhilaratingly honest and direct.
>
> . . . I reflected afterwards that [the seeker] seemed very receptive to this and that it appeared that this acceptance had already occurred in his heart, and we thought that perhaps the next step is to share more of the presentation on a subsequent visit and more explicitly invite him to formally declare. . . .
>
> In essence, although I felt trepidation going into it, the home visit was the highlight of my weekend, and I really felt the confirming and assisting spirit throughout the experience. It has got us thinking about teaching the Faith in a whole new way, and we are really excited that once we incorporate this presentation more fully into our consciousness, we will be able to share it in a variety of contexts.[67]

By the end of the decade, a strong network was established throughout the Bahá'í world as learning emerged in a particular cluster and then flowed to the World Centre and back to nations, regions, and clusters in all parts of the world. Effective methods to translate the guidance into action emerged sometimes quickly from creative initiatives, but often had to be patiently refined over years through constant revision and reflection. Not all efforts led immediately to successful results. Problems arose that obstructed progress in particular areas; these had to be overcome through perseverance and sacrifice, and through unified action. But all new learning of this kind is, in essence, learning how to resolve problems in order to make new advances. While it is impossible to summarize all the lessons learned in the decade from 1996 to 2006, the following examples illustrate how various elements emerged and were combined to shape an integrated pattern of action that has proven its effectiveness in diverse settings worldwide.

- At the start of the Four Year Plan, the House of Justice observed that institutes "must offer courses both at a central location and in the villages and towns so that an appreciable number of believers can enter its programs."[68] No specific approach was described, however, for offering the courses at a distance. By 1998, as a result of the experience in one area, a practical approach was discovered involving the establishment of study circles, groups of some "six to ten believers in the towns and villages throughout the country, who will go through a series of basic courses together with a tutor."[69] Because of their proven effectiveness, study circles soon became a feature of institutes worldwide.

- In 2001, the House of Justice made reference to stages of community building and observed that "among the initial goals for every community should be the establishment of study circles, children's classes, and devotional meetings, open to all the inhabitants of the locality."[70] One year later, as a result of the experience gained by implementing these activities, the House of Justice observed promising indications that went far beyond what was originally envisioned:

> Where a training institute is well established and constantly functioning, three core activities—study circles, devotional meetings, and children's classes—have multiplied with relative ease. Indeed, the increasing participation of seekers in these activities, at the invitation of their Bahá'í friends, has lent a new dimension to their purposes, consequently effecting new enrollments. Here, surely, is a direction of great promise for the teaching work. These core activities, which at the outset were devised principally to benefit the believers themselves, are naturally becoming portals for entry by troops. By combining study circles, devotional meetings and children's classes within the framework of clusters, a model of coherence in lines of action has been put in place and is

already producing welcome results. Worldwide application of this model, we feel confident, holds immense possibilities for the progress of the Cause in the years ahead.[71]

- The experience with some 25 area growth programs in the Twelve Month Plan contributed directly to the specification of propitious conditions for the establishment of intensive programs of growth presented in the Five Year Plan. Yet, in 2001, it was not possible to describe the specific nature of an intensive program of growth, but only to clarify some desirable conditions and outline general principles. "Success will depend on the manner in which lines of action are integrated and on the attitude of learning that is adopted," the House of Justice wrote. "At the core of the program must lie a sound and steady process of expansion, matched by an equally strong process of human resource development," it further explained. "A range of teaching efforts needs to be carried out, involving both activities undertaken by the individual and campaigns promoted by the institutions."[72]

  By the midpoint of the Plan, the features of the intensive program of growth emerged from experience and, by its end, they could be clearly defined. "Conforming well to the vision we presented five years ago," the House of Justice explained, such a program "consists of cycles of activity, in general of three months' duration each, which proceed according to distinct phases of expansion, consolidation, reflection and planning."[73] "The expansion phase," the House of Justice added, "often a period of two weeks, demands the highest level of intensity. Its objective is to widen the circle of those interested in the Faith, to find receptive souls and to teach them."[74] Further, it became clear that institute courses should proceed uninterrupted from cycle to cycle because "When human resources increase in a manner proportionate to the rise in the overall Bahá'í population from cycle to cycle, it is possible not only to sustain but to accelerate growth."[75]

- The role of those who would serve as tutors of institute courses evolved over the course of the entire decade. Veteran believers were initially involved, many having no first hand experience with the materials they were sharing with others. During the Four Year Plan, regular gatherings of tutors in which they could learn about effective methods discovered through experience constituted a significant component of the institute process in many countries. By the start of the Five Year Plan, Book 7 of the Ruhi Institute, *Walking Together on a Path of Service*, which focuses on the service of the tutor, became available; it was developed through the experience of training tutors from many parts of the world rather than Colombia alone. With the addition of this book to the sequence of courses, the number of trained tutors rapidly multiplied. It became increasingly clear that tutors were not to merely assist the friends to move through the courses; it was also important for them to engage in "accompanying participants in their initial attempts to perform acts of service." In outlining the second Five Year Plan launched at Riḍván 2006 the House of Justice referred to such accompaniment: "This particular aspect of the institute process, which serves to multiply the number of active supporters of the Faith in a self-perpetuating manner, holds much promise, and we hope that its potential will be realized in the coming Plan."[76]

- Early in the Five Year Plan, the International Teaching Centre observed that when a sizable number of individuals in a cluster completed the sequence of institute courses, there was a corresponding increase in core activities and a revitalization of the teaching work. In certain clusters, however, the friends, eager to reach these numbers rapidly, left out key elements of the courses, especially those involving the practice of new skills essential to the overall scheme of the process. Guidance to the increasing number of clusters that were determined to move ahead soon incorporated this lesson, as conveyed in the following statement by the International Teaching Centre:

  > In some areas, the eagerness of the believers and institutions to achieve certain targets in the institute process has led them to eliminate portions of the courses, particularly the practice components, which are an essential aspect of training. If the friends are never able to apply the skills they are learning, they will not become effective in carrying out the tasks of expansion and consolidation. It has become clear that to move quickly through the training does not mean reducing the number of hours spent on a course; it means completing

the same course and its practices in their entirety, but in a shorter period of time—perhaps days instead of weeks or weeks instead of months. A balanced approach is needed that avoids the potential pitfalls of rapid training that fails to cultivate skills and multiply activities, or endless training to achieve capacities that would be developed more fully through practical experience.

We have noted that at times the focus on taking 50 or so believers through the sequence of courses has resulted in rigid or overly simplistic perspectives. In some clusters that contained all the needed resources and core activities for intensive growth, initiating a growth program was delayed because there were, for example, only 46 believers who had completed the full sequence. Meanwhile, in clusters where the target of 50 was achieved, there was sometimes the expectation that this would automatically result in growth. In such instances it is important to remember that having 40 to 50 believers complete the sequence is not a magic formula. It is an indicator that has to be viewed in the context of other propitious conditions as well as the success at outreach and teaching already achieved in the cluster.[77]

- In a number of clusters, the temporary yet often unavoidable rigidity that arises during the early implementation of new methods on the one hand, and the apprehension of some to engage fully in unified action on the other, led to a debate on flexibility. Some of the friends seemed to demand that all methods and activities for expansion and consolidation be supported equally. Yet, no learning or advancement can occur when every method and activity is regarded *a priori* as equal to all others. In clusters where the issue became a subject of prolonged debate, the energies of the community were dissipated, and the intensity of action required for progress was not achieved. A better understanding of the importance of maintaining focus was required, and this was eventually provided by the House of Justice in the message dated December 27, 2005 to the Counsellors' conference that introduced the second Five Year Plan.

Perhaps the task that will occupy the attention of you and your auxiliaries above all others is to assist the community in its effort to maintain focus. This ability, slowly acquired through successive Plans, represents one of its most valuable assets, hard won through discipline, commitment and foresight as the friends and their institutions have learned to pursue the single aim of advancing the process of entry by troops. On the one hand, you will find it necessary to discourage the tendency to confuse focus with uniformity or exclusivity. To maintain focus does not imply that special needs and interests are neglected, much less that essential activities are dropped in order to accommodate others. Clearly, there are a host of elements that comprise Baháʼí community life, shaped over the decades, which must be further refined and developed. On the other hand, you will want to take every opportunity to reinforce the disposition to prioritize—one which recognizes that not all activities have the same importance at a given stage of growth, that some must necessarily take precedence over others, that even the most well-intentioned proposals can cause distraction, dissipate energy or impede progress. What should be plainly acknowledged is that the time available for the friends to serve the Faith in every community is not without limits. It is only natural to expect that the preponderating share of this limited resource would be expended in meeting the provisions of the Plan.[78]

- Work with junior youth received impetus from the statement of the Universal House of Justice a few months before the start of the Twelve Month Plan that "Strategies to advance the process of entry by troops cannot ignore children and junior youth, if the victories won in one generation are not to be lost with the passage of time."[79] In most countries, however, junior youth activities continued to be extensions of children's classes. In some cases, junior youth entered prematurely the basic sequence of institute courses. This brought limited results, for most of them, while going through the courses enthusiastically, were not equipped to fully grasp the implications of the concepts being discussed or to undertake the necessary acts of service. During the Five Year Plan, the Office of Social and Economic Development collaborated with a number of Baháʼí and Baháʼí-inspired organizations on literacy projects that eventually led to a primary focus on junior youth and the creation of some effective educational materials. Baháʼí training institutes quickly saw the value of the experience being accumulated in development activities, and began to incorporate the curricular elements available into their programs for junior youth. A new chapter opened in the learning process, with the friends in scores of countries striving for a greater understanding of how to contribute to the spiritual, moral, and social development of youth ages 12-14. Eventually, the materials for training junior youth animators developed through experience in communities around the world led to a reorganization of the basic sequence of courses of the Ruhi Institute. A new Book 5 displaced the previous one for children's class teachers of grade 2, which in turn became a branch course of Book 3. The work with junior youth broadened and by the start of the second Five Year Plan in 2006 the Universal House of Justice wrote:

> What has become especially apparent during the current Five Year Plan is the efficacy of educational programs aimed at the spiritual empowerment of junior youth. When accompanied for three years through a program that enhances their spiritual perception, and encouraged to enter the main sequence of institute courses at the age of fifteen, they represent a vast reservoir of energy and talent that can be devoted to the advancement of spiritual and material civilization. So impressed are we by the results already achieved, and so compelling is the need, that we will urge all National Assemblies to consider the junior youth groups formed through programs implemented by their training institutes a fourth core activity in its own right and to promote its wide-scale multiplication.[80]

▪ As the activities for expansion and consolidation evolved through action and reflection over the course of the decade, administrative arrangements also evolved. In 1997, as a result of "the experience gained in the operation" of various regional bodies, and "from detailed examination of the principles set forth by Shoghi Effendi," the Universal House of Justice decided "to formalize a new element of Bahá'í administration, between the local and national levels, comprising institutions of a special kind, to be designated as 'Regional Bahá'í Councils.'" In explaining this action it stated: "The expansion of the Bahá'í community and the growing complexity of the issues which are facing National Spiritual Assemblies in certain countries have caused us in recent years to examine various aspects of the balance between centralization and decentralization."[81]

At the start of the Five Year Plan, attention focused on institutional capacity at the level of the cluster. The implementation of an intensive program of growth, the House of Justice explained, "will require the close collaboration of the institute, the Auxiliary Board members and their assistants, and an Area Teaching Committee."[82] Gradually, new relationships among the agencies involved in supporting intensive programs of growth, including Local Spiritual Assemblies, began to emerge. In some cases, the rapid growth of the community and the complexity of its activities called for full or part time staff. Change at the cluster level required corresponding changes in national administration, including the structure of National Committees. By the end of the decade, most agencies of Bahá'í administration at all levels were affected by the changes in the approach to growth and development of the Faith.[83]

These examples highlight several areas of learning about growth in the decade from 1996 to 2006. Yet, potential achievements and additional challenges remain for the current and future Plans. In the second year of the Five Year Plan from 2006-2011, for example, great strides were made in the expansion of the Faith through the dissemination of learning from cluster to cluster. Capable individuals from advanced clusters experiencing growth were sent for extended periods as resource persons to share their learning with other areas, while individuals from promising clusters were sent for training and practice to clusters where significant growth was evident. The believers learned to find receptive populations in rural and urban areas and to teach them in a direct and open manner. Coherence in the pattern of activities for expansion and consolidation emerged in which collective teaching efforts were carried out for some two to three weeks during a cycle's expansion phase and were immediately followed by a transition to consolidation through the core activities. This pattern led to scores of new believers in a single cycle, even in areas that had previously demonstrated little potential for success in teaching. It also proved to be a pattern that could begin simply even in the least developed clusters and unfold organically, allowing these areas to achieve in months what had previously taken years in other places. These insights led to another great acceleration in the work: from 1996 to 2006 about 300 intensive programs of growth were initiated, but by 2008 this number passed 600, with a goal of some 1100 by Riḍván 2009. The learning from this period is summarized in the document *Attaining the Dynamics of Growth: Glimpses from Five Continents*, prepared by the International Teaching Centre in 2008.

Looking into the future, the continuing progress of the Faith in the clusters will depend upon learning how to further develop Bahá'í community life, to strengthen Local Spiritual Assemblies, and to address the needs of a growing body of believers and the wider community through greater involvement in the life of society,[84] including projects of social and economic development. Administration at the local, cluster, regional, and national levels has to continue to evolve to sustain growth and to serve large, dynamic communities with all their potential and problems. Of more than 16,000 clusters at the start of the second Five Year Plan in 2006, some 10,000 remained unopened to the Faith and less than 2% were capable of taking on the challenge of growth; even the ambitious goal of establishing at least 1500 intensive programs of growth by 2011 will reach fewer than 10% of the clusters worldwide. Unforeseen obstacles surely lie ahead as well. Yet, by 2006, a clear breakthrough had been achieved, and a path for the progress of cluster after cluster had been charted, to be systematically pursued in future Plans through the year 2021.

Change in Understanding and Practice

The change in culture in the Bahá'í community over the decade that made possible an advance in the process of entry by troops was, in essence, a change in understanding and practice. The Bahá'í community became increasingly involved in a dialogical process combining study, consultation, action and reflection to understand the Writings and the guidance of the Universal House of Justice and translate this understanding into practical and effective action. As the House of Justice described the challenge of the recent Plans:

> Many issues related to the process of growth are complex in nature and can only be clarified in the minds of the friends over time, as they participate in the collective endeavors of their communities. . . .
>
> Of paramount importance . . . is the attitude of learning being adopted by believers and institutions throughout the Bahá'í world. It is necessary for the friends to fully appreciate the change needed and that new ideas not be measured by old modes of thinking,

which, while valuable in many respects, have not been conducive to rapid growth. The challenge for the friends everywhere is to study the guidance issued by the House of Justice, on the one hand, and to learn from experience as they strive to put that guidance into practice, on the other. Such an evolutionary process requires patience and perseverance on the part of all the believers, as we endeavor both individually and collectively to advance the process of entry by troops.[85]

By addressing the challenge of expansion and consolidation through learning, the community was able to overcome the paralysis originating in debates on the best method of teaching and arguments about the success or failure of particular initiatives. It also began to move beyond the freneticism and stagnation that comes from a relativistic tendency to encourage all methods and activities according to personal preference, undermining the critical thought necessary for the cultivation and diffusion of ever-more effective action. The result was an integration of various activities into a vibrant and sustainable pattern of growth, resulting not only in quantitative but also qualitative change. As the Universal House of Justice stated:

> On several occasions we have made reference to the coherence that is brought to the process of growth through the establishment of study circles, devotional meetings and children's classes. The steady multiplication of core activities, propelled by the training institute, creates a sustainable pattern of expansion and consolidation that is at once structured and organic. As seekers join these activities and declare their faith, individual and collective teaching endeavors gather momentum. Through the effort made to ensure that a percentage of the new believers enroll in the institute courses, the pool of human resources required to carry out the work of the Faith swells. When strenuously pursued in a cluster, all of this activity eventually brings about conditions favorable for launching an intensive program of growth.
>
> What a close examination of clusters at this threshold confirms is that the coherence thus achieved extends to various aspects of community life. The study and application of the teachings become a pervasive habit, and the spirit of communal worship generated by devotional meetings begins to permeate the community's collective endeavors. A graceful integration of the arts into diverse activities enhances the surge of energy that mobilizes

the believers. Classes for the spiritual education of children and junior youth serve to strengthen the roots of the Faith in the local population. Even an act of service as simple as visiting the home of a new believer, whether in a village in the Pacific Islands or in a vast metropolitan area like London, reinforces ties of fellowship that bind the members of the community together. Conceived as a means for exposing believers to the fundamentals of the Faith, "home visits" are giving rise to an array of deepening efforts, both individual and collective, in which the friends are delving into the Writings and exploring their implications for their lives.

As the spiritual foundations of the community are fortified in this way, the level of collective discourse is raised, social relations among the friends take on new meaning, and a sense of common purpose inspires their interactions. Little wonder, then, that a study carried out by the International Teaching Centre shows that, in some fifty advanced clusters surveyed, the quality of the Nineteen Day Feast has improved. Other reports indicate that contributions to the Fund have increased as consciousness of its spiritual significance expands and the need for material means is better understood. Reflection meetings at the cluster level are becoming a forum for the discussion of needs and plans, creating a collective identity and strengthening the collective will. Where such advanced clusters are flourishing, the influence they exert begins to spread beyond their own borders to enrich regional events, such as summer and winter schools.[86]

Efforts to advance the process of entry by troops also reflected a proper Bahá'í expression of power and authority. Individuals, whose capacities for advancing the teaching work were enhanced by the educational programs of the training institute, were empowered to take initiative.[87] Institutions learned not to exercise authority in a manner to control or inhibit individual action, but to release it, support it, multiply it, integrate it, and guide it along more effective channels.[88] Institutional arrangements evolved and new ones were created in order to efficiently advance the teaching work.[89]

A more conscious approach to understanding the teachings about growth and translating them into action created change in the pattern of Bahá'í community life and the way in which Bahá'ís interacted with the wider society—a change in social reality. The tendency to be inwardly directed that was unfortunately beginning to achieve prevalence was curbed. Bahá'í practice among individuals, communities, and institutions struggling to overcome ingrained habits reached out to the wider population and cultivated an enriching environment where all were welcome participants. As the House of Justice explained to an individual concerned about the stagnation of the growth of his community:

> Where Bahá'í communities are unable to free themselves from an orientation to Bahá'í life that has long outlived whatever value it once possessed, the teaching work will lack both the systematic character it requires, and the spirit that must animate all effective service to the Cause. To mistakenly identify Bahá'í community life with the mode of religious activity that characterizes the general society—in which the believer is a member of a congregation, leadership comes from an individual or individuals presumed to be qualified for the purpose, and personal participation is fitted into a schedule dominated by concerns of a very different nature— can only have the effect of marginalizing the Faith and robbing the community of the spiritual vitality available to it.
>
> . . . the Four Year Plan, the Twelve Month Plan and the current Five Year Plan have been designed as progressive steps in achieving this change of Bahá'í culture. . . .[90]

Naturally, the achievements of the past decade did not come without difficulties, nor are they yet realized universally in every cluster throughout the world. But the efficacy of the approach since 1996 is irrefutably demonstrated by the widespread capacity and spirit of joy, thanksgiving, and sacrifice evident at the 41 regional conferences marking the midpoint of the Five Year Plan held in all parts of the world from November 2008 to February 2009.[91] As the capacity for learning is extended and nurtured, the relationship between a community of inquirers exploring new frontiers of Bahá'í understanding and practice and the divinely-inspired guidance that flows through the Universal House of Justice becomes clearer. The counsel provided in the Plans is not a formula or rigid set of procedures for what must be done. If, as Bahá'ís, we are not consciously striving, within the framework of the Plan, to understand new concepts and thoughtfully apply principles and approaches through action and reflection in a specific setting, we will not see progress. Further, the guidance we receive is not simply a list of suggestions from which individuals or institutions choose according to their own preferences. The question is not *does* the guidance apply, but rather, *how* does the guidance apply? How is it translated effectively into reality? Without the capacity to think and adapt to discover practical manifestations of the guidance, communities will not see results. And once effective patterns of action are established in any community, the experience can be shared with others. Bahá'í understanding and practice associated with expansion and consolidation will continually evolve throughout the dispensation as the Bahá'í community grows in size, complexity, and influence and learns to make greater and greater contributions to a process of social transformation that is the expression of Bahá'u'lláh's will and purpose for humanity.

4
Contributing to the Advancement of Civilization

T HE FRUIT OF BAHÁ'U'LLÁH'S STUPENDOUS REVELATION, Shoghi Effendi tells us, will be the birth and efflorescence of a global civilization "such as no mortal eye hath ever beheld or human mind conceived."[1] Indeed, central to Bahá'í belief is the doctrine of progressive revelation, which holds that every Manifestation of God has infused the earth with a spirit that disrupts the old order, transforms individuals, and ultimately results in the unfoldment of a new civilization. One of the distinctive features of the age of maturity in humanity's development, however, is that the civilization associated with Bahá'u'lláh's dispensation will not be a mere by-product of the principles and teachings He has revealed. Rather, its unfoldment will be a conscious[2] process in which individuals endowed with a new understanding create new patterns of action to translate His vision into social reality.

To say that the process of building a new civilization is a conscious one does not imply that the outcome depends exclusively on the believers' initiatives. The Writings clearly describe the release of "creative energies" that have "instilled into humanity the capacity to attain" the "final stage in its organic and collective evolution."[3] The great "plan of God" is "tumultuous in its progress, working through mankind as a whole, tearing down barriers to world unity and forging humankind into a unified body in the fires of suffering and experience."[4]

So too, emphasis on the contributions Bahá'ís are to make to the civilization-building process is not intended to diminish the significance of efforts being exerted by others. A host of individuals and institutions contribute to the forces that are propelling social transformation. These include numerous well-intentioned and dedicated protagonists of change whose accomplishments have made progress in every field of human endeavor possible, and from whom Baháʼís have much to learn. "There are many souls who are promoters of peace and reconciliation and are longing for the realization of the oneness and unity of the world of humanity," ʻAbduʼl-Bahá explains. Nevertheless, He reminds us that this intention and effort are in need of a "dynamic power."[5] Baháʼís, then, develop their own capacity to draw on the power of divine assistance in service to humanity while learning to collaborate effectively with like-minded individuals and organizations.

The Baháʼí vision of a new civilization is

> as far removed from current concepts of human well-being and happiness as is possible. We should constantly be on our guard lest the glitter and tinsel of an affluent society should lead us to think that such superficial adjustments to the modern world as are envisioned by humanitarian movements or are publicly proclaimed as the policy of enlightened statesmanship—such as an extension to all members of the human race of the benefits of a high standard of living, of education, medical care, technical knowledge—will of themselves fulfill the glorious mission of Baháʼuʼlláh. Far otherwise. . . . "The principle of the oneness of mankind," [Shoghi Effendi] writes, "implies an organic change in the structure of present-day society, a change such as the world has not yet experienced."[6]

The movement toward a global civilization is, therefore, an organic process in which God's purpose for humanity becomes gradually realized. To the degree that unity of thought on a myriad of concepts is reached, the construction of the social reality that constitutes a new civilization proceeds. Once again, the challenge involves understanding and practice. The promotion of fundamental change in the very structure of society requires that systematic yet informal learning to foster the development of the Baháʼí community, as illustrated in the previous chapter, be complemented by a process of learning that employs more formal methods—involving both religion and science—in which Baháʼuʼlláh's teachings are applied in the diverse fields of human endeavor. Consider, in this respect, the following passages of ʻAbduʼl-Bahá calling for the generation and application of knowledge to recast social reality.

> The aims of the Baháʼís are these: to raise aloft the banner of the Most Great Peace, and to eradicate the causes of war and

conflict in every land; to gather together all nations and peoples within the shadow of the all-embracing Tabernacle of God, and to eliminate prejudice—whether racial, national, religious, sectarian, or political—from the face of the globe; so that all nations merge into one nation. Thus may the world of creation attain unto well-being and repose.[7]

How long shall we drift on the wings of passion and vain desire; how long shall we spend our days like barbarians in the depths of ignorance and abomination? God has given us eyes, that we may look about us at the world, and lay hold of whatsoever will further civilization and the arts of living. He has given us ears, that we may hear and profit by the wisdom of scholars and philosophers and arise to promote and practice it. Senses and faculties have been bestowed upon us, to be devoted to the service of the general good; so that we, distinguished above all other forms of life for perceptiveness and reason, should labor at all times and along all lines, whether the occasion be great or small, ordinary or extraordinary, until all mankind are safely gathered into the impregnable stronghold of knowledge. We should continually be establishing new bases for human happiness and creating and promoting new instrumentalities toward this end. How excellent, how honorable is man if he arises to fulfill his responsibilities; how wretched and contemptible, if he shuts his eyes to the welfare of society and wastes his precious life in pursuing his own selfish interests and personal advantages. Supreme happiness is man's, and he beholds the signs of God in the world and in the human soul, if he urges on the steed of high endeavor in the arena of civilization and justice.[8]

. . . arise with complete sincerity and purity of purpose to educate the masses: to exert the utmost effort to instruct them in the various branches of learning and useful sciences, to encourage the development of modern progress, to widen the scope of commerce, industry and the arts, to further such measures as will increase the people's wealth. For the mass of the population is uninformed as to these vital agencies which would constitute an immediate remedy for society's chronic ills.

It is essential that scholars and the spiritually learned should undertake in all sincerity and purity of intent and for the sake of God alone, to counsel and exhort the masses and clarify their vision with that collyrium which is knowledge.[9]

All blessings are divine in origin, but none can be compared with this power of intellectual investigation and research, which is an eternal gift producing fruits of unending delight.... The man of science is perceiving and endowed with vision, whereas he who is ignorant and neglectful of this development is blind. The investigating mind is attentive, alive; the callous and indifferent mind is deaf and dead. A scientific man is a true index and representative of humanity, for through processes of inductive reasoning and research he is informed of all that appertains to humanity, its status, conditions and happenings. He studies the human body politic, understands social problems and weaves the web and texture of civilization. In fact, science may be likened to a mirror wherein the infinite forms and images of existing things are revealed and reflected. It is the very foundation of all individual and national development. Without this basis of investigation, development is impossible. Therefore, seek with diligent endeavor the knowledge and attainment of all that lies within the power of this wonderful bestowal.[10]

Let your actions cry aloud to the world that you are indeed Bahá'ís, for it is actions that speak to the world and are the cause of the progress of humanity.

If we are true Bahá'ís speech is not needed. Our actions will help on the world, will spread civilization, will help the progress of science, and cause the arts to develop. Without action nothing in the material world can be accomplished, neither can words unaided advance a man in the spiritual Kingdom. It is not through lip-service only that the elect of God have attained to holiness, but by patient lives of active service they have brought light into the world....

This is the work of a true Bahá'í, and this is what is expected of him. If we strive to do all this, then are we true Bahá'ís, but if we neglect it, we are not followers of the Light, and we have no right to the name.[11]

Given the magnitude of the transformation ahead and the scope of human suffering today, the current efforts of the Bahá'í community may appear to be but a mere drop. For a period of time, Bahá'í influence on the social order will obviously be limited. Yet, at least three areas of activity can be immediately identified. Bahá'ís contribute through their work and professions to the generation and application of knowledge in various disciplines. We contribute to the social and economic development of our communities by carrying out specific projects that benefit the general population in their immediate surroundings. And we also participate in humanity's collective discourse, seeking solutions to problems and encouraging action according to insights provided by Bahá'í teachings. A notable example having to do with all of these three areas of activity is emphasis on the education of girls.[12] This is a teaching that Bahá'ís have advocated for decades and the truth of which has now been vindicated in practice and universally recognized in the field of development. Over time, as the Faith grows in size, capacity and experience, its direct role in promoting human welfare will no doubt become increasingly significant.

Engaging in Diverse Fields of Human Endeavor

Bahá'ís are called to engage in all fields of endeavor that are of benefit to humanity. In referring to the arts, crafts and sciences, Bahá'u'lláh states: "Knowledge is as wings to man's life and a ladder for his ascent. Its acquisition is incumbent upon everyone."[13] "Let the loved ones of God," 'Abdu'l-Bahá urges, "whether young or old, whether male or female, each according to his capabilities, bestir themselves and spare no efforts to acquire the various current branches of knowledge, both spiritual and secular, and of the arts."[14] And in another passage He states: "Make every effort to acquire the advanced knowledge of the day, and strain every nerve to carry forward the divine civilization. . . . Included must be promotion of the arts, the discovery of new wonders, the expansion of trade, and the development of industry."[15] Shoghi Effendi explains that "It is just as important for the Bahá'í young boys and girls to become properly educated in colleges of high standing as it is to be spiritually developed."[16] He assigned to Local Assemblies the responsibility to encourage the believers "to make detailed inquiry into the various branches of contemporary learning—arts and sciences alike—and to concentrate their attention on serving the general interests of the people."[17] 'Abdu'l-Bahá and Shoghi Effendi encouraged individuals to study such fields as the sciences, medicine, agriculture, industrial sciences, journalism, philosophy, history, economics, and sociology.

　　Participation in the various fields of human endeavors is an essential aspect of service to humanity. The Universal House of Justice indicates that young Bahá'ís must move towards the front ranks of the professions, trades, arts and crafts which are necessary to the further progress of humankind—this to ensure that the spirit of the Cause will cast its illumination on all these important areas of human endeavor. Moreover, while aiming at mastering the unifying concepts and swiftly advancing technologies of this era of communications, they can, indeed they must, also guarantee the transmittal to the future of those skills which will preserve the marvelous, indispensable achievements of the past. The transformation which is to occur in the functioning of society will certainly depend to a great extent on the effectiveness of the preparations the youth make for the world they will inherit.[18]

The House of Justice cautions youth, however, that they must not merely absorb all they are taught—rather, they face the difficult challenge of evaluating what they learn in the light of the Bahá'í teachings.

The Teachings of Bahá'u'lláh throw light on so many aspects of human life and knowledge that a Bahá'í must learn, earlier than most, to weigh the information that is given to him rather than to accept it blindly. A Bahá'í has the advantage of the Divine Revelation for this Age, which shines like a searchlight on so many problems that baffle modern thinkers; he must therefore develop the ability to learn everything from those around him, showing proper humility before his teachers, but always relating what he hears to the Bahá'í teachings, for they will enable him to sort out the gold from the dross of human error.[19]

The obligation to acquire and apply knowledge to serve humanity and contribute to an ever-advancing civilization applies to all believers without exception. Those with particular capacity for achievement in various disciplines of human knowledge, of course, are called to a higher level of scholarly pursuit. As a letter written on behalf of the Guardian states:

The Cause needs more Bahá'í scholars, people who not only are devoted to it and believe in it and are anxious to tell others about it, but also who have a deep grasp of the Teachings and their significance, and who can correlate its beliefs with the current thoughts and problems of the people of the world.[20]

And as a letter written on behalf of the Universal House of Justice explains:

> As the Baháʾí community grows it will acquire experts in numerous fields—both by Baháʾís becoming experts and by experts becoming Baháʾís. As these experts bring their knowledge and skill to the service of the community and, even more, as they transform their various disciplines by bringing to bear upon them the light of the Divine Teachings, problem after problem now disrupting society will be answered. . . .
>
> In time great Baháʾí institutions of learning, great international and national projects for the betterment of human life will be inaugurated and flourish.[21]

By participating in the diverse fields of human endeavor, Baháʾís help to contribute to the generation and application of knowledge essential for the gradual advance of civilization. ʿAbduʾl-Bahá describes the gradual process of social change in *The Secret of Divine Civilization*:

> The world of politics is like the world of man; he is seed at first, and then passes by degrees to the condition of embryo and fetus, acquiring a bone structure, being clothed with flesh, taking on his own special form, until at last he reaches the plane where he can befittingly fulfill the words: "the most excellent of Makers." Just as this is a requirement of creation and is based on the universal Wisdom, the political world in the same way cannot instantaneously evolve from the nadir of defectiveness to the zenith of rightness and perfection. Rather, qualified individuals must strive by day and by night, using all those means which will conduce to progress, until the government and the people develop along every line from day to day and even from moment to moment.[22]

The Relationship Between Science and Religion

The appeal to young Baháʾís "to weigh the information that is given" and to Baháʾí experts to "transform their various disciplines by bringing to bear upon them the light of the Divine Teachings" is made in light of the understanding that the commonly accepted assumptions and approaches of various fields are subject to debate, investigation, evaluation, and continual refinement in ways that are inherent to scientific and rational inquiry. The engagement of Bahá'ís in all fields of knowledge, then, requires the struggle to draw upon insights from religion and science on theory, method and practice. The efforts of learned Bahá'ís to find an appropriate engagement between religion and science, however, can never be reduced to scholasticism or scientism.

Insights from religion cannot be thrust arbitrarily into the discourse of a particular discipline. It would be unacceptable and completely unconvincing to a scientist, for example, if a quotation from the Bahá'í Writings were used in an attempt to overturn scientific understanding of biological evolution while justifying nonscientific arguments such as intelligent design which are, in fact, theological or philosophical in nature. Whatever the source of inspiration, a hypothesis must be tested according to scientific methods and standards, producing change that can be articulated and justified within the domain of science. So too, insights from various disciplines of human knowledge cannot be arbitrarily imposed on the understanding and practice of the Bahá'í community. A particular tool of scholarly inquiry, for example, such as historical criticism,[23] may be very useful in shedding light on aspects of the teachings. Yet, the scope of the validity of such tools is a topic of discussion even within academia. While they may have value to Bahá'ís engaged in scholarly study of the Faith, they cannot be blindly accepted as instruments that yield "scientific truth" and used to justify propositions that overturn explicit Bahá'í concepts presented in the authoritative Texts.[24]

That religion may be a source of inspiration for art, music, poetry, and architecture is readily apparent. In other fields, such as the trades or natural sciences, any suggestion of a direct contribution from religion may seem invasive or irrelevant—until one contemplates the value of an honest auto mechanic or the damage caused when corporations determine that there is no profit in using science to attack diseases endemic to poor countries. It would seem that particularly in fields that directly address human well-being—education, psychology, economics, sociology, and so on—the insights or principles of religion would be most relevant. While there has been, of course, a traditional tension between science and religion (or more broadly, between the disciplines of human knowledge and religion), Bahá'ís seek a harmony between the two.

In an article entitled "Overview of the Structure of a Scientific Worldview," John J. Carvalho observes that science rests upon certain philosophical assumptions while embracing certain methods for the investigation of reality. Science is engaged in the search for truth—not absolute truth—and as he explains, "science, as a rational enterprise, can gain knowledge about the universe in a systematic, progressive, and meaningful way by acquiring contingent, partial truths the sum total of which provide a reasonable idea of how the world works."[25] According to a large number of thinkers like Carvalho, a scientific worldview is not comprehensive—it cannot answer all the questions of interest to humanity. Where the scope of science ends, philosophy or religion steps in. If a philosophical or religious worldview attempts to be comprehensive, it must accommodate and not contradict the truths of science. As Carvalho states:

> . . . comprehensiveness cannot be achieved by a strictly scientific worldview. Rather, such comprehensiveness needs a philosophical worldview that may have science as a component but not as the element whereby hierarchical tenets are formed. . . . [I]n such a worldview scientific information is used by philosophical theory construction to answer questions that science alone could not solve. The question then becomes whether a philosophical world-view is adequate to explain the sum total of reality or whether a theological perspective is required. This position, one that many nontheist scientists refuse to recognize, is actually the position that must be taken given the scope of any scientific worldview. The methods of science answer scientific questions, and the methods of philosophy and theology answer questions about the ethical implications of scientific information or what can be inferred from scientific information about nonscientific phenomena, such as the possible existence of a divine entity whose status is "supernatural" and therefore beyond the immediate hypothetico-deductive or statistical-relevance methods of science, which deal with objects that are naturally observable. . . .
>
> . . . [A] theological worldview is more extensive than a strictly scientific one, because it asks questions that science alone does not ask. Furthermore, it seems clear that the debate in the science-religion dialogue is between comprehensive philosophical world-views and comprehensive theological worldviews, which act as umbrella world views encompassing noncomprehensive scientific

worldviews. It also is clear that any comprehensive worldview must take into account the modern noncomprehensive scientific worldview for the obvious reason that if it did not, it would be by definition noncomprehensive itself, lacking the questions the scientific worldview asks and effectively answers.[26]

In this light, a perceived clash between science and religion could indeed be a clash between a scientific worldview and a religious worldview that is unscientific, and thus, noncomprehensive. But it could also be between a philosophical worldview in which science is embedded and a comprehensive religious worldview that also includes science. Thus materialism, as a philosophical perspective that encompasses science, seeks to reduce religion to the material realm, described as a mere social phenomena, biochemical impulse, or set of superstitions, thereby invalidating religion's claim to offer comprehensive or even useful contributions to humanity's endless search for meaning. A religious perspective that fully embraces science seeks a harmony between science and religion, and can legitimately challenge philosophical assumptions and conclusions that are imposed upon scientific inquiry or proffered in the guise of scientific truth.

Another useful insight into the relationship between science and religion is provided by Stephen Toulmin in his book, *Cosmopolis*, which traces the evolution of the Enlightenment project over more than three centuries. In reflecting on the relationship between science and religion, Toulmin observes that there was no enduring conflict between these two knowledge systems in the period predating modernity. And in the initial stage of the Enlightenment, religion could readily accommodate Newtonian physics with the conception of God as clockmaker. It was the evolution in thought driven by new scientific insights that over the course of the modern age challenged the founding assumptions of the Enlightenment and gave rise to increasing pressure on religion. Toulmin writes:

> Before the Reformation, Christianity had little investment in doctrines which natural science had any reason to dispute.... The alleged incompatibility of science and theology was thus a conflict *within* Modernity, which arose as the growth of experience gave scientists occasion to question beliefs used by Counter-Reformation Catholics and Protestants alike *after* 1650, in their edifying sermons on the wisdom of God's creation.

> . . . From then on, recurrent controversies . . . pitted a system
> of dogmatic theory against the skeptical testimony of human
> experience, and challenged the position of people whose position
> was less a belief in any particular doctrine than a belief in belief
> itself.[27]

Toulmin's account of the history of modernity offers insight
into certain challenges facing Baháʼís engaged in scholarly activity.
Baháʼís are involved in a new undertaking, but the approach and
the specific language used to explore the relationship between
science and religion has developed within the historical experience
of the encounter between Christianity and an emerging empirical
science in Western thought. Imposing modernity's assumptions
and problems on the Faith produces an impasse. An undercurrent
of concerns juxtaposing fundamentalism and liberalism, authority and evidence, or received doctrines and free investigation
refuel the outworn debate between faith and reason and obscure
the truth that the unfoldment of Baháʼí discourse is not merely
a continuation of the struggles of modernity. Rather, the Baháʼí
teachings address modernity's culmination and beyond. As any
Manifestation must, Baháʼuʼlláh begins His conversation with
humanity within the framework of its ongoing discussions, including that of Enlightenment thought. But He extends these concepts
to create new understandings and to cultivate intersubjective
agreements that are intended to give rise to a new world order and
a new civilization.

In the Enlightenment quest for truth through science and
reason, religion has been gradually set aside into a realm of personal preference. The alternative put forward in the Baháʼí teachings
upholds the validity of scientific inquiry, but enables humanity to
apply the powers of reason and faith to explore systematically a
wider realm of values, human capacity, and spiritual and social
realities so as to contribute to greater understanding and the
progress and well-being of humanity.

The Universal House of Justice has observed that "science and
religion are the two inseparable, reciprocal systems of knowledge
impelling the advancement of civilization."[28] In His talks, ʼAbduʼl-
Bahá described how these two are related, explaining that

> Any religious belief which is not conformable with scientific
> proof and investigation is superstition, for true science is reason
> and reality, and religion is essentially reality and pure reason;

therefore, the two must correspond. Religious teaching which is at variance with science and reason is human invention and imagination unworthy of acceptance, for the antithesis and opposite of knowledge is superstition born of the ignorance of man. If we say religion is opposed to science, we lack knowledge of either true science or true religion, for both are founded upon the premises and conclusions of reason, and both must bear its test.[29]

And He adds:

We may think of science as one wing and religion as the other; a bird needs two wings for flight, one alone would be useless. Any religion that contradicts science or that is opposed to it, is only ignorance—for ignorance is the opposite of knowledge.

Religion which consists only of rites and ceremonies of prejudice is not the truth. Let us earnestly endeavor to be the means of uniting religion and science.

... Whatever the intelligence of man cannot understand, religion ought not to accept. Religion and science walk hand in hand, and any religion contrary to science is not the truth.[30]

These statements indicate that, for Baháʾís, science and religion are not in conflict. Nor are they simply incommensurable, exploring in different ways different domains that are mutually exclusive. The Baháʾí teachings offer an approach to reality that lies beyond the debates arising from modern and postmodern thought, without ignoring the truths or valid criticisms in each. This approach encompasses a scientific worldview but is more comprehensive, addressing a wider range of questions that are essential to human progress.[31]

In chapter 1, three levels of understanding that pertain to spiritual reality were described: 1) reality "as it is," 2) Revelation or the knowledge offered by the Manifestation, and 3) the level of human comprehension of religious belief and practice. In a similar manner, the Baháʾí view of the harmony between science and religion can be illustrated by drawing parallels between physical and spiritual reality. Of course, any effort to convey complex concepts within the confines of a simple table is overly reductionistic. Yet certain insights emerge from a comparison of the levels of comprehending reality; in this instance four levels are proposed in order to distinguish between the levels of theoretical and practical knowledge.[32]

LEVEL 1	Reality *(ontologically objective reality; reality "as it is"; the "mind of God")*	
LEVEL 2	**Revelation (R2)** *(Revelation that can be known; the revealed Word of God; the Book & its authoritative interpretation)*	**the Universe (S2)** *(physical & human reality; facts, patterns & laws of creation that can be known by the human mind)*
LEVEL 3	**knowledge system of religion (R3)** *(the body of religious knowledge, including methods & standards of inquiry and justification)*	**knowledge system of science (S3)** *(the body of scientific knowledge, including methods & standards of inquiry and justification)*
LEVEL 4	**practical knowledge associated with spiritual life & moral social practice (R4)**	**technology & practical knowledge associated with material progress (S4)**

First, as in the case of a religious perspective, there is a level of reality that lies beyond the reach of scientific investigation. Roughly equivalent to the second level, Revelation, are the laws of nature, the facts of the physical world, and the mental and social dimensions of humanity, which we might summarize as "the universe." These are aspects of existence that are potentially discoverable by humanity.[33] Human knowledge can perhaps be divided into two levels that are essentially integrated: a level that represents the knowledge system of science, with a distinct body of knowledge that grows and evolves over time through the application of accepted methods, and a level that represents the technical or practical knowledge derived from the application of scientific knowledge or from practice to contribute to an ever-advancing civilization and which is comparable to religious practice.

The conception of truth varies in relation to each of these levels of comprehension. The truth that is associated with the essential nature of reality is beyond human capacity to even contemplate (level 1). Humanity attempts to investigate the truth that corresponds with reality as manifested in the text of the Revelation (R2) and the physical and human world (S2). Because of the limitations of human capacity, we cannot achieve this level of understanding. Yet, we also cannot avoid the implications of the truths of reality. The mutable knowledge that constitutes the horizon of human comprehension is continually tested against the brute facts of physical reality, through the understanding and methods of the scientific community (S3), and against the verses of Revelation, through the understanding and methods of the religious community (R3). Truth, at this third level, is justified knowledge, and represents humanity's best insight into the universe and Revelation (S2 and R2). Such truths are subject to alteration or refinement over time as more profound understandings that encompass and transcend previous notions emerge through practical action to shape society (S4 and R4).

Without an appreciation of the difference between the mutable nature of knowledge at level 3 and the immutable nature of truth and reality at level 2, a number of errors of reasoning may occur. Fundamentalism is a belief that human religious understanding is equivalent to what is presented in the Revelation (R3 = R2), and that as a result, deductions of religious belief supersede scientific knowledge (R3 > S3) or are even used to reject observable facts of the physical world (R3 > S2). Scientism or positivism equates scientific knowledge with knowledge of physical reality "as it is" (S3 = S2 or even S3 = level 1) and includes the assertion that science can be used to weigh Revelation (S3 > R2). Relativism rejects any preference given to religion or science (R3 or S3) as knowledge systems over any other way of knowing or describing reality, essentially denying the existence of any reality except that constructed by human understanding (essentially denying level 1 or S2 and R2 while permitting innumerable parallels to S3 and S4 and R3 and R4).

The Bahá'í principle of the harmony of science and religion implies that these knowledge systems operate in a parallel and complementary manner. They shed light on aspects of a single reality within which there is no true contradiction (S2 and R2 do not contradict one another).[34] However, at any given point, human knowledge may not be able to transcend a contradiction in its representations of reality—currently held scientific or religious perspectives may clash (S3 vs. R3). In these instances, scientific knowledge (S3) is a means by which we can check our interpretations of Revelation (our religious beliefs, R3), so that they do not degenerate into superstition (in general, S3 > R3, according to the explicit statement of 'Abdu'l-Bahá).[35] True religion is not unscientific, and therefore religious beliefs and practice must be correlated with the understanding of reality derived from science. Yet the Bahá'í Writings also clarify that the meaning of the Text or its authoritative interpretation cannot be judged by limited human standards (S3 $\not\gtrless$ R2).[36] So too, our religious understanding (R3) can guide the manner in which scientific knowledge and technology (S3 or S4) are used to contribute to society, thus preventing them from becoming mere instruments of materialism.[37] The community of practice that is science and the community of practice that is religion engage and influence one another and humanity as a whole; this engagement is most intense in the areas of common concern, such as human nature and behavior, ethics and morality, education, and the domain of the social sciences.

In science, if a sufficient number of observed facts (S2) stand in contradiction to a theory held in the body of scientific knowledge (S3), then that theory may require modification or may be rejected. If certain scientific methods (S3) produce outcomes that conflict with reality (S2), then those methods are in question and are likely to be discarded or modified, or at least used only within the limited range of circumstances in which they produce valid results. The same principle holds true for religion. Methods of individual interpretation or action must produce understanding and practices (R3 or R4) that correspond to the authoritative statements of the Text (R2). The purpose of study and scholarly activity that explores the Revelation is, therefore, to improve understanding and practice (that is, a change in understanding and action with R3 or R4 that expands upon or advances the previous notions of R3 or R4 because it draws us closer to R2). Care must be exercised that personal interpretation does not distort, deny, or contend with the Word or its authorized interpretation or attempt to direct Baháʾí practice along lines that contradict the guidance of the Universal House of Justice.

Moving Beyond Perceived Tensions Between Science and Religion

Even though science and religion are not fundamentally in conflict, tensions or ambiguity will sometimes arise between the involvement of individual Baháʾís in study and action as believers and their engagement in a professional discipline, particularly scientific or scholarly inquiry. How are such tensions resolved?

In the book *Our Practices, Our Selves: Or, What it Means to be Human*, Todd May introduces the concept of a "practice," which he describes as "a regularity (or regularities) of behavior, usually goal-directed, that is socially normatively governed."[38] According to May, practices constitute a large part of what it means to be a human being. Examples of practices include using credit cards, raising children, engaging in a profession, or participating in politics. Communities and even cultures can be understood as practices, such as scientists, church-goers, or members of the legal profession. In these cases, shared participation in a community says something meaningful about the participant's personal identity.

May explains that "To be committed to a practice . . . is to be committed to enough of the claims, findings, and theories of that practice—and particularly its 'central' claims, findings, theories, and so on—as to be reasonably seen as being committed to it."[39] Thus, each practice has its own body of knowledge, its own criteria for justification, and its own methods of investigating reality and discovering truth. Different practices may interact and, through the exchange of ideas, influence one another; but change occurs as a result of a practice affirming new conclusions based on its own criteria. An individual is usually a member of more than one community of practice, and therefore, is able to contribute to change within a particular practice by introducing new insights from others. Different practices are, however, not relativistic groupings free to occupy distinct realms each with their "own" truth, since insights are ultimately checked against reality and must, over time, yield to it. An individual is confronted, therefore, by the tensions that come from the competing truth claims and standards found within the various practices that are embraced.

Bahá'ís, of course, would never limit human capacity merely to its social dimension. And it is possible to describe a Bahá'í approach to the relationship between science and religion in very different terms. Nevertheless, May's approach to practices offers a perspective that may be useful in understanding and resolving any apparent tensions between science and religion that emerge for a Bahá'í engaged in scholarly activity. We can see that Bahá'ís participate in a wide range of social practices in addition to membership in the Bahá'í community. In so doing, we bring insights from Bahá'u'lláh's teachings to those practices and influence them—within the range of the internally accepted standards of that practice. And we can gain insights from these practices and bring them into the Baháʼí community—to the degree that they are acceptable within the range of internal standards of the Baháʼí teachings.

From this perspective, Baháʼí scholarship, as described by the Central Figures of the Faith and the Universal House of Justice, is an internal function of the Baháʼí community of practice; it is not the academic study of the Baháʼí Faith. It is open to all believers according to their capacity, not just Baháʼí academics. It serves the purposes of the Faith. It has its standards of rationality and justification, and its own growing body of knowledge. These are derived from the Baháʼí Writings as well as from validated elements drawn from the wide range of other practices in which Baháʼís engage, including the natural sciences, the social sciences, and the humanities. An academic who is a Baháʼí can, of course, participate in this internal scholarly activity and simultaneously be a member of an academic community of practice.

Disciplines such as economics, philosophy, history or religious studies give rise to their own communities of practice. They have their own bodies of knowledge, standards and methods with which they explore reality and come to understandings that guide judgment and action. Baháʼís who are participants in such academic communities of practice are correct to point out that they are obliged to conform to the accepted range of methods, criteria, and truths. Otherwise, they would never be taken seriously and their arguments would have no influence. There is also a need to acknowledge, however, that academic practices do evolve and that Baháʼís can contribute to that evolution. Within any academic field there is inevitably a range of voices, theories, and approaches, some of which are closer to Baháʼí teachings than others; Baháʼí students and practitioners within a discipline can seek out and build upon compatible approaches. Yet, change within a practice—even revolutionary change—takes place according to its own standards and web of belief, not because ideas are imposed from the outside.

How is it possible to work within two practices that sometimes have divergent assumptions or standards—in particular, the practice of a religion and the practice of the academic study of religion that cannot take into account metaphysical influences? What is a Baháʼí to do? Moojan Momen, in the article "Methodology in Baháʼí Studies," reviews a range of options, including an "interior scholarship" that would take place within the Baháʼí community alone using a "faith-based, revelation-centered methodology," and an "external scholarship," an involvement with the academic world that may require suspending the Bahá'í viewpoint on reality or focusing on areas that are more compatible with Bahá'í principles. He concludes with his own preference: "writing material that satisfies both the academic community and the believing community."[40] Writing in such a manner that is acceptable to the standards of reasonable individuals within both practices seems to resolve the dilemma in most cases.

A problem arises, however, when demands of the two practices cannot be reconciled. Todd May suggests three possible outcomes. First, it is possible to live with ambiguity, anticipating resolution at a future time. Ambiguity is inherent in scientific inquiry; to find it in the engagement between science and religion is, therefore, unsurprising. Reality is one, but our practices, being fallible, involve insights into reality that evolve to become more robust. This is true also of our practice of the Faith, since "practice" in this respect is concerned with the capacity of the believers to understand and act on Bahá'u'lláh's teachings, not with Bahá'u'lláh's capacity or the nature of His Revelation. An entire lifetime may pass—perhaps many lifetimes—before certain questions can be resolved. A second possible outcome is that the understandings from one practice help to shape the other in a manner that eliminates an apparent contradiction. Again, reciprocity is required, in that either practice can influence the other—not by imposing outside standards but by introducing influence or new insights that provoke change from within. If insights from science or other disciplines cause a change in the Bahá'í community, this is a change in the perception of the believers that draws them closer to Bahá'u'lláh's intended meaning and purpose. A final possibility is that an individual, unable to reconcile the two practices and unwilling to tolerate ambiguity, will reject and withdraw from one of the practices. In various statements, the Universal House of Justice has acknowledged all three of these alternatives.[41]

It is not reasonable to assume, however, that an individual who is committed to the investigation of reality and the search for truth and who is involved in both practices, would participate in one while ignoring what has been accepted as true within the other. This is just another face of extreme relativism.[42] It implies living within separate, contradictory worlds, fully embracing each on its own terms without regard for the conflicts and inconsistencies such a life engenders. Far more reasonable, albeit more difficult at times, is to acknowledge the possibility of conclusions that could be reached within religious worldviews, identify discrepancies, and use them as starting points for gaining deeper insights into reality. Thus a Bahá'í historian, for example, may not be able to introduce into the discipline the argument that divine forces influence events; this concept can be set aside while other forces are being examined. Yet a believer's assumptions, arguments and conclusions cannot be identical with those that result from an entirely materialistic worldview, a view that implicitly demands that all historians be materialists while hiding such demand in its apparently innocent requirement that the scholar totally ignore his or her faith when engaged in rational inquiry.

When an individual sees participation in formal processes of the generation and application of knowledge in two or more communities of practice as complementary, the contribution to both acquires special value. The practice of the Bahá'í community is still in an early formative stage. Bahá'í scholarly activity is part of Bahá'í practice and therefore adheres to its methods and standards, including for example its own hermeneutical principles. While it is true that the Revelation does not change, our understanding of the Revelation does change, and therefore the application of the knowledge, methods, and standards of Bahá'í practice evolve throughout the dispensation. Learned Bahá'ís who are members of other communities of practice—historians, sociologists, lawyers, biologists, political scientists, anthropologists, philosophers, educators and so on—can draw upon the insights gained in their fields and propose ideas and methods that are valuable in understanding the teachings and in translating them into action. Those in accord with the Bahá'í community's understanding of the inviolable tenets of the Faith will, in one way or another, be adopted. The progress thus achieved creates more capacity in the Bahá'í community to undertake scholarly activity. This in turn makes it possible for an increasing number of individuals to participate meaningfully in the many fields of human activity and contribute to the generation of knowledge indispensable for the advancement of civilization.

Bahá'í Involvement in Social and Economic Development

A brief account of the evolution of thought and practice in the Bahá'í community regarding the social and economic development of peoples may shed further light on its attempts to contribute to the civilization-building process. While development may more appropriately be considered the outcome of endeavors in such diverse fields as economics, education, health, agriculture, anthropology, international law, and governance, for more than a half century it has been a distinct field of activity, an area of focus involving exhaustive and intensive study and action. From simple beginnings near the start of the dispensation, Baháʼís have combined understanding of Baháʼí teachings relevant to social and economic development with knowledge of the various associated fields, to engage in their own ever-more complex development practice. This insight and experience has served as the basis for an expanding discourse with the wider society.

Baháʼí engagement in development receives its impulse from Baháʼuʼlláhʼs Revelation. As the Universal House of Justice explains:

> From the beginning of His stupendous mission, Baháʼuʼlláh urged upon the attention of nations the necessity of ordering human affairs in such a way as to bring into being a world unified in all the essential aspects of its life. In unnumbered verses and tablets He repeatedly and variously declared the "progress of the world" and the "development of nations" as being among the ordinances of God for this day.[43]

Social and economic development is an aspect of the consolidation of Baháʼí communities. It is that part of community life which is to be associated, in the fullness of time, with the dependencies of the Mashriquʼl-Adhkár, "the spiritual center of every Baháʼí community round which must flourish dependencies dedicated to the social, humanitarian, educational and scientific advancement of mankind."[44] Its watchword is coherence between the material and the spiritual. Its aim is not achieved merely through the delivery of charitable services; its central concern is the building of the capacity of people to guide their own development. A document prepared at the Baháʼí World Centre offers the following definition:

> Central to the capacity of a Baháʼí community to lead a process of transformation is the ability of its members and institutions to apply the Revelation of Baháʼuʼlláh to various aspects of life and thereby establish consistent patterns of change. In fact, learning to apply the Teachings to achieve progress could be taken as the very definition of Baháʼí social and economic development. Such

learning has to occur locally, regionally, nationally and internationally and become the axis around which our development efforts are organized at all levels.

Learning in this sense is not limited to study and evaluation. It comes about in combination with action. The believers must regularly engage in consultation, action, reflection—all in the light of the guidance inherent in the Teachings of the Faith. Such a learning process can occur in a very simple manner at the village and local level, but with greater sophistication by national agencies and institutions. At the international level, it calls for a higher degree of conceptualization, one that takes account of the broader processes of global transformation as described in the Writings and serves to adjust the overall direction of development activities in each country accordingly.[45]

In calling the Bahá'í world to more systematic involvement in development, the House of Justice stated:

> The steps to be taken must necessarily begin in the Bahá'í Community itself, with the friends endeavoring, through their application of spiritual principles, their rectitude of conduct and the practice of the art of consultation, to uplift themselves and thus become self-sufficient and self-reliant. Moreover, these exertions will conduce to the preservation of human honor, so desired by Bahá'u'lláh. In the process and as a consequence, the friends will undoubtedly extend the benefits of their efforts to society as a whole, until all mankind achieves the progress intended by the Lord of the Age.[46]

The principle that development is intended for the well being of all, not just Bahá'ís alone, governs Bahá'í endeavors in this field. 'Abdu'l-Bahá notes that "In all the cycles of the prophets the philanthropic affairs were confined to their respective peoples only—with the exception of small matters, such as charity, which was permissible to extend to others." He indicates, however, that Bahá'í efforts in this regard "are for all humanity, without any exception, because it is the manifestation of the mercifulness of God."[47] Bahá'í development is an act of "disinterested service to the cause of humanity,"[48] and in that light, is an inseparable aspect of what it means to be a Bahá'í. "Do not busy yourselves in your own concerns;" Bahá'u'lláh commands His followers, "let your thoughts be fixed upon that which will rehabilitate the fortunes of mankind."[49]

For more than a century after the birth of the Faith, the number of believers was too small and communities were too weak for Bahá'ís to be systematically engaged in development activities anywhere outside of Iran. The specific experience of the Iranian Bahá'í community, which had received direct guidance from 'Abdu'l-Bahá and Shoghi Effendi, was particularly noteworthy, however. Through diligent work in areas such as education, health, economic development and literacy, the believers achieved a marked advance in two to three generations, creating a community that was in the forefront of many a praiseworthy field of endeavor. Despite widespread opposition, its efforts also had a profound influence upon Iranian society. 'Abdu'l-Bahá and Shoghi Effendi continually exhorted the Bahá'ís to distinctive service to the entire population, as illustrated by the following passage from the Guardian:

> In philanthropic enterprises and acts of charity, in promotion of the general welfare and furtherance of the public good including that of every group without any exceptions whatever, let the beloved of God attract the favorable attention of all, and lead all the rest.
>
> Let them, freely and without charge, open the doors of their schools and their higher institutions for the study of sciences and the liberal arts, to non-Bahá'í children and youth who are poor and in need. . . . At this time, when the nation has awakened out of its sleep of negligence, and the Government has begun to consider the promotion and expansion of its educational establishment, let the Bahá'í representatives in that country arise in such a manner that as a result of their high endeavors in every hamlet, village and town, of every province and district, preliminary measures will be taken for the setting up of institutions for the study of sciences, the liberal arts and religion. Let Bahá'í children without any exceptions learn the fundamentals of reading and writing and familiarize themselves with the rules of conduct, the customs, practices and laws as set forth in the Book of God; and let them, in the new branches of knowledge, in the arts and technology of the day, in pure and praiseworthy characteristics—Bahá'í conduct, the Bahá'í way of life—become so distinguished above the rest that all other communities, whether Islamic, Zoroastrian, Christian, Judaic or materialist, will of their own volition and most gladly enter their children in such advanced Bahá'í institutions of learning and entrust them to the care of Bahá'í instructors.[50]

The year 1983 saw the beginning of a new phase in the evolution of the Bahá'í community. In its message of 20 October, the Universal House of Justice explained that "the community of the Greatest Name has grown to the stage at which the processes of [social and economic] development must be incorporated into its regular pursuits." Action was particularly "compelled by the expansion of the Faith in Third World countries where the vast majority of its adherents reside."[51] Development activity became a fundamental aspect of the plans of Bahá'í communities worldwide.

The first decade of involvement in social and economic development included a wide variety of activities; it constituted "a period of experimentation, characterized simultaneously by enthusiasm and trepidation, thoughtful planning and haphazard action, achievements and setbacks."[52] In 1993, an analysis of the experience to date was conducted and new strategies formulated. These were presented in "Bahá'í Social and Economic Development: Prospects for the Future," a statement prepared in August 1993 at the Bahá'í World Centre and approved by the Universal House of Justice. Among the measures to be taken to systematize Bahá'í development work, the document suggested that the Office of Social and Economic Development at the Bahá'í World Centre, created "to promote and coordinate the activities of the friends throughout the world," develop the capacity to "facilitate learning about development by fostering and supporting action, reflection on action, study, consultation, the gathering and systematization of experience, conceptualization, and training—all carried out in the light of the Teachings of the Faith."[53]

Since 1993, additional documents have been written on the subject of development.[54] These include "The Prosperity of Humankind," prepared by the Bahá'í International Community and three items prepared by the Office of Social and Economic Development at the Bahá'í World Centre: "The Evolution of Institutional Capacity for Social and Economic Development," "A Clarification of Some Issues Concerning Social and Economic Development in Local and National Communities," and *For the Betterment of the World*. The purpose of the first document is to foster understanding about global prosperity within the Bahá'í community. The second outlines the emergence of strong institutions for guiding development projects. The third addresses a range of questions that had arisen since the strategies in the "Prospects" document were implemented, including the relationship between teaching and development, and the role of training institutes in development. The fourth provides an overview of the Bahá'í approach to development illustrated by examples of specific projects. Taken together, these documents are a reflection on practical experience, a response to emerging challenges, and an overview of vision, strategies, and lines of action that will guide the course of Bahá'í development activities in the coming decades.

After the first quarter century of systematic development activity, there are several thousand social and economic development activities conducted by Bahá'ís in more than 100 countries. They span such diverse domains as agriculture, education, microenterprise, governance, environment, vocational training, technology, rural development, literacy, health, race unity, children's rights, youth empowerment, and the advancement of women. The vast majority of these are fairly simple activities of limited duration in which Bahá'ís in villages and towns around the world are beginning to address the challenges facing their localities. More than 500 are sustained projects, many with permanent administrative structures, while some 50 organizations have evolved to the point where they have relatively complex programmatic structures and significant spheres of influence.[55]

Beyond specific Bahá'í projects, thousands of believers participate professionally and as volunteers in other development efforts. The House of Justice has encouraged such individuals to "participate in worthy endeavors outside the Faith in order to influence their professional fields and infuse them with the teachings of Bahá'u'lláh" for "this is, in and of itself, a tremendous service to the Cause" and they should "not feel that they are serving the Faith only if they dedicate themselves directly to Bahá'í projects."[56]

The nascent character of current Bahá'í development activities cannot be overemphasized. Yet Bahá'ís are striving to increase the number and complexity of projects through which we can apply Bahá'í teachings in diverse fields and at increasingly higher levels of sophistication. As has been the case with the expansion and consolidation of the Faith, here too the emphasis is on learning and the generation of knowledge. The approach being promoted by the Office of Social and Economic Development centers on two complementary undertakings. The first involves building institutional capacity to guide the learning of the people of a region to become the protagonists of their own progress, which includes the development of human resources through formal educational programs. The second involves consolidating the learning experience of these institutions and disseminating it effectively to other communities.

Every Bahá'í development project—even the smallest effort at the grassroots—may be considered, and should strive to become, a center of learning on how to achieve human prosperity. Most projects begin by addressing specific challenges facing a population in simple ways. As the work advances, however, the need for increased institutional capacity becomes apparent, the capacity to assess social forces and conditions, create a vision of possible action, devise well-defined strategies, manage resources, and implement one or more lines of action. In time, lines of action need to be integrated so that the problems of local communities and regions can be addressed in a coherent, interdisciplinary manner. In this way, a population can, over time, reflect upon, modify, and restate its vision, adapt its responses, and advance.

The training institute, by now a well-established feature of the Bahá'í community, is essential to the creation of capacity in the people of a region to become protagonists of their own social and economic development. The spiritual insights it offers in its courses prove indispensable to a development process that seeks coherence between the spiritual and material, and the attitudes and skills of service it helps develop enhance the ability of its participants to become engaged in sustained social action. In fact, there is every indication that many of the branch courses emerging from such sustained action will be concerned with training in one or another aspect of social and economic development. The Universal House of Justice has explained, that training institutes can develop human resources for participation in activities for social and economic development and can even run development projects.

> It is understood that the institute will be an agency for the development of human resources for activities of expansion and consolidation, as well as for projects of social and economic development. . . . In this latter context, it could also gradually take on the administration of the development projects. . . . The institute can establish a clear-cut organizational structure that has various departments and sections, each of which is dedicated to one of its programs—a health program, a literacy program, and so on—as well as those for training human resources for expansion and consolidation.[57]

Because of the many challenges facing training institutes in the development of human resources for expansion and consolidation, by the end of the Five Year Plan in 2006, only a small number had some level of involvement with development activities. These institutes explored how development efforts emerge and are integrated with activities of the community in a rapidly growing cluster, involving activities such as tutorial schools, radio stations, or programs for primary health educators.

Institutional capacity to engage in social and economic development activity in the Baháʼí world today lies mostly in Baháʼí-inspired, non-governmental, not-for-profit organizations each created by a group of believers who share a common vision. The multiplication and strengthening of these organizations is a highly promising and significant area of Baháʼí endeavor. A letter written on behalf of the Universal House of Justice explains:

> As a national community grows, the activities undertaken by its members also increase in number and diversity. Some of these activities will be initiated and administered by the Baháʼí institutions. Others will fall in the realm of private initiative. . . .
>
> The private initiatives of believers need not, however, be limited to business ventures. The laws of most societies allow for the establishment of non-profit organizations which, while private, are subject to special regulations and enjoy certain privileges. Customarily a board of trustees is responsible for all the affairs of such an organization and must ensure that its income is spent for the purpose stipulated in its by-laws. This board also oversees the functioning of the projects of the organization and the work of those who are in charge of them. An increasing number of believers around the world are taking advantage of this possibility and creating organizations dedicated to the application of Baháʼuʼlláhʼs teachings to the analysis and resolution of important social and economic issues. The House of Justice looks with keen interest on this growing phenomenon in the Baháʼí world.[58]

As Baháʼí development agencies increase their capacity to guide action and learning, each in one or more regions, they accumulate experience that can be analyzed and distilled. Eventually, either from the proven experience of a single organization, or from the combination of lessons from various agencies, enough knowledge is gathered to be shared with a wide range of organizations in diverse countries to accumulate further experience. When the process of revision based on action and reflection is sufficiently advanced, a program begins to emerge that Bahá'í agencies and development organizations around the world can adopt, and implement according to local circumstances. This consolidation and dissemination of learning may even lead to projects involving collaboration with national governments or international agencies.

Today's worldwide Bahá'í activity directed towards the spiritual empowerment of junior youth is the result of this approach to the systematization of experience. In 1994, the Office of Social and Economic Development at the Bahá'í World Centre invited a number of individuals to come together and analyze Bahá'í experience in the promotion of literacy to date. Drawing on the lessons learned in Bahá'í projects and on the knowledge of experts outside the community, they proposed three pilot projects to be launched in Cambodia, the Central African Republic, and Guyana in order to accelerate the learning process in this field. In 1996, the effort was extended to an additional six countries in Asia, Africa, and Latin America. When in 2002 the results of efforts through which over 2000 facilitators had been trained and over 10,000 students had been reached were analyzed, one feature stood out: the contrast between the extraordinary receptivity of junior youth to these programs and the difficulty of maintaining effective projects of adult literacy which did not have some other dimension, microfinance for example.

A new arena for systematic learning had emerged from experience. The focus shifted from mere literacy to the empowerment of junior youth—an effort to endow them with the capacity to conquer the word and unravel its meaning, both for their own spiritual upliftment and as a basis for social action. The range of content expanded to include science and mathematics and service to humanity. The experience gained from the pilot projects laid the foundation for the preparation of various materials that were gradually shared with interested national communities, enabling them to initiate their own projects. During the Five Year Plan from 2001-2006, the accumulating results prompted a number of training institutes to incorporate the curricular materials into their programs for junior youth. By the end of the Plan, the work with junior youth broadened beyond efforts for social and economic development to become a fourth core activity for Bahá'í communities, incorporating the training of animators of junior youth groups in the institute program. Presently, the Office of Social and Economic Development, now confident in the efficacy of its approach, is promoting the systematization of experience in a few other areas such as health, community banking, and primary and secondary education.

Method and Learning

This brief examination of the evolution of thought in the context of Bahá'í social and economic development underscores the importance of search for appropriate methods for the generation and application of knowledge as the Bahá'í community tries to increase its capacity to contribute to the advancement of civilization. The most fruitful approach up to now continues to be one of action, reflection on action, consultation, conceptualization, and the study of both the text of science and the text of religion, in this case the Bahá'í teachings. But in a field that touches on so many academic disciplines, methodological concerns cannot remain at this level of generality. Specific methods of learning have to be explored as dictated by the nature of the problems being addressed. The experience of one Bahá'í-inspired organization, La Fundación para la Aplicación y Enseñanza de las Ciencias (Foundation for the Application and Teaching of the Sciences, FUNDAEC) helps illustrate the nature of this methodological exploration.

FUNDAEC[59] was established in Colombia in 1974 through the efforts of a number of individuals, many who were not Bahá'ís but all of whom had agreed on fundamental Bahá'í principles to govern their endeavors. Presently, it is a well-known organization in the field of development with its educational programs reaching thousands of students in various countries.

The concept of learning has been central to the evolution of FUNDAEC. As described by one of its long time collaborators, Haleh Arbab:

> Those who join the organization belong to various intellectual traditions in the natural and social sciences and the humanities and are well versed in some set of theories prevalent in their fields. A question that arose early in the life of our organization was how to employ these theories, given that they did not constitute a consistent body of knowledge and often led to conflicting approaches to development work. What we saw in the operation of similar groups over the years was not encouraging. There

seems to be a tendency to become too attached to one or another theoretical position and try everything possible to make reality fit the provisions of that theory. Under such circumstances, an entire organization may become a slave to a set of predetermined prescriptions and lose the freedom of enquiry. When we add to this the difficulties arising from the short life of most social theories, the field of development begins to appear like a series of fads, and not a scientific process of learning about how to build a better world and bring an acceptable level of prosperity to the great masses of humanity.

The problem actually runs deeper. As David Bohm, the well-known physicist and philosopher, has pointed out, the way most intellectual disciplines treat theory today is intimately connected with the fragmentation of thought that is prevalent in society. At the most fundamental level, this fragmentation arises, he argues, from our insistence that our theories correspond to "reality as it is" rather than being manageable models of limited sets of phenomena occurring within an objective reality that is infinitely complex. Since our theories are necessarily fragmented, by considering them replicas of "reality as it is," we end up assuming that reality itself is fragmented. And so we miss the interconnectedness of all things. . . .

Theories, of course, are constantly evolving, but as Bohm suggests, instead of assuming that "older theories are falsified at a certain point of time," we should accept that we are "continually developing new forms of insight, which are clear up to a point and then tend to become unclear." This conception of theory, namely, "theories as sources of insight" has helped us immensely at FUNDAEC in advancing our various lines of action. It has allowed us to study freely and gain insights from a wide range of scientific theories, without falling into the trap of undue theoretical debate. These insights guide us in our endeavors all of which are concerned in one way or another with capacity building—in individuals, in communities, and in institutions. This we do through a process of action, reflection on action, research, and study all focused on learning how to bring about desired change to some aspect of society. Treating theory in this way has also helped us to avoid, to a reasonable extent, the usual dichotomy between theoretical elaboration and practice. It has assisted us in dealing with theory and practice as two inseparable parts of one whole, each feeding and being fed by the other.

The degree of detachment from theory that we have tried to achieve is not without its dangers. For, it could readily lead us to haphazard and frenetic activity. But development cannot be the result of a series of disconnected interventions. Social action needs to be consistent and coherent. The way we have tried to achieve such coherence is to ensure that our action and research occur within an evolving conceptual framework, which we examine often, taking the necessary time and energy to make it explicit. This conceptual framework consists of series of elements related to the way we interpret the world around us, our assumptions, our ideals, our aims, our values, our approach to life, and our methodological perspective. Our understanding of these elements grows organically as we apply them and use them to shape our programs of action. We could not say at any given moment that this framework is complete, but it does manage to give consistency to our endeavors.[60]

FUNDAEC emerged in response to the perceived limitations of the development discourse and practice of the day. Social and economic development in the mid-1970s was being conceived, it felt, as a series of packages to be presented from the "developed" to the "undeveloped." Even discussions about participation centered on how a population would receive the prepared package, and rarely on how it would contribute fully to the consultation on and planning of its affairs. Rural education, to take an example, when available, provided students with a curriculum mirroring that of industrialized nations, which held little meaning for the rural populations of a developing nation. Thus graduates would abandon their farms and villages to flock to the margins of urban areas. During its first years of its existence, FUNDAEC focused on one rural area near the city of Cali and tried to understand how the population of the region could benefit from science and religion as two complementary systems of knowledge and practice in order to generate and apply knowledge to address their specific problems and concerns.

The central institution of the population of the region, as conceived by FUNDAEC, was the "Rural University," which was to set in motion and catalyze processes that would contribute to the region's continual progress. Such a university was to develop human resources through formal and non-formal programs, strengthen the scientific and technological capacities of the rural population, and study the processes of community life and the corresponding institutional arrangements in such areas as primary and secondary production, marketing, flow of information, socialization of the young, health and sanitation, and governance. After about a decade of experience in the region near Cali, FUNDAEC's focus shifted away from a rural area per se to various microregions each consisting of villages, towns and even one or two large urban centers. The concept of a Rural University also changed into that of a University for Integral Development which serves as a "social space" connecting individuals and institutions in a microregion and providing the means for the population to learn systematically about the changes taking place within it, while drawing from the universe of knowledge—modern and traditional—and from the experiences of other populations facing similar challenges.

FUNDAEC's methodology of a continual process of action and reflection within an evolving conceptual framework replaced the elaborate analysis and planning typical of development interventions. Coherent sets of activity would be set in motion within a population one after the other, each involving reflection and analysis, the sharing of experiences among different groups, consultation about results in the light of other experiences and theories, and systematization of the knowledge being generated in order to advance the framework of all participating groups. Haleh Arbab explains:

> The University for Integral Development establishes its operations in a region of a country through an agreement between FUNDAEC and an indigenous non-governmental organization. The region usually enjoys a more or less well-defined ecological, cultural and political identity, and includes a sizeable rural area of many villages. It may also embrace several towns and possibly one or two cities. In this combination of rural and urban settings, the University identifies those practices—individual, group and community—that together define the social, economic, political and cultural life of the inhabitants of the region. It sets in motion, one by one, learning processes that would help transform these practices so as to improve the welfare of the entire population. In learning about socially significant undertakings and their transformation, the University places great importance on the creation of human resources and the enhancement of institutional capacity, both necessary if a given population is to gradually become the true protagonist of its own development.

Learning processes are formally designed and involve action, research and training woven into one coherent set of activities. These are to occur in the very social spaces where the population engages in the multitude of undertakings essential to its progress. The University is to be present in almost every instance of social action, accompanying the population, organizing existing knowledge, generating new knowledge, and offering the fruits of systematic learning to the community and its institutions. A few examples will illustrate the approach being described here.

In a typical region where the University for Integral Development would operate, a set of practices defines the production of crops and animals in small family farms. The institutions that sustain this type of production include land tenure, the extended family, markets, and government extension services. The practices themselves consist of those resting on a traditional knowledge system evolved over centuries and newer ones adopted under the pressures of modernization. . . . In a disintegrating village economy, however, this mode of production is incapable of holding its own, and the University is bound to find the small farms of the region in profound crisis. The crisis manifests itself in a range of phenomena. Some are easily identified such as the deterioration of soils and intensification of pests; others are more subtle, for example, the loss of genetic potential and the weakening of the bonds of solidarity and of connection to nature. . . . The University for Integral Development sets in motion in the region a learning process—action, research and training—to search for alternative systems of small farm production.

The search for alternative production systems is not a romantic inquiry into the past. The purpose is not to preserve traditional practices for the sake of preservation. But nor does activity consist of the mere introduction of the latest technological packages, perhaps tested on a few farms of the region according to the more enlightened methods of extension. The task is to help evolve a new and dynamic rationality of production that carries over the desirable elements of the previous one but is shaped according to the exigencies of a new life into which all of humanity must enter. As such a rationality is being built, a combination of technological and social research is vigorously pursued in order to discover the appropriate systems of production, to determine the appropriate technology, and to create and strengthen the appropriate institutional arrangements. Research and action are carried out with the participation of the population itself. Experiments are designed and implemented together by the professionals from the University and the farmers in order to develop individual subsystems that can then be put together according to the conditions on each farm in the region. The development, adaptation, and application of specific technology, however, are not the only objects of research. The entire scientific and technological culture of the population must advance, and this is the context within which the learning process is set in motion. Furthermore, although the immediate concern of this process is material culture, the University is cognizant that all technological choices are dictated by a system of values. Action, research and training, then, are undertaken in the light of a discourse on the implications of spirituality for individual and social life that the University helps initiate and nurtures in the region. . . .

Yet another learning process set in motion by the University for Integral Development in a typical region is directed towards the strengthening of local economies. Here attention is focused on small-scale economic activity—in agricultural and animal production, in processing, in manufacturing, and in various types of services and support including marketing. Those engaged in activity of this kind, and the small enterprises with which they are associated, are victims of social and economic forces far too strong to be overcome by haphazard and uncoordinated remedial action. What is needed is the establishment of institutions and processes that embody the spirit of human solidarity. As a learning process, the strengthening of local economies seeks to discover systematically the modes of operation of such institutions and to determine the shape of various types of economic activity.[61]

For more than thirty years the University for Integral Development has applied the above methodology to engage in a wide range of investigations. For each of the major processes of community development in various microregions, a research agenda has been established and carried out. Depending on the nature of the problems and on the opportunities available, some activities have begun as modest research projects, some as simple actions at the community level, and some as courses for small groups of students. Often they have evolved into rather complex lines of action which have resulted in the moral and intellectual empowerment of thousands of people. Rather than being "objects"

of study, the individuals from the local population who have par-
ticipated in the University for Integral Development have become
active agents in research, reflection, and action. They have freed
themselves from the dichotomy of the traditional and modern, a
major cause of confusion throughout the planet, and have fully
engaged in the elaboration of a vision of progress for the realization
of which they have learned to work systematically.

Interestingly, FUNDAEC has made little use of academic publications for the diffusion of its findings. Rather, the textbooks of
its formal educational programs have been the main depositories
of the knowledge it has generated. One such program, the Tutorial
Learning System—SAT (Sistema de Aprendizaje Tutorial)—has
become an alternative secondary rural education program recognized by the government of Colombia, has reached over 50,000
students in 22 provinces of that country, and is gradually spreading
to other countries in Latin America, Africa and Asia. The 74 units
to be studied by the students of this program are not only based
on the research carried out by FUNDAEC over the years, but also
guide the students—the new participants in the University for
Integral Development—to continue the process of generation
and application of knowledge. Building on SAT, FUNDAEC has
gone on to develop other educational programs, degree courses in
rural education and the administration of local economies and a
postgraduate program on education for development. Haleh Arbab
describes FUNDAEC's educational aims:

> One of the concerns that originally led to the creation of the
> University for Integral Development is the increasing superfi-
> ciality of the education received by the majority of the children
> and youth in the world today. In most cases the result of such
> education is the fragmentation of the student's mind and its
> final outcome compliance with the social and spiritual vacuum
> that characterizes present-day society. The object of the learning
> process, then, is to create an educational alternative for the region
> which would endow the students with a twofold moral purpose: to
> take charge of their own personal intellectual and spiritual growth
> and to contribute meaningfully to the transformation of society.
>
> In most educational systems, students attend classes orga-
> nized by subject matters that in one way or another are based on
> the division of knowledge into distinct disciplines. This division
> is seen as inherent to knowledge itself, which is defined in terms

of its fragments—as the sum of all the disciplines in natural and social sciences, arts and humanities, and professional fields such as engineering and medicine. Students accumulate, year after year, aggregates of information about each subject matter without an adequate understanding of the concepts that give structure to the corresponding discipline. And, even if they are fortunate enough to achieve a reasonable level of understanding in one subject—usually through the efforts of a talented teacher—they rarely get a glimpse of knowledge as one interconnected whole or develop a mind structured enough to investigate reality and become partners in its continual recreation. The problem is not circumscribed to traditional systems founded on rote learning; it is even more apparent in the dozens of competing approaches considered to be modern, in which enormous effort goes into building self-confidence not on solid knowledge and real competence but on the thin air of illusion.

The learning process in question, then, seeks to design and put into practice curricula for various educational levels—preschool, basic, high school, and university—which foster creativity and the will to act in a structured and disciplined way. In the design of curricula, particularly for the first three levels, traditional subject matters are set aside; educational activities integrate knowledge from various disciplines in a way that is conducive to profound understanding and the cultivation of noble qualities of the human soul. They focus on the development of those capabilities—scientific, artistic, technical, social, moral and spiritual—that enable the students to vigorously pursue, according to the exigencies of each stage of life, their twofold moral purpose. In general, they are intellectually more challenging than comparable activities in educational systems prevalent in most countries. They achieve great success among populations who are considered by some culturally unprepared for rigorous scientific training.[62]

The approach adopted by FUNDAEC illustrates ongoing search for valid methodologies of social action that incorporate spiritual principles and, particularly Bahá'u'lláh's teachings, into rigorous processes of research and action in order to find practical solutions to the problems faced by the peoples of the world. Applying Bahá'í teachings in efforts that address specific development challenges implies much more than a quick reading of selected texts. FUNDAEC's experience is valuable largely because of its attempt to create a framework within which it can act and generate knowledge. This evolving framework is built of insights from the various fields of human learning, particularly science, and of certain beliefs, practices, and principles, drawn largely from the Revelation—the oneness of humankind, consultation, justice, the equality of men and women, and so on. The values present in this framework are incorporated in all endeavors, for example, in technological choice, in pedagogy and in the way human beings are mobilized to participate in the search for and application of solutions. The methodology clearly depends on the inter-penetration of the twin knowledge systems of science and religion, as explained by one of FUNDAEC's founders, Farzam Arbab, in the context of an international effort to promote a discourse on science, religion and development:

> Science in its broadest sense, embracing a wide range of phenomena in both nature and society, admits a variety of approaches and methods each suitable to the character of the specific object of inquiry. In the study of innumerable systems and processes, questions related to the existence of God or the spiritual dimension of life simply do not arise; proper method must necessarily exclude them from consideration, if for no other reason than the preservation of scientific rigor. Yet when such exclusion becomes a rule to be applied dogmatically across the board, an inflexibility sets in that robs science of some of its powers. Rigidly "scientific" approaches make it difficult to weigh science's own assumptions in balance with belief systems lying outside it. They allow the study of religion, but usually as a psychic or social phenomenon created by the interactions of human beings among themselves and with their environment, interactions that, in the final analysis, are thought to occur among aggregates of atoms and molecules each behaving in strict compliance with the measure of complexity accorded it by nature. That this is not the view of the vast majority of humanity who, everyone agrees, will have to participate fully in the process of social transformation, and whose cultures, beliefs and values are to be incorporated into the design and implementation of development activity, poses a contradiction that severely limits the usefulness of development studies carried out according to narrow definitions of the "scientific method."
>
> I take it to be a premise of our research program that it is possible to explore issues of religious belief rigorously without trivializing them and explaining them away, without relegating

matters of faith only to the private and isolated world of the individual, and without confining religious practice to the domain of ritual legitimized by the needs of humanity as a social species. This, of course, is not a new premise; it underlies the work of social scientists and theologians of various schools. Unfortunately, it has not had a significant influence on the kind of thinking that, in the past few decades, has shaped the field of development.

Furthermore, it appears unavoidable that in order to deal properly with the difficulties of methodological choice, our approach to this research should remain measured and judicious. Thus, I hope that for some time to come the emphasis will continue to be on the formulation of a discourse on the theme of science, religion, and development, and not shift to elaborate studies or the articulation of hypotheses. Naturally, to be scientific, our discourse would have to fulfill certain conditions. For example, its language must strive to be rational, unambiguous, and objective. The challenge before us is to achieve this when the object of inquiry touches so intimately on each participant's own faith.

I find quite inadequate the approach to the study of religion according to which the researcher is divided into two separate entities, the scientist and the believer, the first bound to the rules of academia and the second obliged to ignore the absurdities that this duality introduces into his or her belief system. That so untenable an approach should have achieved widespread acceptance is due to the impositions of secularism acting as a kind of fundamentalist creed. As a result, much of the reality of science, religion and the forces that transform society has ended up hidden behind a veil created by false objectivity.

The alternative to the prevailing situation is not apologetics or sectarian controversy. What is called for is a new look at the interpenetration of reason and faith, as well as a systematic exploration of rational approaches that are not tied to materialism. While such a thorough exploration is not part of the mandate of the present project, acknowledgement of its absolute necessity is important to our frame of reference.

An immediate consequence of this realization, it could be argued, is to require the researcher in certain fields to make explicit relevant aspects of his or her own belief and experience. To do so in a meaningful way, one must be convinced that it is possible to be firm in one's convictions without being judgmental. Although the statement "if I believe something to be right, then he whose opinions differ from mine must be wrong" passes the tests of formal logic, and although it is applicable in countless situations, its usefulness vanishes once the object of discussion becomes relatively complex. It is not that "A" and "not A" can both be true, but that the vastness of truth does not allow most matters of belief, if there is any depth to them at all, to be reduced to such comparisons. The only options this simplistic posture finally leaves open are either religious and ideological fanaticism or the brand of relativism that does away with faith, embraces skepticism, and idolizes doubt. It is instructive to note how the assaults of such relativism on belief, initially launched against religion, have been directed in the postmodern era to the very foundations of science.[63]

Contributing to Humanity's Collective Discourse

A third aspect of the contributions Bahá'ís make to the civilization-building process is through participation in humanity's collective discourse on the challenges and opportunities facing the world. This occurs at all levels of society, but more particularly through efforts to reach leaders of thought. Such participation includes individual Bahá'ís who contribute as experts in their fields, or through their involvement in governmental or non-governmental organization, as well as Bahá'í-inspired initiatives. It also involves the direct contributions of Bahá'í institutions, especially through the Bahá'í International Community at the United Nations.

For example, as the number of Bahá'í social and economic development organizations and their body of experience has increased, the Bahá'í world has been able to expand its involvement in the global discourse on development. One channel has been the publications of individual Bahá'ís who are experts in related fields. The Universal House of Justice notes that "As the friends gain experience in social and economic development, and as they advance in their studies of various branches of learning or in their professional fields, individuals arise in every continent who have expertise in some aspect of development work. . . ."[64] Another channel is the establishment of the Institute for Studies in Global Prosperity at the Bahá'í World Centre. As its first initiative, the Institute launched a program to promote a discourse on science, religion, and development. The activities of the program began in India with a colloquium held in New Delhi in November 2000 that brought together more than a hundred representatives of non-governmental organizations from all regions of the country. The warm reception by individuals and agencies in India to this gathering has prompted steps to promote similar efforts in Africa and Latin America.

Another way in which Bahá'ís attempt to contribute to humanity's discourse for the betterment of the world is through external affairs activities, particularly in such areas as human rights, the status of women, global prosperity, and moral development. The efforts of the Bahá'í International Community to share the Bahá'í perspective is summarized as follows:

> At the general level, the Bahá'í International Community (BIC) has participated in a number of major international summits and nongovernmental forums. Notable among them have been the United Nations Conference on Environment and Development (the "Earth Summit") in Rio de Janeiro in 1992, the World Summit for Social Development in Copenhagen in 1995, and the Fourth World Congress on Women in Beijing that same year, as well as the World Conference Against Racism in 2001 and the World Summit for Sustainable Development in 2002, both held in South Africa, and the 2005 Annual Meeting of the World Economic Forum in Davos, Switzerland.
>
> Because of the worldview deriving from the Bahá'í system of belief, the community has taken a particularly keen interest in discussions that explore the contribution of religion to questions of development. These have included the "World Faiths and Development Dialogue," cosponsored by the World Bank and the Archbishop of Canterbury held in Lambert Palace, London, in 1998, and the Parliament of World Religions held in South Africa in 1999. Especially enriching has been the involvement, from 1995 to 2000, in a project sponsored by the International Development Research Centre (IDRC) in Canada, which explored the relationship between science, religion, and development.
>
> The community has found in this series of activities welcome opportunities to give expression to the central conviction animating Bahá'í work in the development field. As early as the Earth Summit, a statement submitted by the BIC to the plenary session, on behalf of all religious nongovernmental organizations, concluded: "The profound and far-reaching changes, the unity and unprecedented cooperation required to reorient the world toward an environmentally sustainable and just future, will only

be possible by touching the human spirit, by appealing to those universal values which alone can empower individuals and peoples to act in accordance with the long-term interests of the planet and humanity as a whole."[65]

A steady flow of documents from the Bahá'í International Community and from National Assemblies have presented the Bahá'í perspective to a variety of audiences. Among these are the aforementioned *The Prosperity of Humankind*, distributed at the World Summit on Social Development, and the document *Valuing Spirituality in Development: Initial Considerations Regarding the Creation of Spiritually Based Indicators for Development*, prepared as a follow-up to the World Faiths and Development Dialogue. The latter discusses five principles—unity in diversity, equity and justice, the equality of the sexes, trustworthiness and moral leadership, and the independent investigation of truth—that may offer a measurable means for assessing the impact of values on development. In some cases, the Universal House of Justice has directly addressed problems confronting humanity, for example in the statement on peace to the peoples of the world in July 1985, and more recently, in a message to religious leaders April 2002.

The success of the initial involvement of the Bahá'í community in some of the discourses of the wider society points to the need to cultivate, over time, a greater involvement of Bahá'ís in all fields of human endeavor. Drawing from the insights provided by the teachings and reinforced by the growing experiences of Bahá'ís working for social justice and the common good, institutions and individuals can engage others and become effective participants in the search for constructive solutions to human problems.

The Nature of Bahá'í Intellectual Activity

Bahá'u'lláh and 'Abdu'l-Bahá, as well as the Guardian and the Universal House of Justice, leave no room for doubt regarding the essential value of Bahá'í intellectual activity. No romantic notions, no appeal to mystical insight, nor any apposite principles associated with obedience, unity, or spirituality can call into question the attainments of the mind and the vital role of the truly learned in this dispensation.

"The man of consummate learning and the sage endowed with penetrating wisdom are the two eyes to the body of mankind,"[66]

Bahá'u'lláh states. And He adds: "Righteous men of learning who dedicate themselves to the guidance of others and are freed and well guarded from the promptings of a base and covetous nature are, in the sight of Him Who is the Desire of the world, stars of the heaven of true knowledge."[67] "There are certain pillars which have been established as the unshakeable supports of the Faith of God," 'Abdu'l-Bahá explains. "The mightiest of these is learning and the use of the mind, the expansion of consciousness, and insight into the realities of the universe and the hidden mysteries of Almighty God. To promote knowledge is thus an inescapable duty imposed on every one of the friends of God."[68]

Shoghi Effendi urges the Bahá'ís "to accord honor, veneration and respect to—and endorse the efforts of—exponents of the arts and sciences, and to esteem and revere those who are possessed of extensive knowledge and scholarly erudition."[69] And the Universal House of Justice observes that Bahá'ís have been "encouraged from the time of the Faith's inception to pursue knowledge in all its forms and to excel in such attainments"[70] and it "regards Bahá'í scholarship as of great potential importance for the development and consolidation of the Bahá'í community as it emerges from obscurity."[71]

Such emphatic and repeated authoritative statements should be sufficient to ensure that the body of the believers and the national and local institutions do not succumb to a reactionary anti-intellectualism or superstitious spiritualism that have corrupted religious practice in past dispensations. Nor should the sincere efforts of those who labor in scholarly disciplines—and who as human beings will inevitably err—be confused with the actions of a handful of "unwise or malicious"[72] individuals, who, immovably attached to their own views, attempt to impose them on the community.

To appreciate the nature of the praise bestowed on the learned so lavishly in the Bahá'í Writings, one must also be aware of Bahá'u'lláh's warning against the dangers of the kind of learning that results in arrogance and separation from the divine purpose. "Amongst the people is he whose learning hath made him proud . . . who, when he heareth the tread of sandals following behind him, waxeth greater in his own esteem."[73] And He states: "True learning is that which is conducive to the well-being of the world, not to pride and self-conceit, or to tyranny, violence and pillage."[74] It is for such reasons that 'Abdu'l-Bahá admonished the learned, citing the authoritative Islamic tradition, "'As for him who is one of the learned: he must guard himself, defend his faith, oppose his passions and obey the commandments of his Lord.'" "Whoever is lacking in these divine qualifications and does not demonstrate these inescapable requirements in his own life," He concludes, "should not be referred to as learned."[75]

> For desire is a flame that has reduced to ashes uncounted lifetime harvests of the learned, a devouring fire that even the vast sea of their accumulated knowledge could never quench. How often has it happened that an individual who was graced with every attribute of humanity and wore the jewel of true understanding, nevertheless followed after his passions until his excellent qualities passed beyond moderation and he was forced into excess. His pure intentions changed to evil ones, his attributes were no longer put to uses worthy of them, and the power of his desires turned him aside from righteousness and its rewards into ways that were dangerous and dark.[76]

Knowledge can be a veil. It can prevent one from recognizing the Manifestation of God. But the history of the Faith also demonstrates that those who recognize the Manifestation are not immune to such dangers and, seduced by their own views, can follow a destructive course. 'Abdu'l-Bahá warns:

> O ye loved ones of the Lord! Open the ear of inner understanding and refrain from all manner of mischief. Should ye perceive the odor of sedition from any soul, even though to outward seeming he be a prominent personage or a peerless man of learning, know ye of a certainty that he is an antichrist amongst men, an opponent of the religion of the All-Glorious, an enemy of the reality of the Almighty, a destroyer of the edifice of God, a violator of His Covenant and Testament, and an outcast from the threshold of the merciful Lord. One who is possessed of true knowledge and insight is even as a shining lamp and is the cause of the well-being and advancement of the dwellers of both the lesser and the greater worlds. Prompted by his faith and by his allegiance to the Covenant, such a soul striveth for the good of humanity and seeketh the peace and tranquility of mankind.[77]

Guarded by humility, by a deep and thoughtful appreciation of the mutable and limited nature of their views, and by the obligation to be firm in the Covenant and preserve unity, those who engage in

Bahá'í scholarly activity explore new perspectives, examine aspects of the community's understanding and practices, and propose promising avenues for a fuller expression of the potentialities latent in Bahá'u'lláh's Revelation. As participants in all fields of human endeavor, they bring insights from sciences and the Bahá'í teachings to bear upon various questions, thereby contributing to the evolution of thought and action that leads to social transformation and well-being. When attitude and method are sound, errors and false starts are nothing more than natural occurrences in the process of the investigation of reality. A variety of metaphors help clarify the role of a learned Bahá'í in contributing to the progress of the Bahá'í community.

The learned Bahá'í is not a "gatekeeper" or "priest." While the effective work of trained, knowledgeable, and insightful individuals shed light on the context and meaning of the Writings in many ways, the community of believers is not dependent upon a body of specialists in order to understand the meaning of the Text. The Word of God is accessible to all believers, according to their capacity. The experience of the community derived from practice, the growing understanding of the implications and meaning of the Text over time, and above all, the guidance of the Universal House of Justice contribute to shaping both the believers' understanding as well as the perspective and direction of scholarly activity.

The learned Bahá'í is not an "anthropologist" of the Bahá'í community. The purpose of Bahá'í scholarship is not merely to explain the community at a moment in history and present the resulting picture as its reality. Bahá'ís recognize that, at any point, the community is far from that which Bahá'u'lláh has envisioned. It is "less Bahá'í" now than what it will become in future.

The learned Bahá'í is not an "archeologist." The "true" meaning of the Faith is not lost somewhere in the past, to be recaptured by excavating layers of erroneous interpretation and practice. Such an approach is especially problematic if it is used to justify a search for the meaning of the Faith in Bahá'u'lláh's Writings alone, while ignoring the role of the authoritative institutions He established to guide His Faith.

The learned Bahá'í is not an "artist" who is free to shape the teachings according to some criteria of personal choice or creativity. The teachings of Bahá'u'lláh have an intended meaning and an intended aim. Unity—even unity in diversity—emerges by seeking out and conforming to this meaning. One cannot select, rearrange, or craft from the teachings, according to subjective standards, a particular narrative or design. If such an approach were pursued, the Faith would become nothing more than an individual or cultural adornment.

The learned Bahá'í is not an "impartial observer." The resolution of important questions requires more than the application of methods of the natural sciences. It is not possible to stand apart from the community to study it without influencing it or being influenced by it.

Perhaps the learned Bahá'í is more like the "scout" who helps to guide an expedition on a journey into unexplored territory. This role involves investigating the unknown and generating and applying knowledge to contribute to the success of the mission at hand. It is someone who participates actively in the journey, but whose specialized knowledge, skills, and experience informs various aspects of the struggle to make progress: constructive perspectives into the past, present, and future; insight and technical capacity for ongoing study of the Text; problem posing and problem solving; the defining of culture and intercultural relations. On this journey, the learned individual/scout does not have authority, and, while making a vital contribution, like any other participant is fallible and learns over time.

One of the distinctions often made between the natural and social sciences is that in the natural sciences, the study is of objects; in the social sciences the study is of people—"the object is a subject."[78] This presents a special challenge to the social sciences because not only are researchers attempting to make sense of their studies, but the people they are attempting to understand are also continually engaged in an ever-changing process of interpretation and action. The implication of this specific challenge is not that one cannot conduct research in areas that pertain to human beings, but rather, that in doing so one must be aware of the inherent limitations and potential consequences in order to determine how best to be effective.

Bahá'ís engaging in scholarly activity have to confront the problems that arise from these two levels of interpretation—especially those concerned with studies that focus on the Faith itself. The researcher's knowledge, attitudes, choices, assertions, and assumptions have a bearing on the outcome of a particular study. And they influence and are influenced by the knowledge, attitudes, choices, responses, assertions, and assumptions of the community members who are the objects and active recipients of that study. A Bahá'í researcher cannot, when operating within the framework of Bahá'í practice, suspend Bahá'í principles, methods or knowledge without consequences. Those consequences are not diminished, but are even compounded, when a Bahá'í acts from within another practice—that of a particular academic field—while studying some aspect of the Faith.

The problem of framing categories of liberals and fundamentalists in the Bahá'í community is an example of this problem.[79] One cannot propose the existence of these categories solely as an instrument of academic study without simultaneously introducing them as an aspect of social reality lived by the believers and the institutions. Selecting and refining the methods appropriate to Bahá'í scholarly activity must take into account this hidden, but weighty concern.[80]

It is for this reason that Bahá'í who are specialists in a particular field cannot separate themselves into two distinct persons, believer and scholar. The Writings and ideas of the scholar will, especially if they distort the teachings in an effort to conform to the demands of a particular academic discipline, have consequences for the community of believers. This does not prevent Bahá'ís from having successful professional or academic careers, but creates a challenge for how to bridge the tensions that sometimes arise from participation in both communities.

The scholarly activity carried out within the Bahá'í community of practice requires consciousness of the difference between studying the Faith as an object, to collaborating in the movement toward its aims and purpose within the framework of the Covenant.[81] Bahá'ís endowed with intellectual capacity direct their energies toward the transformative aims of the Faith. The teachings of God are intended for the masses of humanity; the goal is a new race of human beings and a world order that reflects the oneness of humanity. The learned followers of Bahá'u'lláh stand with the peoples of the world and are protagonists serving the forces of change toward justice and unity.

Bahá'í scholarly activity is vital to the progress of the Faith and its engagement with the wider society. The fruits, however, will only be abundantly realized as the culture of learning that is beginning to emerge in the fields of teaching and development also takes root in such efforts. Any existing tensions have to give way to a community of inquirers using sound hermeneutical principles; involved in consultation, action, and reflection; conscious of their role and influence as an integral part of the Bahá'í community and in the other practices in which they participate; imbued with qualities, attitudes, and behaviors shaped by the teachings; and operating in harmony with the teachings of the Faith and the guidance of the Universal House of Justice. This culture of learning will be characterized by error and achievement and by periods of ambiguity or of consensus punctuated by valuable new insights. In a culture of learning, Bahá'í specialists will find personal fulfillment in their chosen discipline and will contribute their share to the progress of the Cause and of society.

Understanding and Action and the Building of a New World

At this early stage in the Faith's development, Bahá'ís must learn how to engage in a process of understanding and practice that translates the teachings into reality, so as to weave the tapestry of Bahá'í life and gradually, of social reality, that reveals Bahá'u'lláh's intended design. The Faith must labor under the gaze of a skeptical world; other interested parties—religious, academic, political, social—will not hesitate to pick at the threads of our tapestry, trying to influence its design to conform to their own picture of reality. It is true that, on occasion, part of what we have accepted to be "Bahá'í" is in error; in such cases reweaving is required. But for the most part, we have yet to systematically create the Bahá'í community as it should be; the requisite threads lie expectantly on the floor. Here lies the opportunity before all Bahá'ís, particularly those of learning: to contribute to the progress of the Cause, true to the insights of the teachings and of science and reason; to defend it against the self-interest of others and the potentially distorting standards inadvertently imposed on the Faith by well meaning believers unduly influenced by their fields; and to learn how the community collaborates with all peoples in the construction of a world that reflects Bahá'u'lláh's highest aims—the Most Great Peace and a global civilization that embodies the oneness of humankind.

"Ye are the stars of the heaven of understanding, the breeze that stirreth at the break of day, the soft-flowing waters upon which must depend the very life of all men, the letters inscribed upon His sacred scroll,"[82] Bahá'u'lláh assures His followers. An ever more effective process of understanding and practice is to give rise to a community of people who will act without self-interest for the common good. It is a community of individuals distinguished by moral virtue who are striving for justice, unity, and peace. It is a community of those who, in forgetting themselves, become a leaven that will help lift humanity to a new stage in its development. All are invited to join this community and contribute to its mission; with all those that choose a different path, Bahá'ís consort with friendliness and fellowship, and collaborate in working for the betterment of the world. The following statement of 'Abdu'l-Bahá succinctly captures the aim of understanding and practice in the Bahá'í community:

> O army of God! Today, in this world, every people is wandering astray in its own desert, moving here and there according to the dictates of its fancies and whims, pursuing its own particular caprice. Amongst all the teeming masses of the earth, only this community of the Most Great Name is free and clear of human schemes and hath no selfish purpose to promote. Alone amongst them all, this people hath arisen with aims purified of self, following the Teachings of God, most eagerly toiling and striving toward a single goal: to turn this nether dust into high heaven, to make of this world a mirror for the Kingdom, to change this world into a different world, and cause all humankind to adopt the ways of righteousness and a new manner of life.
>
> O army of God! Through the protection and help vouchsafed by the Blessed Beauty—may my life be a sacrifice to His loved ones—ye must conduct yourselves in such a manner that ye may stand out distinguished and brilliant as the sun among other souls. Should any one of you enter a city, he should become a centre of attraction by reason of his sincerity, his faithfulness and love, his honesty and fidelity, his truthfulness and loving-kindness towards all the peoples of the world, so that the people of that city may cry out and say: "This man is unquestionably a Bahá'í, for his manners, his behavior, his conduct, his morals, his nature, and disposition reflect the attributes of the Bahá'ís." Not until ye attain this station can ye be said to have been faithful to the Covenant and Testament of God. For He hath, through irrefutable Texts, entered into a binding Covenant with us all, requiring us to act in accordance with His sacred instructions and counsels.
>
> O army of God! The time hath come for the effects and perfections of the Most Great Name to be made manifest in this excellent

age, so as to establish, beyond any doubt, that this era is the era of Bahá'u'lláh, and this age is distinguished above all other ages.

O army of God! Whensoever ye behold a person whose entire attention is directed toward the Cause of God; whose only aim is this, to make the Word of God to take effect; who, day and night, with pure intent, is rendering service to the Cause; from whose behavior not the slightest trace of egotism or private motives is discerned—who, rather, wandereth distracted in the wilderness of the love of God, and drinketh only from the cup of the knowledge of God, and is utterly engrossed in spreading the sweet savors of God, and is enamored of the holy verses of the Kingdom of God—know ye for a certainty that this individual will be supported and reinforced by heaven; that like unto the morning star, he will forever gleam brightly out of the skies of eternal grace. But if he show the slightest taint of selfish desires and self love, his efforts will lead to nothing and he will be destroyed and left hopeless at the last.

O army of God! Praise be to God, Bahá'u'lláh hath lifted the chains from off the necks of humankind, and hath set man free from all that trammeled him, and told him: Ye are the fruits of one tree and the leaves of one branch; be ye compassionate and kind to all the human race. Deal ye with strangers the same as with friends, cherish ye others just as ye would your own. See foes as friends; see demons as angels; give to the tyrant the same great love ye show the loyal and true, and even as gazelles from the scented cities of Khatá and Khutan offer up sweet musk to the ravening wolf. Be ye a refuge to the fearful; bring ye rest and peace to the disturbed; make ye a provision for the destitute; be a treasury of riches for the poor; be a healing medicine for those who suffer pain; be ye doctor and nurse to the ailing; promote ye friendship, and honor, and conciliation, and devotion to God, in this world of non-existence.

O army of God! Make ye a mighty effort: perchance ye can flood this earth with light, that this mud hut, the world, may become the Abhá Paradise. The dark hath taken over, and the brute traits prevail. This world of man is now an arena for wild beasts, a field where the ignorant, the heedless, seize their chance. The souls of men are ravening wolves and animals with blinded eyes, they are either deadly poison or useless weeds—all except for a very few who indeed do nurture altruistic aims and plans for the well-being of their fellow men: but ye must in this matter—that is, the serving of humankind—lay down your very lives, and as ye yield yourselves, rejoice.

O army of God! The Exalted One, the Báb, gave up His life. The Blessed Perfection gave up a hundred lives at every breath. He bore calamities. He suffered anguish. He was imprisoned. He was chained. He was made homeless and was banished to distant lands. Finally, then, He lived out His days in the Most Great Prison. Likewise, a great multitude of the lovers of God who followed this path have tasted the honey of martyrdom and they gave up everything—life, possessions, kindred—all they had. How many homes were reduced to rubble; how many dwellings were broken into and pillaged; how many a noble building went to the ground; how many a palace was battered into a tomb. And all this came about that humankind might be illumined, that ignorance might yield to knowledge, that men of earth might become men of heaven, that discord and dissension might be torn out by the roots, and the Kingdom of Peace become established over all the world. Strive ye now that this bounty become manifest, and this best-beloved of all hopes be realized in splendor throughout the community of man.[83]

PART II

Additional Considerations

5
A Problem of Knowledge

FROM THE DISCUSSION IN PART I, it should be clear that there is a process of understanding and action in which the Bahá'í community explores reality, grows in comprehension and knowledge, unifies thought, and contributes to transforming the world in accordance with the truths expressed in Bahá'u'lláh's Revelation. However, there are certain predominant perspectives in contemporary thought that clash with this approach to understanding and action, viewing it as hopelessly naïve, as rigid and fundamentalistic, or as potentially oppressive. It is useful, therefore, to enquire into these perspectives and explore Bahá'í understanding and practice in more depth. This will not only assist in developing a response to certain types of criticism of the Bahá'í community, but will provide an opportunity for additional insights into the teachings. It is crucial, also, for weighing how these contemporary perspectives influence our own thinking.

Since the Enlightenment, humanity (more particularly, Western thought) has sought universal and objective standards for the investigation of reality and discovery of truth so that understanding and practice could be freed from subjective influences. In this perspective, knowledge—a true understanding of reality—serves to defeat superstition and the arbitrary imposition of power that produces tyranny and oppression. The appeal to authority drawn from traditional beliefs is to be displaced by rationality and empirical evidence undistorted by bias or sectarian values. Through institutions like the state, power struggles among individuals are to be restrained; foundational theories of justice and liberty are to define proper social order. In this expansion of rationalism, religion is relegated to the category of subjective belief and progressively dissociated from questions of what is true and what is right. Given time, it is believed, science and reason will solve the problems of humanity and release it from ignorance and superstition, globalization will rationalize the international political and economic order, and universal human rights will be extended to all humanity.

In the past several decades, however, the assumptions, aims, and methods of modernity that have driven humanity's progress for centuries have been increasingly challenged by postmodern thought. The meaning of postmodernism has been presented in diverse and often contradictory ways, with sharp differences about its value, if any. In its extreme form, postmodernism is synonymous with nihilism and relativism—any standards for discriminating between divergent claims to truth or morality are rejected. Postmodern thought has fostered doubt and skepticism. It objected to what it perceives as the positivistic foundations of science and provoked a sharp exchange between the natural and social sciences that became known as the "science wars." It introduced profound changes in the field of philosophy, what some see as a collapse of reason, or failure of epistemology. It contributed to the transformation of journalism from a quest for objective facts to a consumer market suited to subjective tastes—one person's terrorist becomes another's freedom fighter. In undermining the authority previously granted to foundational truths of science and universal values, it appears to have opened the door to endless, adversarial criticism and struggle for power among rival relativistic perspectives.

The clash between modernism and postmodernism centers on questions of knowledge and power. Most branches of study have been touched by this contest, some radically transformed and others stubbornly resistant. But while some have seen this as a struggle of irreconcilable views, an intellectual war that threatens reason and the modern worldview, it seems possible to take a more moderate and constructive perspective.

One of the pivotal voices in postmodern thought, Jean-Francois Lyotard, in "simplifying to the extreme," defined postmodernism as "incredulity toward metanarratives." Nicholas C. Burbules comments on this definition:

> Nearly everyone focuses here on the idea of metanarratives, our attempts to offer general and encompassing accounts of truth, value, and reality. Postmodernism seems to be about denying the possibility of these, and rejecting as monolithic and hegemonic the ones that Western traditions have embraced. But the key term in this phrase (in translation at least) is "incredulity"—a fascinating

and unexpected word. Incredulity is not denial or rejection or refutation; it is an inability to believe. In this difference I think we see what is most distinctive and penetrating in the postmodern insight. . . .

Now we have moved into a strange terrain: one that replaces notions such as "denial" and "refutation" with notions such as "doubt," "displacement," "instability," and "uncertainty." This shift introduces a different notion of "critique." Denial or refutation place one outside of the view being rejected, beyond and above it. But what is our stance to be toward ways of thinking that for us are necessary, that we do not know how to live entirely without—but in which an unshakable confidence is no longer possible? Language, science, ethics, reason and justice are features of the modern world in ways that appear unavoidable: what would the alternatives be, really? But the Enlightenment faith that particular forms of beliefs and practices can gain universal acquiescence as the correct ones, and that through these will come the amelioration of human ignorance and other ills, is impossible to believe any longer, for reasons that have become all too evident in the social and historical events of the modern era. We who are creatures of modernity must confront a crisis of faith in its notions of progress and universal social betterment. It seems, instead, that we have exchanged older problems for newer ones, and if our ways of living are unquestionably better now in some ways, they are worse in others.[1]

From this perspective, postmodern thought can be seen not as an attempt to reject modernity, but as an interrogation of its weaknesses that opens the way for a new, more effective orientation if the consensus required for collective human endeavor can be re-established. It is an effort to provide greater respect for "the other" and an opening in the social realm for voices that had been suppressed or marginalized.[2] Modern thought sought methods and ideals that would provide a sure basis for prosperity and justice. Postmodern thought challenges these assumptions and approaches, but cannot provide a satisfactory alternative.

The tension between modern and postmodern ideas can be seen as part of what is more commonly understood by Bahá'ís as the breakdown of the old world order. The assumptions and intersubjective agreements that formed the basis of the social reality that became the modern world have been challenged, contributing to the process of disintegration that is tearing asunder institutions, belief systems and social relationships. New understandings, new agreements, new behaviors, and new social structures are needed. Postmodern critique is, in a way, an effort to define the crisis of the old world order. Bahá'u'lláh's teachings are concerned with the resolution of this crisis, addressing what needs to be done during the period of transition to establish a new order.

Insights such as these about modernism and postmodernism have implications for the understanding and practice of the Bahá'í community. We cannot completely escape the influence of culture or the breakdown of the old world order. We need to be aware of the ways that traditional religious practice, modern thought, and postmodern thought influence our consciousness and our approach to the Revelation if we are to acquire a deeper understanding of how Bahá'u'lláh expects us to read the Sacred Text and translate His guidance into action. As we increasingly gain a better under-standing for ourselves, we will also be in a position to engage the wider society in an increasingly more constructive dialogue. Two challenges face us in this respect.

The first challenge centers on the question of knowledge. What is knowledge? How do human beings know? How do we determine what is true? How reliable is knowledge derived from religion or from science? Is there some foundation upon which human knowledge rests, or are we forever left with uncertainty and doubt? How do we know that our understanding of the Bahá'í teachings is correct? Must we accept every statement of the Text as equal to any other? When it comes to knowledge, why have religious communities typically divided along the lines of liberalism and fundamentalism? Must this fate inevitably befall the Bahá'í Faith?

The second challenge concerns the question of power as it pertains to the relationship between individuals and groups. What perspective can be drawn from the Bahá'í teachings about the con-temporary discourse on power? What are the relationships among individuals and between individuals and institutions that make the exercise of power possible? How is it determined which practical measures are to be taken? Is unity and peace dependent upon the control of power? What is the relationship between power and free-dom? Is Bahá'í consultation an example of power-free discourse? How do we interact with other individuals and communities without imposing our views, values, and judgments upon them? How do we balance the competing claims of personal conscience and collective action, of independent investigation and obedience, of critical thought and unity? Such questions are particularly important when matters pertaining to knowledge are unsettled. For if we have no reliable means of ascertaining truth and discovering knowledge, does this mean that what happens inside and outside the Baháʼí community is merely the imposition of power?

The problem of knowledge will be addressed in this chapter, the problem of power in the final one.

The False Choice Between Liberalism and Fundamentalism

The deceptively simple question, "How do we know reality?" has been a vital and perplexing concern of humanity for thousands of years. In religious thought, this question has centered on how to understand the sacred teachings, which informs action. This line of inquiry, taken to its extreme, has led to the clash between liberalism and fundamentalism. The postmodern emphasis on relativism exacerbates this divide.

Generally speaking, the fundamentalist, or conservative, clings to the scripture as absolute truth, assumes that the Text means what it plainly says and asserts that the world must be shaped by this truth. Emphasis is placed on individual salvation or on the purity of the community of believers apart from a world that is suffering because it has failed to embrace the truth. The liberal believes that the understanding of scripture must be adapted to the needs of a changing world, asserts that the Book is largely metaphorical in its meaning, works to modify religious forms and communities to fit changing conditions, and is often concerned with social action before individual salvation or sectarian interests. Further, these two perspectives are considered by some to represent different modes of thought, different ways in which human beings know. Depending on how a person's mind works, he or she sees the world one way or another, and gravitates toward one group or the other. The fundamentalist sees sharp distinctions; there is truth and there is error. The liberal sees a range of options and complex, even unique, circumstances in every situation; reality is many shades of gray. In this sense, rather than being associated with religion alone, liberalism and fundamentalism are believed to characterize a framework for rationality that infuses all aspects of life.[3]

The traditions of western thought, specifically, and religious thought, generally, make it tempting to apply the perspective of liberalism and fundamentalism to the Bahá'í community. Attempts in this direction, however, prove to be entirely inadequate. Viewing the Faith in this manner imposes a dichotomy that the teachings of Bahá'u'lláh, by their very nature, have transcended. It suggests that two camps, composed respectively of liberals and fundamentalists, have to emerge as the result of the differences of human minds. Individuals in each camp are bound to interpret and act on the teachings in their distinct ways, with specific implications for the study of the Text, administration, application of laws, education, the teaching work, involvement with society, and a host of other matters. Presumably, changes in the evolution of the Faith, in the action of the center of authority, or in the external environment create conditions for either the liberal or the fundamentalist position to gain ascendancy for a period of time, either within a particular Bahá'í community or at the global level. The only distinction between the expression of this problem in other religions and within the Faith, it might seem, is that the Bahá'ís are preserved from division through the Covenant and loyalty to a single center.

Yet, liberalism and fundamentalism, no matter how moderately presented, insist on specific requirements for understanding that are completely foreign to Bahá'í thought and action. This is not to deny that individual Bahá'ís think differently or that their personal views sometimes clash, but to emphatically reject the assumption that these differences have to crystallize into contending positions. The liberal-fundamentalist dichotomy is a schema, a lens, through which reality is perceived. However, in certain situations a lens will enhance sight, in others it will distort it.

It is clear from the Writings of the Central Figures that Bahá'ís are to see themselves as one community—indeed, as a single soul. The believers commit themselves precisely to learning how to treat diversity in a way that does not lead to conflict or division. In letters written on his behalf, Shoghi Effendi unequivocally repudiates any attempt to label and divide the community:

> The believers should be careful not to deviate, even a hair-breadth, from the Teachings. Their supreme consideration should be to safeguard the purity of the principles, tenets and laws of the Faith. It is only by this means that they can hope to maintain the organic unity of the Cause. There can and should be no liberals or

conservatives, no moderates or extremes in the Cause. For they are all subject to the one and the same law which is the Law of God. This law transcends all differences, all personal or local tendencies, moods and aspirations.[4]

> He urges you to exert your utmost to get the . . . Bahá'ís to put aside such obnoxious terms as "radical," "conservative," "progressive," "enemies of the Cause," "squelching the teachings," etc. If they paused for one moment to think for what purpose the Báb and the Martyrs gave their lives, and Bahá'u'lláh and the Master accepted so much suffering, they would never let such definitions and accusations cross their lips when speaking of each other. As long as the friends quarrel amongst themselves their efforts will not be blessed for they are disobeying God.[5]

Bahá'ís strive to be one so that they can contribute to the establishment of a social order based on the principle of the oneness of humanity—the aim of the Revelation of Bahá'u'lláh. Any model that proposes the sustained existence of antagonistic schools of thought within the community is by definition antithetical to its goals and methods. The attempt to divide the community into liberals and fundamentalists, despite any claim to a value-free distinction, is encumbered by value judgments that immediately pit the two "groups" against one another. The term "fundamentalist" in a Bahá'í context is pejorative. For while the understanding of some Bahá'ís might lead them to eagerly embrace the label "liberal," none would be as favorably inclined toward being identified as a "fundamentalist" because of the contradiction with explicit Bahá'í teachings. Even substituting the less problematic label "conservative" would not ameliorate the negative connotation that lies at the heart of a "liberal" need to define "the other." Such labeling invites aggrieved individuals to try their hand at defining the two contending perspectives. So, for example, the division between the two camps is redrawn between "those who hold a sound understanding of the teachings" and "those who distort its meaning." Labeling that assigns believers to contending groups makes unity impossible.

Another essential contradiction that arises from imposing a liberal-fundamentalist framework onto the Faith is that it locks individuals into conflicts that can never reach resolution. Bahá'ís are encouraged by Bahá'u'lláh to "be united in counsel, be one in thought."[6] We have been given principles of consultation as a means of achieving unity of thought and action, and have been exhorted to avoid clinging to personal views and to consult without rancor. The spirit of true consultation is captured in a prayer of 'Abdu'l-Bahá's for Assemblies:

> We have gathered in this Spiritual Assembly, united in our views and thoughts, with our purposes harmonized to exalt Thy Word amidst mankind. . . . O God! Make our souls dependent upon the Verses of Thy Divine Unity, our hearts cheered with the outpourings of Thy Grace, that we may unite even as the waves of one sea and become merged together as the rays of Thy effulgent Light; that our thoughts, our views, our feelings may become as one reality, manifesting the spirit of union throughout the world.[7]

Dividing the community into two camps reduces such teachings to empty words. Rather than using diverse viewpoints to enhance consultation and then collectively draw closer to the meaning and purpose of the Revelation over time, "liberals" and "fundamentalists" stubbornly hold to predetermined positions. Indeed, whether one considers the problem to be lack of flexibility or too much flexibility in approaching the Bahá'í Writings, the parameters of the debate are fixed and the style is always contentious. Any attempt to impose a liberal-fundamentalist divide on Bahá'í discourse produces the same type of intractable moral arguments that plague society as a whole.[8]

A liberal-fundamentalist framework further contradicts Bahá'í practice through a misdiagnosis of challenges and incorrect prescriptions for action. When individuals and institutions presented their problems to Shoghi Effendi, he repeatedly encouraged them to be patient and persevering, since most problems resulted from the immature practice of the teachings and administrative principles.

> The Guardian feels very strongly that everywhere, throughout the entire Bahá'í world, the believers have got to master and follow the principles of their divinely laid down Administrative Order. They will never solve their problems by departing from the correct procedure. . . . The Bahá'ís have got to learn to live up to the laws of Bahá'u'lláh, which are infinitely higher, more exacting and more perfect than those the world is at present familiar with. Running away, fighting with each other, fostering dissension, is not going to advance . . . [any] Community; all it is going to do is to bring Bahá'u'lláh's plans and work to a standstill until such time as the

believers unite to serve Him, or new and more dedicated souls arise to take their place.[9]

A liberal-fundamentalist mindset does not assess challenges from this perspective, but views problems as inherent to structure. A particular Assembly, for example, may have a tendency to be rigid and controlling in its actions. Rather than seeing this as the immature practice of one group of Bahá'í administrators that requires correction through education, measured feedback, and encouragement, it is argued that the Assembly's action is the result of a "fundamentalist approach" to administrative practice that must be overcome by constant criticism or outright opposition, or by voting for "liberals" to replace the "fundamentalists." It may even lead to recommendations to alter the design of Bahá'í administration to build in artificial checks and balances perceived necessary to prevent fundamentalist "domination." Viewed through the tinted lens of the liberal-fundamentalist dichotomy, the Bahá'í world is a different place indeed. Are we to question whether those with whom we consult are liberals or fundamentalists? Is "our" goal to debate with "them" and have "our" views win out? Do we now factor such considerations into Bahá'í elections? Are there liberal and fundamentalist methods of teaching the Faith? Or, perhaps, we are to conclude that liberals are so accepting of the views of others they see no need to teach, while fundamentalists are determined to pursue their triumphalist schemes of indoctrination. Considerations such as these are the antithesis of the Bahá'í teachings.

Shoghi Effendi explains that "Nothing short of the spirit of a true Bahá'í can hope to reconcile the principles of mercy and justice, of freedom and submission, of the sanctity of the right of the individual and of self-surrender, of vigilance, discretion and prudence on the one hand, and fellowship, candor, and courage on the other."[10] If a so-called "liberal Bahá'í" possesses certain liberal virtues that are compatible with the teachings, then all Bahá'ís ought to possess these virtues. If a so-called "fundamentalist Bahá'í" possesses harmful attributes that are counter to Bahá'u'lláh's teachings, then no Bahá'í should possess them. The reverse is also true. In this sense, both the "liberal" and "conservative" may be perceived as an immature believer lacking in some desirable characteristics or failing to achieve a balance between the virtues that are to distinguish the "true Bahá'í." While no believer may ever achieve the standard described by the Guardian, we cannot aim for anything less. It is the obligation to strive to move past liberalism and fundamentalism, not the claim that we have completely done so, that makes such a framework unacceptable when applied to the Bahá'í community.

If we are to learn how to practice the Faith as Bahá'u'lláh intends in order to achieve His purpose, we also have to learn to try to understand it as He intends, acknowledging that we will struggle a lifetime toward this aim. We cannot even begin this endeavor, however, without releasing ourselves from preconceived notions and their associated patterns of action. As 'Abdu'l-Bahá states:

> Just as the thoughts and hypotheses of past ages are fruitless today, likewise dogmas and codes of human invention are obsolete and barren of product in religion. Nay, it is true that they are the cause of enmity and conducive to strife in the world of humanity; war and bloodshed proceed from them, and the oneness of mankind finds no recognition in their observance.[11]

While the framework of liberalism and fundamentalism may be useful for an analysis of religion as it has often been practiced, or even for an analysis of the adolescent stage of human thought, it is inadequate for understanding a new stage in the spiritual evolution of humanity. A different framework for human rationality is required.

One insight is provided by Richard J. Bernstein in the book, *Beyond Objectivism and Relativism: Science, Hermeneutics, and Praxis*. Bernstein is of the opinion that modern intellectual and cultural life is affected by an uneasiness that has spread to almost every discipline and every aspect of society. The source of this uneasiness, he suggests, is the opposition between objectivism—the view that knowledge must be grounded on a particular basis—and relativism—the view that any claim to truth, knowledge or morality are not absolute but exist only in relation to a particular culture, society, or historical context.

Bernstein describes objectivism as "the basic conviction that there is or must be some permanent, ahistorical matrix or framework to which we can ultimately appeal in determining the nature of rationality, knowledge, truth, reality, goodness, or rightness."[12] There are closely related variations of this argument in different contexts,[13] but all basically come down to the idea that we can have a way of obtaining certain knowledge about the world around us. At different times in history, human beings had different ideas about what constitutes this basis of knowledge. At one time, it was believed that the proper use of pure reason through philosophy would enable humanity to determine what was true. In recent times, science has become the authoritative source of knowledge about reality. It won this position because of its proven ability to uncover secrets of the physical world and to produce technologies that provide mastery over nature.

History, Bernstein asserts, has demonstrated that claims made on behalf of any particular foundation for knowledge have eventually failed. Objectivism has, therefore, always been followed by doubt and skepticism as to whether we can ever be certain about what we know. Such doubts give rise to the second perspective, relativism, which he describes as "the basic conviction that when we turn to the examination of those concepts that philosophers have taken to be the most fundamental—whether it is the concept of rationality, truth, reality, right, the good, or norms—we are forced to recognize that in the final analysis all such concepts must be understood as relative to a specific conceptual scheme, theoretical framework, paradigm, form of life, society, or culture."[14] Relativism, according to Bernstein, avers that there are no universal principles or absolute standards of truth or reliable methods for discovering knowledge; rather, there is only uncertainty and different, contending viewpoints that are "incommensurate"—as incomparable as apples and oranges. There is no escaping from "our" and "their" ways of knowing; no one way of knowing can be considered to be better or more effective than another. Thus, from the perspective of relativism, it is argued that cultures possess different ways of knowing and the values and beliefs of one cannot be judged by the standards of another.

Over time, Bernstein explains, the pendulum has swung between objectivism and relativism. "Each time that an objectivist has come up with what he or she takes to be a firm foundation, an ontological grounding, a fixed categorical scheme, someone else has challenged such claims and has argued that what is supposed to be fixed, eternal, ultimate, necessary or indubitable is open to doubt and questioning."[15] A secure foundation for knowledge is accepted for a period of time, but then its weaknesses are eventually exposed and it falls from favor, plunging humanity into doubt. Relativism reigns. Then a proposal for a new foundation emerges and gradually gains support until it is widely accepted. Eventually it too is discredited.

This line of thought embellished over the centuries has led, according to Bernstein, to "a grand and seductive Either/Or." "Either there is some support for our being, a fixed foundation for our knowledge, or we cannot escape the forces of darkness that envelop us with madness, with intellectual and moral chaos."[16] It is the choice between objectivism and relativism. However, he views this dichotomy as "misleading and distortive."

Having described the problem, Bernstein calls for an alternative approach to human rationality that seeks a way beyond objectivism and relativism. Drawing upon the work of a number of individuals, he proposes an approach whose features include the importance of dialogue among a community of inquirers, practical reasoning born of experience, and an ability to refine human understanding through action over time. He draws upon Aristotle's description of phronēsis, or practical reasoning, in contrast to epistmē (scientific or theoretical reasoning) and technē (technical or methodological reasoning).[17] The action of a community is guided and directed by phronēsis, which involves reasoning through dialogue, an exchange of differing opinions, interpretation, judgment, and decision-making. It includes practical application of principles to particular situations—a kind of ethical know-how. While reasons do not prove something absolutely, they support judgment. When consensus in a community breaks down, as in the case of questions of rightness or appropriateness, then this type of practical discourse is needed to re-establish the collective agreement upon which further action depends.

Bernstein's analysis portrays human beings as investigators of reality, seeking to interpret and understand the world, and then acting on that understanding to achieve the consensus that shapes social reality. Such an approach is similar to that of a number of scholars that are attempting to find an adequate response to the problem of knowledge arising from the clash between objectivism and relativism, between modernism and postmodernism. Knowledge, in this perspective, involves a shift from epistemology—the branch of philosophy that attempts to define a reliable means for generating knowledge—to hermeneutics—the principles of interpretation used to unravel communication and human understanding. Knowledge is not conceived as an exact description of reality, but involves insights into reality[18] that can guide effective practice. It is not a bedrock, but as a rope in which insights are like fibers, that "may be ever so slender, provided they are sufficiently numerous and intimately connected."[19] It holds, in common with objectivism, a sense that we can know something about reality and can make progress in knowing, but at the same time rejects any claim to certainty that can lead to superstition or oppression. It holds, in common with relativism, a sense of uncertainty about how much we can know and an appreciation for different points of view, but rejects wholesale skepticism that results in unrestricted individualism or nihilism.

This insight into human rationality is similar to what some others have described as a "nonfoundational" approach to questions of knowledge.[20] Whereas foundationalism—what Bernstein refers to as objectivism—seeks a sure means for securing certain knowledge and relativism rejects all such claims, thereby effectively equating knowledge with opinion (or perhaps more specifically, eliminating the concept of knowledge altogether and replacing it with a pluralistic range of equally valid viewpoints), a nonfoundational worldview holds that knowledge is mutable. In a nonfoundational perspective, reality does exist, but human beings are limited in their capacity for understanding and, therefore, must struggle over time to derive more useful descriptions and insights about reality that can guide more effective and productive action in the world.

Knowledge, in a nonfoundational sense, is not an object that can be possessed. It is not accurate information or a correct set of facts that perfectly reflects reality as it is. But neither are all views equal, or all ways of knowing as valid as any other. Many beliefs do not correspond to reality. Certain human practices, buttressed by particular bodies of knowledge, are more conducive to well-being than others. Knowledge that is nonfoundational is intimately tied to language, justification, intersubjective agreement, and relations of power; it is not something that stands apart from human beings. It is ever-evolving. It is tied to experience and is sensitive to context. Knowledge is also tied to theory and universal norms that are attuned to reality, but however robust and reliably predictive, such general understandings are merely insights to be transcended when their limits are eventually exposed. The human enterprise is, then, the never ending investigation of reality, the search for truth, the quest for knowledge, and as important, the application of knowledge to achieve progress, the betterment of the world, and the prosperity of its peoples.

The metaphor of foundationalism is that of building on a rock. If any piece of the foundation of knowledge is seriously compromised, the whole structure falls and doubt reigns supreme. A suitable metaphor of nonfoundational thought is standing on a raft. There is no anchor for knowledge, so change is a constant. With the generation of new insights and new beliefs, it is necessary to regularly alter some essential elements of understanding—to replace pieces of the raft. However, we cannot revise all aspects of our knowledge at the same time—we need some reliable piece of the raft on which to stand to replace other parts.[21]

Human Rationality and the Bahá'í Teachings

Observers may seek to impose a liberal-fundamentalist dichotomy (or relativist-foundationalist) when assessing the development of the Bahá'í Faith. So too, without caution, the tension between liberal and fundamentalist influences can enter the Bahá'í community, shaping attitudes and understanding, and ensnaring Bahá'ís in competing claims made about the nature of Revelation, of knowledge, and of truth. Legitimate questions, posed out of context, create the illusion of irreconcilable differences.

Does not the Revelation provide us with the source of truth? Should we not weigh within the context of the Revelation the standards and methods of humanity? Is not Bahá'u'lláh, as the Manifestation of God, the source of truth? Has not this source of truth been preserved through the Covenant by means of the infallible interpretations of 'Abdu'l-Bahá and Shoghi Effendi and the infallible guidance of the Universal House of Justice? Is it not imperative for the body of believers to understand and be united around certain truths within the Revelation? Does not submission to the will of God mean that an individual should abide by the teachings, rather than attempting to redefine His will to conform to personal conscience and opinion?

Or, is it not true that the meaning of the Revelation can never be exhausted, and that holding only to its literal meaning is misleading? Does 'Abdu'l-Bahá not say that any religion that fails to be accord with science is superstition? Does Shoghi Effendi not assure us that religious truth is relative? Should not Bahá'ís use reason and the best scholarly methods to understand the Sacred Text? Is not every believer entitled to the independent investigation of truth, and freedom of conscience and expression, and the right to formulate personal interpretations of the Writings?

The Bahá'í teachings, however, resolve the apparent contradictions among these questions by transcending the grand "either/or" of foundationalism verses relativism. "It is not for anyone to exceed the limits laid down by God and His law, nor should anyone follow his own idle imaginings," Bahá'u'lláh states.[22] As previously mentioned, Shoghi Effendi warned against both extremes in the development of the Cause.

> It is our primary task to keep the most vigilant eye on the manner and character of its growth . . . lest extreme orthodoxy on one hand, and irresponsible freedom on the other, cause it to deviate from that Straight Path which alone can lead it to success.[23]

Another message, written on his behalf, again emphasizes an alternative to two extremes.

> We believe in balance in all things; we believe in moderation in all things. . . . [W]e must not be too emotional, nor cut and dried and lacking in feeling, we must not be so liberal as to cease to preserve the character and unity of our Bahá'í system, nor fanatical and dogmatic.[24]

The "Straight Path" that avoids the two extremes referred to by the Guardian constitutes a distinct, nonfoundational, option. The Bahá'í Writings place definite limits on understanding. 'Abdu'l-Bahá explains that human beings cannot know the essence of a thing, but only its qualities.[25] He also states that all ways of human knowing—reason, tradition, the senses, and inspiration—are fallible, and therefore must be checked against one another.[26] Science, then, is extolled for its powers of empirical investigation and reason, but its limitations are also acknowledged. Religion takes its place along with science as a means for investigating reality, educating humanity, and contributing to the advancement of civilization. Yet, rejecting scientific positivism does not become a justification for religious foundationalism.

It may appear strange to suggest that religion can be associated with a nonfoundational perspective. Indeed, religion has traditionally been considered to be the archetype of foundational thought. Jesus extols the individual who grounds life in the Word of God: "He is like a man which built an house, and digged deep, and laid the foundation on a rock: and when the flood arose, the stream beat vehemently upon that house, and could not shake it: for it was founded upon a rock," as opposed to "he that heareth,

and doeth not," who "is like a man that without a foundation
built an house upon the earth; against which the stream did beat
vehemently, and immediately it fell; and the ruin of that house
was great."[27] Bahá'u'lláh too, in certain passages appears to support
foundationalism:

> This is the straight Path, the fixed and immovable foundation.
> Whatsoever is raised on this foundation, the changes and chances
> of the world can never impair its strength, nor will the revolution
> of countless centuries undermine its structure.[28]

Nevertheless, a review of a range of passages from the Bahá'í
Writings, including those presented above, leads to a broader perspective. The absolutist dimensions of foundationalism are absent
in the Bahá'í conception of knowledge. Indeed, in one instance
Bahá'u'lláh even associates the consciousness of the limitation of
human capacity to know with the pinnacle of understanding:

> Consider the rational faculty with which God hath endowed
> the essence of man. Examine thine own self, and behold how thy
> motion and stillness, thy will and purpose, thy sight and hearing,
> thy sense of smell and power of speech, and whatever else is related
> to, or transcendeth, thy physical senses or spiritual perceptions, all
> proceed from, and owe their existence to, this same faculty. . . .
>
> Wert thou to ponder in thine heart, from now until the end
> that hath no end, and with all the concentrated intelligence and
> understanding which the greatest minds have attained in the
> past or will attain in the future, this divinely ordained and subtle
> Reality, this sign of the revelation of the All-Abiding, All-Glorious
> God, thou wilt fail to comprehend its mystery or to appraise
> its virtue. Having recognized thy powerlessness to attain to an
> adequate understanding of that Reality which abideth within
> thee, thou wilt readily admit the futility of such efforts as may be
> attempted by thee, or by any of the created things, to fathom the
> mystery of the Living God, the Day Star of unfading glory, the
> Ancient of everlasting days. This confession of helplessness which
> mature contemplation must eventually impel every mind to make
> is in itself the acme of human understanding, and marketh the
> culmination of man's development.[29]

The inability to achieve rational certainty can be distinguished,
of course, from the attainment of spiritual certitude. Certainty
implies an ability to acquire absolute knowledge, a knowledge that

corresponds exactly to reality, a knowledge that rests upon unassailable evidence or immutable fact. Certitude, in contrast, involves unshakable belief supported by justifiable proofs and evidences that are accessible to human capacity. To have certitude that Baháʼuʼlláh is the Manifestation of God for this day and to act with steadfastness is very different than having "certain" knowledge of reality.

It may be tempting to embrace relativism as a Baháʼí approach to knowledge particularly when considering metaphysics.[30] In this context, relativism provides a welcome and much needed alternative to an oversimplified perspective in which the Baháʼí teachings on metaphysical themes such as the nature of God are presented as truth against which the error of other religion doctrines must be measured. It offers a way of moving beyond the problem of a "Baháʼí" foundationalism that would not only foreclose any dialogue with other religious communities but would contradict the Baháʼí concept of the oneness of religion. In discussing metaphysics, a realm in which the limitations of both physical reality and words themselves are exposed, a relativism that arises out of the diversity of approaches that originate from the limitations of the human mind would seem to be essential.

Nevertheless, there are limits to a relativistic perspective, even in the case of metaphysics. For it is not merely the human mind that is at work, but also the active intervention of the Manifestation of God in assessing human capacity to grasp dimensions of reality in a given age. Thus, the choices made by the Manifestations in defining and describing aspects of Their teachings are the starting point for what has become the metaphysical diversity of religious traditions. The approach given emphasis in a particular age is rooted in the Manifestation's innate comprehension of reality as it is, in the necessity of speaking to the beliefs and assumptions of a particular society, and in the intended aim and purpose for individual and collective transformation in that age. Furthermore, relativism would seem to be suitable for Baháʼís only when dealing with texturally supported approaches to metaphysics, such as monism or dualism. Relativism is inadequate as a means of evaluating the merits of pantheism, which is granted a conditional validity in Baháʼí teachings, nor does it allow for rejecting certain approaches, such as a reductionistic materialism or a superstitious spiritualism.

In any case, whatever the merits of relativism in addressing metaphysical concerns, it is nonfoundationalism, not relativism, that most closely correlates with the Baháʾí teachings on knowledge when dealing with the contingent world. A nonfoundational approach to knowledge, like relativism, recognizes the legitimacy of different points of view and the limitations on certainty. Unlike a relativistic approach, however, it permits judgments about inadequacy or error.

While the Baháʾí teachings indicate that human capacity for comprehending reality is circumscribed, they also make it clear that the mind does have access to reliable knowledge. It is possible to acquire insights into reality and into the meaning of the Revelation that guide action so that, over time, an individual or society can make progress. Baháʾuʾlláh has expressed His will and purpose through His teachings, and Baháʾís will struggle over the course of the dispensation to understand these teachings more fully and to translate them into practical action in order to change social reality. Among the many aspects of a Baháʾí approach to human understanding found in the teachings that correspond with a nonfoundational approach to knowledge are the following.

Truth and the Baháʾí Teachings

The Baháʾí Writings about the nature of truth, taken as a whole, reject a strict foundationalist or relativistic position. "This day is the Lord of all days," Baháʾuʾlláh states, "and whatsoever hath been revealed therein by the Source of divine revelation is the truth and the essence of all principles."[31] However, human beings cannot judge the validity of the truths of the Revelation, for "He doeth what He willeth and ordaineth whatsoever He pleaseth" and "none is given the right to question His authority."[32] There is a clear distinction between the mind of God, or more particularly that of His Manifestation, as expressed in Revelation and human understanding of the meaning of the Text. For whatever comes from the Manifestation is "identical with the truth, and conformable to reality,"[33] while all human "criteria or avenues of knowledge" are "faulty and unreliable."[34] "That which is in the hands of people, that which they believe," ʿAbduʾl-Bahá states, "is liable to error." This extends to understanding the Word of God, for the Text itself is apprehended through the limited instrument of human reason.[35] Religious beliefs may even degenerate into superstition. It is the appreciation of the eternal gap between Revelation and our ability to fully comprehend Revelation that proscribes fundamentalism and demands a humble and continual investigation of reality through the knowledge systems of science and religion.

The Bahá'í Writings are equally clear that Bahá'u'lláh "does not ask us to follow Him blindly."[36] The right to freedom of individual conscience and individual interpretation are preserved. All are encouraged to investigate truth. Yet this freedom is not license. There are boundaries. The believers must obey every injunction of the Text, they may not contend with its authoritative interpretation, and they must adhere to the decisions of the Universal House of Justice. Truth does exist—and so does error. "Truth is one, although its manifestations may be very different," 'Abdu'l-Bahá explains.[37] And the Guardian indicates: "The more we read the Writings the more truths we can find in them and the more we will see that our previous notions were erroneous."[38] The Revelation is the expression of the will of God, and we are expected to submit to that will in order to transform ourselves and the society around us. To what does one adhere if personal opinion is the only arbiter of truth? This does not in any way imply that truth is easy to find, but it does point out the contradiction implicit in an extreme relativistic position: the categorical assertion that all views, being contextual, are therefore incommensurable and equally valid or justifiable, is just another form of absolutism.

Thus, the Bahá'í teachings indicate that our grasp of truth lacks the assurance of certainty necessary for foundationalism, or extreme orthodoxy, as well as the arbitrariness implicit in relativism, or irresponsible freedom. The Bahá'í principle of the independent investigation of truth confirms this assertion. The fact that truth must be investigated presumes both that we must continually search it out, but also, that it can be found. Progress in understanding aspects of truth about reality is infinite: even at the end of a dispensation God gives us a fresh measure of truth in a new Revelation. The principle, however, is not an endorsement of subjective belief systems. 'Abdu'l-Bahá clearly foresaw the independent, unprejudiced investigation of truth as leading to common understanding.

> Being one, truth cannot be divided, and the differences that appear to exist among the nations only result from their attachment to prejudice. If only men would search out truth, they would find themselves united.[39]

Human Minds Differ

"It is clear," 'Abdu'l-Bahá states, "that the reality of mankind is diverse, that opinions are various and sentiments different; and this difference of opinions, of thoughts, of intelligence, of sentiments among the human species arises from essential necessity."[40] It is the difference in human minds that gives rise to the debate between foundationalism and relativism. Some are inclined to seek a basis for truth and identify it as a concrete reality; they appreciate the strength provided by certainty. Others see the elusiveness of truth, its shades of gray, and the urgent requirement for free exchange in order to pursue new avenues to acquire truth; they are suspicious of any attempt to rest upon what is already known. However, there is a spectrum of human thought along these lines, not simply two camps. And such differences, if they are allowed to degenerate into conflict and stubborn attachment to personal opinion, will, 'Abdu'l-Bahá assures us, only obscure the truth.[41] But if varying perspectives are harmonized, they become a resource for the investigation of reality. "The diversity in the human family should be the cause of love and harmony as it is in music where many different notes blend together in the making of a perfect chord."[42] 'Abdu'l-Bahá further explains:

> Thus when that unifying force, the penetrating influence of the Word of God, taketh effect, the difference of customs, manners, habits, ideas, opinions and dispositions embellisheth the world of humanity. This diversity, this difference is like the naturally created dissimilarity and variety of the limbs and organs of the human body, for each one contributeth to the beauty, efficiency and perfection of the whole. When these different limbs and organs come under the influence of man's sovereign soul, and the soul's power pervadeth the limbs and members, veins and arteries of the body, then difference reinforceth harmony, diversity strengtheneth love, and multiplicity is the greatest factor for coordination.[43]

Rejecting the false dichotomy of liberalism and fundamentalism, therefore, does not impose uniformity or diminish the diversity of views in the Bahá'í community; rather, it preserves the entire spectrum of individual interpretation as an asset in the search for truth. All views are welcome save those that persist in extremes of orthodoxy or irresponsible freedom, since these extremes are in themselves threats to the process of free investigation. Individuals do not have to subscribe to the hegemony of a particular ideological perspective; instead opinions can vary across a range of practical concerns within differing contexts. In consultation, there is the freedom to say what one thinks and the freedom to give up one's opinion after hearing the ideas of others. In this way, diverse views are harmonized to achieve unity of thought and action.

An Evolving Bahá'í Culture

As it grows and develops, the Bahá'í community accumulates beliefs, knowledge, methods, habits, and practices. This culture, or tradition,[44] shapes the believers, and through their experiences they in turn contribute to modifying the tradition. Thus, generation after generation, the Bahá'í culture grows and evolves. In the long term, there is within the culture a closing of the gap between what the believers bring into the Faith and what Bahá'u'lláh intends—a movement toward the realization of the will of God.

For example, for most of the early part of the twentieth century, many western believers held an inaccurate belief about the station of 'Abdu'l-Bahá, convinced that He was the return of Christ, or at least that He held a higher station than that of the Báb. Shoghi Effendi corrected this perspective in "The Dispensation of Bahá'u'lláh," written in 1934. Thus, today, even a child learns the proper station of each of the Central Figures, an understanding that eluded many prominent believers of an earlier age.

The practice of the Nineteen Day Feast provides another example of cultural progress. Bahá'í pioneers who spread to all parts of the globe carried with them an understanding of what constituted a "proper" Bahá'í Feast. This understanding, however, was a mingling of statements in the Text and cultural practice. After consultations at the International Convention in 1988 on seeking ways to make the Feast more efficacious, the Universal House of Justice prepared a new compilation on the subject and encouraged Bahá'í national and local communities to explore a wide range of experiences in the practical implementation of that guidance. The nature of the Feast changed further, becoming more dynamic and more integrated with development and progress in those communities witnessing significant growth during the Five Year Plan from 2001-2006. Most assuredly, it will continue to evolve in future.

Yet another example of the evolution of culture can be found in the community's understanding of the process of teaching.

Shoghi Effendi explained that the teaching work will go through a series of stages, from a steady flow of fresh recruits, to entry by troops, and eventually, to mass conversion.[45] He even appears to have modified his guidance concerning the enrollment process, encouraging caution when the Faith was still small,[46] and then emphasizing a more relaxed attitude as a more mature Bahá'í community began to experience accelerated expansion.[47] Nevertheless, many Bahá'í communities struggled with accepting the validity of the process of large-scale growth when it began in the 1950s and gathered momentum throughout subsequent decades. These difficulties retarded the development of effective teaching methods. In 1996, with the advent of the Four Year Plan, the Universal House of Justice began to move the Bahá'í world toward a change in culture that was characterized by systematic action and learning about expansion and consolidation.

The philosopher Hans-Georg Gadamer has written about the emergence of a tradition and its influence on understanding. Tradition, he observes, is not the dead weight of the past, it is a living thing that informs and shapes thought and is, itself, evolving. As a tradition emerges, it shapes the community, and there is a future projection of understanding—an anticipation of meaning—that guides future interpretation and action. This new interpretation and action, in turn, gradually reshapes the tradition. When a tradition is static, unchanging, then it is no longer viable. A community of thinkers operates within a common tradition, such as science, in which the tradition consists of the accumulated body of scientific knowledge and evolving standards and methods validated by the consensus of scientists. Gadamer speaks about meaning emerging over time. It is not possible to go back in time and acquire an objective understanding of the thoughts of a previous period. The passage of time is, rather, an aid to understanding because there is a progressive clarification of meaning cultivated within a living tradition. He explains that "the discovery of the true meaning of a text or a work of art is never finished; it is in fact an infinite process. Not only are fresh sources of error constantly excluded, so that the true meaning has filtered out of it all kinds of things that obscure it, but there emerge continually new sources of understanding which reveal unsuspected elements of meaning."[48]

So, too, the passage of time is a vital factor in obtaining a greater understanding of the implications of the Bahá'í teachings.[49] The Sacred Text has an intended meaning. We can never fully grasp it. But at any given moment in history, we are interpreting and responding to it. Who we are at that moment leads us to ask certain questions and draw out meanings so we can make further progress toward that which Bahá'u'lláh intends for us. Thus, Bahá'u'lláh's statement that the meaning of the Word is never exhausted can be seen in terms of its implications related to time—the progressive revelation of the meaning of the Word as the Faith unfolds and as civilization progresses—and not as a form of relativism—that conflicting understandings of the Text are equally possible or correct.

Consultation and the Community

Central to the Bahá'í teachings on the investigation of truth is Bahá'u'lláh's exhortation to consult on all things, for consultation is the "lamp of guidance which leadeth the way" and the "bestower of understanding."[50] He further states:

> Consultation bestoweth greater awareness and transmuteth conjecture into certitude. It is a shining light which, in a dark world, leadeth the way and guideth. For everything there is and will continue to be a station of perfection and maturity. The maturity of the gift of understanding is made manifest through consultation.[51]

Bahá'u'lláh makes the establishment of communities that are engaged in dialogue the very starting-point of His world order. He places the affairs of His Cause and of humanity in the hands of consultative bodies and indicates that "Even in their ordinary affairs the individual members of society should consult."[52] The capacity to engage in effective consultation comes over time through experience and through the commitment, born of faith and religious obligation, to adhere to its spiritual and practical prerequisites. Thus, the Manifestation of God, with an innate understanding of the human condition, has, in this age of maturity, established a system for social order that perfectly correlates with humanity's inherent capacity to investigate reality and act in the world.

By engaging in ongoing consultation about how to understand the teachings while simultaneously engaging in ongoing exploration of how to translate these teachings into action, the Bahá'í world gradually learns how to contribute to the building of spiritual civilization, the Kingdom of God on earth. There is not "one way" to do things, yet at the same time, we cannot indiscriminately support all activities and all methods. There has to be a capacity to learn how one approach or idea is superior to another so that knowledge can advance. Discovering the meaning of the teachings, therefore, emerges through interplay between the understanding of the Text and individual and collective actions in the community.[53]

The Bahá'í Writings provide principles and methods for guiding the community in a discourse that constantly refines collective understanding and behavior to move them progressively closer to truth and effective action. Through simultaneous efforts to weigh personal views in the balance of the Revelation, to consult, and to learn in united action, diverse points of view are harmonized to contribute to the discovery of truth. Humility, love, frankness, selflessness, justice, unity, and detachment are among the qualities necessary for thorough exploration of views. Even if all of these principles and methods are properly implemented, there still may be differences of opinion. In such cases, individuals are not asked to compromise their beliefs. They have to learn to avoid conflict and contention, reassured that problems will be resolved over time. Thus, it can be seen that learning—consultation, action, and reflection in light of the guidance—is indispensable for achieving the personal and collective transformation that are the intended aims of the Cause.

The Covenant and the Process of Learning

The investigation of truth unfolds over time through a living tradition and a community engaged in study, consultation, reflection, and action. At the start of a new enterprise, a framework for action can be derived, based upon current understanding, concepts and attitudes derived from the Writings, and the most effective experience of the community to date. Insights from relevant fields of human knowledge may contribute to it. Such a framework evolves over time based on experience. As progress unfolds and experience accumulates, differences of opinion over problems will arise that cannot be immediately resolved; an eventual solution depends upon the degree to which the community's capacity for discussion and investigation can be safeguarded. In establishing a community capable of such learning and progress, Bahá'u'lláh has empowered it through the guidance found within the Texts, and has established the Covenant to preserve the necessary and proper relationships on which progress depends.

The purpose of the Covenant, Shoghi Effendi explains, is "to perpetuate the influence of [the] Faith, insure its integrity, safeguard it from schism, and stimulate its world-wide expansion."[54] In discharging its responsibilities under the Covenant, the Universal House of Justice acts, in part, to protect the Faith from the extremes of both foundationalism and relativism and to nurture the discourse that is essential for learning. A letter written on behalf of the Universal House of Justice explains:

> Independent investigation of truth does not imply that Bahá'ís should question the validity of the very divine revelation which enjoins it, and firm belief in which is the very reason that they are Bahá'ís—such a concept would be entirely illogical. Independent investigation of truth recognizes that no human being can have a full and correct understanding of the revelation of God; it places upon each individual the duty to strive for an ever greater understanding of the Teachings of Bahá'u'lláh, to apply them to the whole of his life; it is the mainspring of mature consultation, by which all the affairs of the community are conducted; it leads men to discover the secrets of the universe and promote the sciences. As you point out, this will produce great diversity of views on a wide variety of subjects, and this is excellent. What it cannot and must not do is to produce "sects" in relation to the Teachings of the Faith; the Covenant provides the center of guidance which is to prevent such a degeneration.[55]

The Covenant, however, does more than simply preserve the unity of the community. The activity of the Bahá'í community is not random. Bahá'ís have a mission to spread the divine teachings, to raise the administrative order that is the nucleus and pattern of a new world order, and to contribute to progress toward a world civilization. This mission is presented in the Tablets of the Divine Plan by 'Abdu'l-Bahá, and it is implemented in stages through the sequence of Plans carried out first under the direction of the Guardian and now under the direction of the Universal House of Justice. These Plans will unfold over "successive epochs reaching as far as the fringes of [the] Golden Age."[56] The Universal House of Justice continually sets the direction for the community's organic development by defining these Plans, adjusting them to the needs and capacities of the believers and the conditions in the world at large. Learning through consultation, action, and reflection takes place within each locality and flows to all parts of the world.

Learning about growth and the progress of the community's mission prevents stagnation and accelerates movement as the believers gain experience and as knowledgeable and capable individuals are continually attracted to the Faith.[57]

An Overview of Understanding and Action in the Bahá'í Community

The ideas presented offer the general outlines of an approach to understanding and applying the Revelation of Bahá'u'lláh that stands in sharp contrast to a fundamentalist-liberal, foundationalist-relativist, or modern-postmodern dichotomy. Its basic features are as follows:

- *The Bahá'í world community walks a "Straight Path" from the dawn of the Revelation to its Golden Age.* Extreme orthodoxy and unfettered freedom are proscribed, yet, minds differ, and the believers represent a wide continuum of opinion, thought, and sentiment that is harmonized in the context of the Revelation.

- *Progress on the path is made by "translating that which hath been written into reality and action."* The creation of the Kingdom of God on earth, the transformation of society in accordance with the will of God, requires the believers to be engaged in an integrated process striving for greater understanding and improving practice. Their understanding of reality is shaped by the knowledge systems of science (the reading of the book of creation) and religion (the reading of the book of religion). Action is necessary to test the truth of any interpretive insights. Over the course of the dispensation, Bahá'ís draw closer to achieving Bahá'u'lláh's intended will and purpose.

- *As the believers walk the "Straight Path" they advance through learning: a systematic, dialogical process involving study, consultation, action and reflection in the light of divine guidance.* Over a lifetime, one investigates reality and attempts to replace erroneous beliefs and practices; the community similarly advances in its collective understanding and development. The process of consultation assists Bahá'ís to harmonize divergent views in the search for truth and in the application of principles in diverse and often ambiguous contexts. Once a decision is reached, all support it, for in this way, 'Abdu'l-Bahá explains, even if the decision is wrong, the foundation of unity is preserved, the truth will be revealed, and the wrong made right. Latitude for initiative and tolerance of mistakes is needed. Reflection on action is indispensable, and, in this regard, constructive criticism is a welcome and essential aspect of learning.

- *At certain times in history, it is not possible to validate a single understanding or course of action.* Standards for making such judgments may emerge at a later date. At best, it may be possible to bracket a range of possible alternatives, ruling out some options and defining a legitimate selection of others according to current criteria for understanding and action. Thus, the believers are free to hold their own views yet they do not impose them on others or contend with the center of authority. They need to be comfortable with ambiguity and allow time, experience, consultation informed by differing perspectives, and the guidance of the Universal House of Justice to gradually resolve of all questions associated with achieving the aims of the Faith.

- *As the community engages in dialogue and systematic learning, a culture, or tradition, emerges and evolves over time, moving toward a fuller expression of Bahá'u'lláh's will and purpose.* This process has unfolded since the beginning of the dispensation and will continue through its Golden Age. The tradition has both universal and particular aspects across the diverse peoples of the Bahá'í world. Among the aspects of the tradition are practices (such as a particular approach to the Feast), a body of knowledge (such as our understanding of 'Abdu'l-Bahá's station), methods (such as firesides or teaching projects), institutional arrangements (such as the organization and operation of training institutes), and a view of history (such as one conveyed in a historical piece from a particular period). The believers of each new generation are educated within the tradition and, in turn, are enabled to contribute to it and gradually reshape and advance it through their understanding and action so that it may reflect more and more Bahá'u'lláh's meaning and purpose—all within limits defined by the Covenant.

- *The Covenant preserves the conditions necessary to guarantee steady progress, to protect against extremes, and to provide proper orientation for progress on the path.* The two authoritative centers are the Book, with its authorized Interpreter, and the guidance of the Universal House of Justice.[58] The House of Justice, by framing the successive stages of 'Abdu'l-Bahá's Divine Plan, directs the believers toward actions appropriate to the current stage of the Faith's organic unfoldment, while guiding progress along the "Straight Path." Although it does not interpret the text, the House of Justice preserves its purity by directing the collective action of the community in response to the writings and by preventing individual interpretations from being imposed on the community. There is an integral relationship between the learning undertaken by the believers and the guidance provided by the House of Justice.

Any attempt to impose a foundationalist or relativist perspective on the Bahá'í community must ultimately fail. Bahá'ís will, no doubt, prepare an adequate response to criticisms raised from outside the community. Yet, we are not immune from the dominant forces of humanity's intellectual life—the temptations of liberalism and fundamentalism in various forms beckon. While we have resisted, and will no doubt continue as a result of the Covenant to resist extreme divisions and sectarianism, such tensions can manifest themselves not only in the intellectual life of the community, but also, for example, in such basic activities as growth or administration, when consultation and a learning attitude are disrupted by disputes among the friends over the meaning of the guidance on some issue.

As described in Greek mythology, sailors steered a treacherous course between Scylla, a fierce sea-monster, and Charybdis, a huge whirlpool. The effort to avoid the former placed one in jeopardy from the latter. In response to a perceived rigidity of thought associated with some administrative practice, interpretation of Text, or scientific or historical analysis, it is understandable that some fair-minded believers would attempt to steer clear of the extreme manifestations of foundationalism or orthodoxy. It is also understandable that other devoted individuals, responding to what they perceive to be attacks on the truths of the Faith, would steer away from extreme expressions of relativism or irresponsible freedom. But in so doing, each is exposed to the opposite danger. The efforts of individuals to redefine concepts and practices—in either direction—may overstep boundaries set in the Bahá'í teachings that prohibit personal opinions from being imposed on the community. This error is compounded when, meeting resistance to their criticisms, a few take excessive measures in an attempt to repudiate aspects of the Bahá'í teachings that do not conform to their personal views.

We need to become conscious that any contemporary understanding of an evolving Faith must be to some degree imperfect; that over time, through the processes that Bahá'u'lláh has put into place, we can create a community more closely attuned to His will and purpose—and indeed we must constantly struggle and sacrifice in order to do so; that the acquisition of knowledge through science and religion is the motive force driving progress; and that acquisition of knowledge must be associated with action and reflection on action. We face, therefore, not the contending alternatives of liberalism and fundamentalism, each of which contains aspects that contradict the teachings; rather, we are collectively attempting, under the guidance of the Universal House of Justice, to define a course along the "Straight Path" that avoids the dangers of "irresponsible freedom" and "extreme orthodoxy." What is necessary, as we increasingly elucidate and refine understanding and practice in the Bahá'í community, is to recognize that Scylla and Charybdis are, after all, myths.

6

A Problem of Power

HAVING EXAMINED THE QUESTION of knowledge, it is now possible to explore the closely related question of power. While there are alternative definitions, power is understood as that condition arising from human relationships that causes or enables individuals to act in a certain way. A person may exercise power to choose how to act, or power may be exerted by other individuals, groups or institutions to cause a person to perform particular actions. The problem of power involves the political order, but, more broadly, it is concerned with how individuals relate to one another, how society impacts individuals, and how the various institutions and structures within society interact.

If there is a way to obtain knowledge that is certain, then knowledge is power, because truth would serve as a means for keeping the abuse of power in check. Those who wish to impose authority and force matters in a direction of their own choosing would have to yield to knowledge that proves their views wrong. The integrity of correct practice would be upheld by certain knowledge. However, if there is no unfailing access to knowledge and relativism reigns, then all that remains is the eternal struggle of one against another without any source of truth or good or right to restrain or direct power.

The previous chapter examined how dialogue and agreement are critical for the generation of the partial, mutable, evolving body of knowledge accessible to humanity that avoids the extremes of foundationalism and relativism. While this approach helps to resolve concerns associated with the problem of knowledge, it creates new challenges in relation to the question of power. The delicate dialogical framework in which understanding and action are conjoined can be easily manipulated. To preserve this framework there must be constant effort. Otherwise, "truth" is merely the product of power, and individuals and diverse communities who possess power are free to rationalize their own actions and impose their subjective views on others. The results of scientific studies supported by funds from the tobacco industry that find no link between cigarette smoking and cancer is a good example of such manipulation. Thus, as a number of thinkers have observed, power deforms practice. Where there is no agreement about universal principles or the means to distinguish between truth and opinion, there can be no basis for rational discussion that can resolve problems or apply principles to specific cases and contexts.

As with knowledge, the concept of power is far-reaching. The scope of this chapter, like the last one, however, must necessarily be circumscribed. It is not a comprehensive Baháʼí approach to the question of power, but merely a response to certain fundamental challenges that could be directed toward the Baháʼí community in light of contemporary thought.

How does the Baháʼí community bring its understanding and action over time into conformity with Baháʼuʼlláh's will and purpose? How do we determine what action should be taken? How do we resolve the tension between the rights of the individual and the responsibilities toward the common good—between individual freedom and unity? As we learn to resolve this tension ever more effectively within our own community, how do we relate to other communities? Do the Baháʼí teachings give us a standard by which to judge the beliefs of others or do they oblige us to simultaneously uphold the validity of a multiplicity of cultures and traditions that maintain conflicting beliefs and practices? How do we engage and appropriately influence the peoples of the world without falling into the pitfalls of dominance or oppression? To be able to answer such questions, we need to explore the relations of power among individuals and institutions that govern human action.

One word of caution before undertaking this exercise. The contemporary discourse on power arises from a particular way of looking at reality that does not fully correspond with—indeed, often stands in contrast to—the Baháʼí teachings. For example, the meaning of the term "religion" in the Baháʼí teachings is markedly different from that which is current in much of society today. So too, any attempt to analyze the Baháʼí teachings from current perspectives on power will distort what Baháʼís mean by human agency and relationships.

A significant portion of the contemporary discourse is concerned with issues of power that arise from tension or competition in various aspects of human relationships—between individuals, between the individual and society, or between one group and another. In these relationships, the term power implies a zero sum game in which the power of one side is derived at the expense of the other. A survey of the Bahá'í teachings, however, presents power as a force that is infused into a relationship or emerges from it once there is a certain harmony within. There is, for example, discussion of the power of love, the power of unity, the power of the Covenant, the power of God, and the creative power of the Word of God. "So powerful is the light of unity that it can illuminate the whole earth," Bahá'u'lláh states.[1] "In the world of existence there is indeed no greater power than the power of love," 'Abdu'l-Bahá explains, for when "the heart of man is aglow with the flame of love, he is ready to sacrifice all—even his life."[2] And again He states: "the Word of God hath infused such awesome power into the inmost essence of humankind that He hath stripped men's human qualities of all effect, and hath, with His all-conquering might, unified the peoples in a vast sea of oneness."[3]

In the Bahá'í teachings, the proper relationships governing individuals, groups, and society are described with the help of the metaphor of the human body. All of the cells, organs and systems have a part to play and when all are in harmony, the full capacity of the body is manifest. In this perspective, it makes no sense to speak of the power of a cell in contrast to the power of an organ or of the body as a whole. Even when taking into account human agency, the aim of the individual or purpose of a social structure is to achieve unity and harmony through cooperation and complementarity. In reflecting upon the relationship between a mother and child, one may address issues such as love, care, mutual responsibility, education, maturation, mentoring and the like. Once a discourse of power is imposed, however, the relationship takes on a very different character, in which the primary considerations are authority, control, criticism, discipline, monitoring, freedom, and a struggle for autonomy. The introduction of the language of power does not further the understanding of harmonious relationships; it does the opposite. When such relationships fail, when it is impossible to address differences through discussion, then one takes recourse to an analysis of power. Perhaps the current discourse on power is a discourse of pathology, not of health. It brings to focus certain concerns but, in the process, distorts significantly other important aspects of reality. In undertaking the task set forth in this chapter then, we should recognize that it does not present a Bahá'í perspective on society or on power, nor does it aver that the Bahá'í teachings are necessarily in accord with any particular perspective on power offered in contemporary thought.

Contemporary Perspectives on Power

The Bahá'í teachings offer a vision of a new world order and promise the establishment of universal peace. They declare that the struggle for power among individuals and communities will be supplanted by relationships governed by the principle of the oneness of humanity. In making such bold claims, however, Bahá'ís need to be sensitive not only to the advances of modern political thought, but also to contemporary, postmodern voices that have radically altered the general consensus on power.

Over the centuries, Western thought primarily approached power in terms of the capacity of institutions to compel individuals to conform to certain patterns of behavior, either through oppression and tyranny or by the rule of law within a just social order. In this perspective, the institutions of the state, and to a lesser degree, religious and economic institutions, possess power. A just political system has been sought in a number of ways—following, for example theological, secular liberal, or socialist reasoning—and attempts are made to ground these views on secure foundations buttressed by unassailable truth, whether metaphysical, philosophical, or scientific. Justice has often been given the task of defining parameters for the exercise of power by institutions in order to establish equality and maximize freedom. The contest between political systems has played itself out on the world stage, resulting in the ascent of liberal democracy.

Recent thinkers have addressed the problem of power from a modernist perspective by considering not only the structures of society, but also the role of the individual. For example, the German philosopher Jürgen Habermas offers a theory of communicative rationality that explains how to strive for objective meaning while exposing the errors of tradition and the limitations of language in social practice. He sets forward a number of precepts for achieving a principled, open dialogue—the "unconstrained, unifying, consensus-building force of argumentative speech."[4] Habermas envisions that it is possible to establish a kind of collective self-reflection that exposes hidden power relations and reverses the damaging influences of ideology, thereby using critical reasoning to ground claims to truth and morality. The British sociologist Anthony Giddens put forward a theory of structuration, which proposes that it is not simply social structures that constrain or compel individual action, but that individuals, despite their limited knowledge, also act in a manner that can gradually change these structures. "Social structures," he states, "are both constituted by human agency, and yet at the same time are the very medium of this constitution."[5] Giddens indicates that the structures of society can constrain action, but they can also enable action by providing a common framework of meaning.

Postmodern thought calls into question the modern perspective on power. Power is seen to be ubiquitous: all, at least potentially, exercise power, and they do so for their own ends. There is a constant struggle, expressed individually and through institutions, to exert will to realize personal views and desires. Humanity is left with no choice but to deal with these power relations that are an inherent aspect of the human condition. In this context, the assertion that it is possible to base political and ethical judgments upon a tenable foundation is regarded with suspicion. The belief that there are methods, principles, or conditions of rationality that can be used to transcend tradition or day-to-day circumstances in order to achieve a universal standpoint is rejected. Appeals to morality are considered a disguised form of self-interest. The call for international peace is said to be a utopian illusion or, more likely, a cover for totalitarian impulses. The premise that human beings can engage in dialogue without selfish motives is considered naïve, foolish, and even dangerous.

The work of French philosopher Michael Foucault offers insight into the postmodern perspective on power. "Power," Foucault explains, "is not an institution, and not a structure; neither is it a certain strength we are endowed with; it is the name that one attributes to a complex strategical situation in a particular society."[6] According to Foucault, power is everywhere. It lies in the hands of individuals and groups as well as with government. It is not possible for the state to contain or even to place adequate checks upon power relations, nor can political institutions or legislation guarantee freedom. Power is a "multiplicity of force relations" within a given sphere of operations that have their own organization; it is a process, which, through "struggles and confrontations, supports, transforms, or reverses these force relations."[7]

Foucault is concerned with the critique of power. Since, for him, power is central to defining what we believe and what we ought to do, he seeks to expose the workings of power, especially as it takes form in truth, ethics or knowledge. The Enlightenment tradition suggests that knowledge is achieved by suspending power, as in the quest for objective truth. It is in this context that "knowledge is power," because once knowledge is obtained, argument and action must submit and conform to truth. Foucault, however, asserts that it is power that produces the standards and conditions that define what constitutes "reality," "justice," "evidence," and "the facts." Power is knowledge.[8] We are, therefore, left with no option except to make a continual effort to expose the workings of power and challenge its implications. A "power-free" society or "power-free" discourse is impossible. Talk of it is utopian and dangerous, because such an approach merely cloaks the desires of those making the claim and opens the door to oppression. Foucault warns against a "tyranny of globalizing discourses," a danger in universal claims or comprehensive (totalizing) explanations.[9] Appeals to peace, freedom, justice or any other ideal are merely the workings of power to exert control or to legitimize the status quo.

Foucault never attempts to provide a theory of justice or a secure basis upon which a critique of society can rest. According to his views, this would be impossible, and the effort would merely amount to constructing another competing manifestation of power. Instead, he lays particular emphasis on thought as a means of analyzing practice. Through reflection one can challenge existing ways of doing things and learn to act differently. Foucault puts forward his argument by historical investigations, or "genealogies," of how power has operated in the world. In one prominent work, *Discipline and Punish*, he explores the modern prison system—how society punishes and attempts to get those outside the boundaries of acceptable behavior to conform. In this book, Foucault draws upon the concept of the panopticon, a hypothetical prison designed to expose inmates to constant surveillance, or, at least, to the belief that they may be under constant surveillance, as a means of inducing proper behavior. Foucault sees the panopticon as a metaphor for the restraints imposed by modern society. A web of disciplinary procedures—the manifestations of power—surround and control individuals, making them adapt themselves to "normal" behavior. These procedures include modest admonishments, such as parking tickets, but also the measuring and testing to establish norms common in economics, academics, medicine, or psychiatry. For Foucault, critique provides freedom, because it provides the means to continually challenge the imposition of dominant expressions of power in order to make room for local or particular expressions of knowledge and truth that would otherwise be subjugated. Oppression is combated not by emancipatory theories but by criticism that exposes its workings and by local action.

The aim here, of course, is not to exhaustively describe the postmodern perspective on power or to suggest that Foucault's views are fully representative of such concerns. It is only to point out certain tensions that exist in contemporary thought that require a careful consideration of the Bahá'í teachings, so that they do not unduly influence Bahá'í discourse and so that we might get a better sense of how Bahá'ís are to present themselves to a skeptical world. Some writers find in postmodernism's rejection of the privileged position of science a new opening for religious contributions to social discourse;[10] others challenge any role for religious or metaphysical contributions because of the presumably unwarranted assertion that there is a foundation for truth and justice.[11] In any case, from the perspective of postmodernism, religion—as well as natural or social sciences, movements for social change, political parties, or any other source of claims to truth or meaning—must be subject to an unrelenting critique to prevent an imposition and abuse of power.

The brief consideration of the contrast between modern and postmodern approaches offers only a glimpse into the complex debate on the nature of power.[12] Yet it illustrates that the problem of power is intertwined with the problem of knowledge discussed in the previous chapter. The tension between foundationalism and relativism weighs heavily on the ethical-political dimension of social relations. Does knowledge restrain power, or does the exercise of power corrupt any attempt to generate and apply knowledge? Are there universal values that are believed to apply to the human condition in such a way that the actions of human beings in all cultures and in all times can be judged by and expected to conform to this set of values? Or are values dependent on local perspectives? Perhaps, in an extreme relativistic view, "values" have nothing to do with ideals of human character at all, but are merely the self-serving constructs that represent the opinions and desires of a particular group of people. Is it possible, then, as modernism assumes, to find a theory of justice, a sound social contract such as a constitution or charter, or a scientific explanation—biological or psychological—for human behavior that provides a foundation for action in the social realm and on the basis of which a just political order, freedom, peace, and human prosperity and well-being can be established? Or is reality far more complex and uncertain, so that there is no alternative to doubt, criticism, struggle, and a constant unmasking of value and knowledge claims as a means of fending off oppression and ensuring there is room for freedom and local expressions of belief?

A traditional foundationalist approach to religion that sets the parameters for power relations might be summarized as follows. God is the all-Powerful and all-Knowing Creator of the Universe. From this absolute position, God reveals to humanity the Word of God, encompassing a complete understanding of human nature and physical reality and presenting the divine laws, teachings and principles—and perhaps even the administrative arrangements—that tell human beings how they should conduct their individual and collective lives. Humanity must first, accept this standard of truth, morality, and justice and second, act on it to improve society and forge a just social order: the Kingdom of God. God's plan for the ordering of human relations is given to us; we are to accept and obey.

Those whose conviction is derived from revealed religion may readily acknowledge the truth in this statement. But a moment's reflection on the horrors perpetrated in the name of religion leads to the sad but unavoidable admission that such acts were justified by similar arguments. An exploration of the Bahá'í teachings that pertain to power and ethical-political relations should avoid over-simplified, reductionistic positions that impose a choice between idealized social systems and unrestricted individual freedom.

Reflect upon some of the questions pertaining to power that might arise in a critique of the Bahá'í community. How do we define power? What are the relationships of power that exist among individuals and between individuals and institutions? How is power exercised in the Bahá'í community? Is there a formal, procedural approach to the use of power? What is the role of criticism? Not only are internal processes to be analyzed, but also our relationship to other communities and peoples. How do Bahá'ís interact with others? Is humanity to be judged by Bahá'í standards and values, or do we assume a relativistic or pluralistic perspective toward other communities? When it comes to our view of a spiritual civilization, the Kingdom of God on earth, how do we avoid charges of naïveté, moralizing, or totalitarianism? We must learn to respond to such questions without distorting our own understanding or conveying an inaccurate view of the Faith.

The Bahá'í teachings associated with contemporary considerations of power, from one perspective, can be correlated with certain modernist aims. Consultation is the method of Bahá'í discourse that allows decisions to be made from the bottom-up and enacted, to the extent possible through rational, dispassionate, and just means, while minimizing personal machinations, argumentation, or self-interested manipulation. Opinions are shared, then modified in the search for truth; a consensus about reality is sought upon which collective action is based and progress made. A system for administering the affairs of the Faith, a set of laws that must be obeyed, and the designation of universal principles that govern human relations, can all be seen as elements of a systematic approach to addressing matters of freedom, morals, justice, and social order.

The Bahá'í teachings, from another perspective, can be correlated with certain postmodern concerns about power. The faults of human beings are readily admitted, including the tendency toward the perpetual struggle to advance oneself over another. Power belongs not only to institutions but also to individuals, who are to exercise initiative and not merely wait for instructions before taking action. Critical thought is acknowledged as imperative for human progress, the individual is entitled to personal understanding and freedom of expression, and there is an obligation to work to transform repressive social structures. If the proper channels for critical and creative thought are obstructed, then some believers may resort to backbiting or become inactive, devoting their energies to other areas. The Bahá'í teachings do not concentrate only on abstract principles of consultation, but also on the practical problems that arise when individuals attempt to impose their opinions and personal agendas. In appreciating that the problem of power can never be entirely eliminated, the Bahá'í community is restrained in various ways from arbitrarily imposing its views on others; therefore, in a world strongly influenced by postmodern doubt, the Bahá'í position cannot simply be dismissed as naïve—the quest for a power-free world—or as totalitarian—the imposition of Bahá'í morality disguised as an appeal for universal values, peace, and justice.

Thus, in the Bahá'í teachings, the quest for order and rationality is complemented by equally important elements of critical thought, learning, diversity, and attention to local context. Unbending rules of behavior and overcentralization of authority belong to the age of humanity's childhood; similarly, unchecked freedom and unrelenting criticism are representative of the age of adolescence. New insights on power are required for the age of human maturity.

As observed in the last chapter, the only way to avoid an endless debate between foundationalism and relativism is to reject the dichotomy and search for a richer, though more nuanced approach. In relation to questions of power, a nonfoundational perspective is also possible. It acknowledges that there is no formula or absolute set of procedures, no theory of justice or political organization upon which we can completely rely for ideal results. But neither is social interaction reduced to circular polemics, relentless criticism, and a never-ending struggle for dominance. Instead, practical judgments can be made about how things should be done in specific circumstances and, over time and through experience, approaches can be improved to yield more effective insights and practices. It is in this context that we can examine more closely the Bahá'í teachings related to the question of power.

Some Bahá'í Teachings Relevant to Human Relationships

For Bahá'ís, the social and ethical arrangements that govern relations among individuals, groups and society from which the question of power arises are forged in every age by the Manifestation of God, Who brings the divine teachings adapted to the prevailing contingencies of human reality—both the capacity of human beings to understand and the degree of human social progress to date. Religious truth, Shoghi Effendi declares, is in this sense "relative" and not absolute.[13] When a new Manifestation of God appears, the book of Revelation is rewritten: certain truths are affirmed while others are illumined in a new context to the extent that, in some cases, what was night becomes day, what was forbidden becomes lawful. The elements of the "raft" of human understanding are restructured.

A new Revelation is not merely the transmission of new truths that humanity could not understand in a previous age. It is a complex response to human culture and capacity, involving a compromise with human limitation. In *The Secret of Divine Civilization*, 'Abdu'l-Bahá analyzes an aspect of divine law in the time of Muhammad.

It is moreover a matter of record in the books of the various Islamic schools and the writings of leading divines and historians, that after the Light of the World had risen over Ḥijáz, flooding all mankind with Its brilliance, and creating through the revelation of a new divine Law, new principles and institutions, a fundamental change throughout the world—holy laws were revealed which in some cases conformed to the practices of the Days of Ignorance. Among these, Muhammad respected the months of religious truce, retained the prohibition of swine's flesh, continued the use of the lunar calendar and the names of the months and so on. There is a considerable number of such laws specifically enumerated in the texts. . . .

Can one, God forbid, assume that because some of the divine laws resemble the practices of the Days of Ignorance, the customs of a people abhorred by all nations, it follows that there is a defect in these laws? Or can one, God forbid, imagine that the Omnipotent Lord was moved to comply with the opinions of the heathen? The divine wisdom takes many forms. Would it have been impossible for Muhammad to reveal a Law which bore no resemblance whatever to any practice current in the Days of Ignorance? Rather, the purpose of His consummate wisdom was to free the people from the chains of fanaticism which had bound them hand and foot, and to forestall those very objections which today confuse the mind and trouble the conscience of the simple and helpless.[14]

Furthermore, Bahá'u'lláh offers the following explanation in response to a question concerning why certain prohibitions differ among religions:

. . . "The All-knowing Physician hath His finger on the pulse of mankind" was, and remaineth, the answer to his question. He further saith: "Be anxiously concerned with the needs of the age ye live in, and center your deliberations on its exigencies and requirements." That is, fix your gaze upon the commandments of God, for whatsoever He should ordain in this day and pronounce as lawful is indeed lawful and representeth the very truth. It is incumbent upon all to turn their gaze towards the Cause of God and to observe that which hath dawned above the horizon of His Will, since it is through the potency of His name that the banner of "He doeth what He willeth" hath been unfurled and the standard of "He ordaineth what He pleaseth" hath been raised aloft. For instance, were He to pronounce water itself to be unlawful, it would indeed become unlawful, and the converse holdeth equally true. For upon no thing hath it been inscribed "this is lawful" or "this is unlawful"; nay rather, whatsoever hath been or will be revealed is by virtue of the Word of God, exalted be His glory.

These matters are sufficiently clear and require no further elaboration. Even so, certain groups believe that all the ordinances current amongst them are unalterable, that they have ever been valid, and that they will forever remain so. Consider a further passage, glorified and exalted be He: "These words are being uttered in due measure, that the newly born may thrive and the tender shoot flourish. Milk must be given in suitable proportion, that the children of the world may attain to the station of maturity and abide in the court of oneness." For instance, some believe that wine hath ever been and shall remain forbidden. Now, were one to inform them that it might one day be made lawful, they would arise in protest and opposition. In truth, the people of the world have yet not grasped the meaning of "He doeth whatsoever He willeth," nor have they comprehended the significance of Supreme Infallibility. The suckling child must be nourished with milk. If it be given meat it will assuredly perish, and this would be naught but sheer injustice and unwisdom.[15]

Thus, from a Bahá'í perspective, divine law does not take an absolute form that is grounded upon an absolute reality. God appears in this sense to be quite pragmatic: taking various kinds of action within specific contexts to achieve desirable results.

Indeed, the very concept "He doeth whatsoever He willeth"[16] implies a judgment born of understanding, adapted to circumstance and with the intention of achieving a purpose, rather than a statement of absolute truth that is reached after an objective assessment of reality. The standard of the Most Great Infallibility is not, "He says what is true" or "He does what is right." Instead, something is true or right *because* the Manifestation of God says so; His Word is the expression of God's will and purpose. "Were He to pronounce water to be wine or heaven to be earth or light to be fire, He speaketh the truth and no doubt would there be about it; and unto no one is given the right to question His authority or to say why or wherefore."[17] "Were He to pronounce right to be wrong or denial to be belief, He speaketh the truth as bidden by God."[18] However, the Manifestation does not speak in an arbitrary or circumscribed way, which would be characteristic of relativism. What is said has meaning and purpose, it is intended for all humanity, it must be obeyed, it produces practical results, and it cannot be altered until the next dispensation. Bahá'u'lláh explains that the Manifestation of God is "The All-Knowing Physician" that has "His finger on the pulse of mankind." He perceives the disease and prescribes the remedy, a remedy for "present-day afflictions" that "can never be the same as that which a subsequent age may require."[19] "Mankind in its entirety must firmly adhere to whatsoever hath been revealed and vouchsafed unto it. Then and only then will it attain unto true liberty."[20] At the same time, the Revelation is suited to the capacity of the hearer. "All that I have revealed unto thee with the tongue of power, and have written for thee with the pen of might," Bahá'u'lláh states, "hath been in accordance with thy capacity and understanding, not with My state and the melody of My voice."[21]

Just as the divine standard of Revelation stands apart from foundationalism and relativism, so too, the effort to understand and apply it should avoid these extremes. The laws, principles, and exhortations are not translated into practice in a fixed and inflexible manner, a code that determines what must be done in every circumstance.

> The human tendency in past Dispensations has been to want every question answered and to arrive at a binding decision affecting every small detail of belief or practice. The tendency in the Bahá'í Dispensation, from the time of Bahá'u'lláh Himself, has been to clarify the governing principles, to make binding pronouncements on details which are considered essential, but to leave a wide area to the conscience of the individual.[22]

In response to an inquiry by a Bahá'í youth about how to apply the teachings in daily life, a letter written by the Universal House of Justice explains:

> It is neither possible nor desirable for the Universal House of Justice to set forth a set of rules covering every situation. Rather is it the task of the individual believer to determine, according to his own prayerful understanding of the Writings, precisely what his course of conduct should be in relation to situations which he encounters in his daily life. If he is to fulfill his true mission in life as a follower of the Blessed Perfection, he will pattern his life according to the Teachings. The believer cannot attain this

objective merely by living according to a set of rigid regulations. When his life is oriented toward service to Bahá'u'lláh, and when every conscious act is performed within this frame of reference, he will not fail to achieve the true purpose of his life.

Therefore, every believer must continually study the sacred Writings and the instructions of the beloved Guardian, striving always to attain a new and better understanding of their import to him and to his society. He should pray fervently for Divine Guidance, wisdom and strength to do what is pleasing to God, and to serve Him at all times and to the best of his ability.[23]

"Think not that We have revealed unto you a mere code of laws," Bahá'u'lláh states. "Nay, rather, We have unsealed the choice Wine with the fingers of might and power."[24] The understanding and application of the Bahá'í teachings requires an appreciation for the spirit that underlies the letter of the Text, the need for an appropriate measure of flexibility based on context, and the cultivation of capacity to respond more fully over time.

The flexibility present in individual practice has a corresponding expression in the collective realm. Organic development and maturation are consistently taken into account. Within the Bahá'í dispensation, divine law is applied progressively, at different times in different places. An example is the law of Ḥuqúqu'lláh, which was not applied to the generality of the believers until 1992. Each community, to take another example, is challenged to gradually eliminate those characteristics of the wider society that are not in keeping with Bahá'í concepts. Shoghi Effendi called upon the believers in North America to "weed out, by every means in their power, those faults, habits, and tendencies which they have inherited from their own nation,"[25] while, in a message to Africa, the Universal House of Justice wrote that "people everywhere have customs which must be abandoned so as to clear the path along which their societies must evolve towards that glorious, new civilization which is to be the fruit of Bahá'u'lláh's stupendous Revelation."[26]

The concept of flexibility in applying the teachings should not be confused with amorality or license, or with a malleability or arbitrariness that conforms to relativism. The teachings are not practiced in a discretionary or partial manner.

> The first duty prescribed by God for His servants is the recognition of Him Who is the Dayspring of His Revelation and the Fountain of His laws, Who representeth the Godhead in both the

Kingdom of His Cause and the world of creation. . . . It behoveth every one who reacheth this most sublime station, this summit of transcendent glory, to observe every ordinance of Him Who is the Desire of the world. These twin duties are inseparable. Neither is acceptable without the other.[27]

To be a Bahá'í is to accept the Cause in its entirety. To take exception to one basic principle is to deny the authority and sovereignty of Bahá'u'lláh, and therefore is to deny the Cause.[28]

The Bahá'í community is an association of individuals who have voluntarily come together, on recognizing Bahá'u'lláh's claim to be the Manifestation of God for this age, to establish certain patterns of personal and social behavior and to build the institutions that are to promote these patterns. There are numerous individuals who share the ideals of the Faith and draw inspiration from its Teachings, while disagreeing with certain of its features, but those who actually enter the Bahá'í community have accepted, by their own free will, to follow the Teachings in their entirety, understanding that, if doubts and disagreements arise in the process of translating the Teachings into practice, the final arbiter is, by the explicit authority of the Revealed Text, the Universal House of Justice.[29]

Once applied, a law is not repealed. Explicit ordinances cannot be transgressed. Divine law demarcates edifying and injurious behavior. Within the boundary marked by the divine laws there is a wide range for human action—the freedom to utilize personal powers as an expression of the potentialities that God has placed within each individual. To live a Bahá'í life is to internalize the teachings to such a degree as to be able to respond to the rich, contextual and ever-changing dimensions of daily life and historical social evolution by applying the principles and teachings to specific situations in a creative and constructive manner. It involves not only surmounting faults, but also balancing dissimilar virtues.[30] This process unfolds over a lifetime, and is characterized by challenges and setbacks, crisis and victory. A letter written on behalf of Shoghi Effendi distills the essence of this challenge: "if we are ever in any doubt as to how we should conduct ourselves as Bahá'ís we should think of 'Abdu'l-Bahá and study His life and ask ourselves what would He have done, for He is our perfect example in every way."[31]

As the teachings are applied, imperfections will be evident in individual believers and institutions, requiring love, tolerance, patience, prayer, and mutual support to create an environment conducive to progress. Mistakes are understood to be an unavoidable dimension of learning how to apply the teachings. Often, believers in a given age will face problems that cannot be resolved at that time, requiring an ability to deal with ambiguity. Yet, progress will occur, and the believers of the future will be "a hundred times more mature, better balanced, more exemplary in their conduct."[32]

Application of the teachings also applies to interaction with those who are not a part of the community. Bahá'ís certainly make an effort to exert an influence, either by teaching the Faith and giving people an opportunity to accept it, or by sharing the principles in the hope of shaping thought and action. However, the Bahá'í standard is not imposed.

> It is not our purpose to impose Bahá'í teachings upon others by persuading the powers that be to enact laws enforcing Bahá'í principles, nor to join movements which have such legislation as their aim. The guidance that Bahá'í institutions offer to mankind does not comprise a series of specific answers to current problems, but rather the illumination of an entirely new way of life. Without this way of life the problems are insoluble; with it they will either not arise or, if they arise, can be resolved.[33]

The Bahá'í concept of wisdom is yet another illustration of how, in matters associated with power, the Faith has a more nuanced approach that avoids foundationalism and relativism. The concept of truth, derived from the Enlightenment tradition, suggests that an individual should strive for objective truth, and then act to uphold that truth in all circumstances. The upholder of truth must depend upon personal conscience as the sole guide; must be unafraid to speak truth to power (that is, to some institution that holds power); and must completely disclose the truth without concern for consequences (since partial disclosure is dishonest). The Bahá'í Writings appeal for an approach that is more sensitive to context and that appreciates human limitations. Truth is always partially grasped. Conscience is shaped by many forces. Power is exercised not only through the decisions of institutions but also through the speech and action of individuals. Most importantly, the consequences of one's assertion of "truth" must be considered and, as a result, action must at times be moderated, not in order to censor or to manipulate the outcome of an exchange of views, but to preserve the conditions necessary for the search for truth, for the appreciation and acceptance of truth, and for the unified action in response to truth. Truth and values—"is" and "ought"—cannot be completely dissociated. For all these reasons, wisdom must govern the use of knowledge and the expression of human agency. 'Abdu'l-Bahá explains:

> Follow thou the way of thy Lord, and say not that which the ears cannot bear to hear, for such speech is like luscious food given to small children. However palatable, rare and rich the food may be, it cannot be assimilated by the digestive organs of a suckling child. Therefore unto every one who hath a right, let his settled measure be given.
>
> "Not everything that a man knoweth can be disclosed, nor can everything that he can disclose be regarded as timely, nor can every timely utterance be considered as suited to the capacity of those who hear it." Such is the consummate wisdom to be observed in thy pursuits. Be not oblivious thereof, if thou wishest to be a man of action under all conditions. First diagnose the disease and identify the malady, then prescribe the remedy, for such is the perfect method of the skilful physician.[34]

Wisdom is not dissimulation. It is not artifice. It is that capacity of reason that balances knowledge, action, values, and context.

All of these examples affirm that, although the Bahá'í Faith is a revealed religion, it does not take an absolutist approach to humanity's ethical-political life. Paradoxically, "absolute" adherence to the Revelation seems to demand that one take a nonfoundational, rather than foundational approach to reality. The Bahá'í teachings are oriented to the limited, ambiguous world of human understanding and practice. Humanity's grasp of reality is always partial, its moral behavior fallible. In the Bahá'í community, at the practical level of translating the teachings into action, the concern with law, administrative systems, universal principles, and consultative methods that echo modern thought are complemented by the thoughtful criticism, reflection, learning, sensitivity to context, and appreciation of human weakness characteristic of postmodern concerns.

The Bahá'í teachings address the strengths and weaknesses present in both perspectives. There can be ways of arranging relationships that are constructive and which increase human well-being, that transcend tendencies toward absolutism and repressive systems on the one hand, and toward skepticism and endless conflict on the other. While threats from error or from the abuse of power always exist, they are addressed in a manner that seeks to harmonize relations through dialogue, practical experience, and the application of principles within well-defined contexts. Unity, for Bahá'ís, is both the goal and the operating principle in relations of power pertaining to individuals and institutions. It is a lived struggle to find harmony in human relationships in an effort to canalize power toward constructive ends. "Let us take the inhabitants of a city," 'Abdu'l-Bahá explains, "if they establish the strongest bonds of unity among themselves, how far they will progress, even in a brief period and what power they will exert."[35] Humanity has learned increasingly more complex relations in its social evolution from tribes to nations; there is no reason to doubt, therefore, that other, more productive and beneficial relations will be gradually discovered and employed.

Power, Freedom, and the Individual

The Bahá'í teachings are compatible with the postmodern consensus that power is ubiquitous and that human beings do not attain or aspire to a "power-free" state. So, too, Bahá'ís would agree that human beings have a lower nature and a capacity to be deceitful and self-serving, exercising power for their own ends. As 'Abdu'l-Bahá states: "You find, for example, that an individual seeking to further his own petty and personal concerns, will block the advancement of an entire people. To turn his own water mill, he will let the farms and fields of all the others parch and wither. To maintain his own leadership, he will everlastingly direct the masses toward that prejudice and fanaticism which subvert the very base of civilization."[36]

In the Bahá'í teachings, however, human agency is not analyzed in the context of self-interest. It is to be directed toward aims such as serving the common good, promoting human honor, or contributing to prosperity and happiness. In this light, justice is not obtained merely through the constraint of power, but through the beneficial arrangements that cultivate human character and capacity. This aim is not the result of a strict application of rules or the realization of some ideal theory, but the practical, incremental outcome of awareness and effort to act in an ever more constructive manner. In the liberal perspective, freedom begins where the power of institutions to compel individual behavior ends. For Baháʼís, freedom is found in an escape from self-serving behavior to the expression of initiative that contributes to social well-being and the development of human potentialities. ʼAbduʼl-Bahá states:

> And among the teachings of Baháʼuʼlláh is manʼs freedom, that through the ideal Power he should be free and emancipated from the captivity of the world of nature; for as long as man is captive to nature he is a ferocious animal, as the struggle for existence is one of the exigencies of the world of nature.[37]

He also states:

> . . . the moderate freedom which guarantees the welfare of the world of mankind and maintains and preserves the universal relationships, is found in its fullest power and extension in the teachings of Baháʼuʼlláh.[38]

From a Baháʼí perspective, the human relationships that give rise to considerations of power cannot simply be reduced to a continual struggle between competing interests, but may be so arranged as to constructively shape human character and contribute to beneficial social outcomes. This is not a naïve belief that human beings can become perfect, but a rejection of an absolute assertion that all behavioral choices are equally acceptable, that no progress is possible, and that all acts must be self-serving. Instead, Baháʼís affirm that altruistic action is possible and individual behavior can improve. One outcome can be more productive for humanity than another and it is possible to choose between the two. The very existence of a democratic form of society, as opposed to oppressive alternatives, demonstrates that choice is available and that some ways of doing things have historically proven to be more beneficial than others.

At the heart of all of these considerations is self-discipline and individual effort. Religion is concerned with forces intended to mold human action. In the Baháʼí teachings, discipline is not primarily imposed from the outside, but through personal struggle and self-mastery, as a believer exerts an effort to conform to the teachings in daily life. The spiritual disciplines of prayer, fasting, study of the Writings, and taking account of personal actions each day, are intended to cultivate the capacity to conquer the self, to live a life that is pleasing to God, and to join with other believers and with humanity as a whole to contribute to social progress. An individual cannot reach the state of perfection and will inevitably fall short of the divine standard in many ways. But this frank acknowledgement of the human condition does not justify surrender to lower impulses. Spiritual progress and moral behavior are won by degrees, in incrementally better actions day by day, in an incrementally better world generation after generation.

Shaping the individual to undertake constructive initiative is a recurrent theme in the Bahá'í Writings. Indeed, Bahá'u'lláh has indicated that the "task of converting satanic strength into heavenly power is one that We have been empowered to accomplish" and that "The Word of God, alone, can claim the distinction of being endowed with the capacity required for so great and far-reaching a change."[39] 'Abdu'l-Bahá explains that "good character must be taught." "The individual must be educated to such a high degree that he would rather have his throat cut than tell a lie, and would think it easier to be slashed with a sword or pierced with a spear than to utter calumny or be carried away by wrath."[40] He further observes that "material civilization, through the power of punitive and retaliatory laws, restraineth the people from criminal acts," while divine civilization "so traineth every member of society that no one, with the exception of a negligible few, will undertake to commit a crime," but instead, will "become enamored of human perfections, and will consecrate their lives to whatever will bring light to the world."[41]

In the Bahá'í teachings, the question of human agency is, of course, not completely divorced from extrinsic discipline and restraint. Certain Bahá'í laws are prohibitions or restrictions intended to inhibit certain destructive kinds of action. Such restraints, however, are not perceived to be an imposition on the prerogatives of the individual but are the source of God's grace. They govern only a small portion of human actions. And, as mentioned above, divine law is intended to set boundaries; it defines a wide expanse within which human beings are free and secure to act. As 'Abdu'l-Bahá explains,

> freedom is that which is born of obedience to the laws and ordinances of the Almighty. This is the freedom of the human world, where man severs his affections from all things. When he does so, he becomes immune to all hardship and sorrow. Wealth or material power will not deflect him from moderation and fairness, neither will poverty or need inhibit him from showing

forth happiness and tranquility. The more the conscience of man develops, the more will his heart be free and his soul attain unto happiness. In the religion of God, there is freedom of thought because God, alone, controls the human conscience, but this freedom should not go beyond courtesy. In the religion of God, there is no freedom of action outside the law of God. Man may not transgress this law, even though no harm is inflicted on one's neighbor. This is because the purpose of Divine law is the education of all—others as well as oneself—and, in the sight of God, the harm done to one individual or to his neighbor is the same and is reprehensible in both cases.[42]

Within the boundaries of law, human beings are not inert and submissive, but empowered to make their mark on the world. An active good is required, rather than a passive good that is merely the result of not doing bad things. This positive effort is cultivated by at least three influences: education, attraction, and reflection.

Through education, the individual's character is formed and virtues are acquired, noble goals are cultivated including commitment to the betterment of the world, and attitudes such as tolerance, trustworthiness, love, and freedom from prejudice that are necessary for human solidarity are fostered. These developments result from specific training, but also from acculturation when an individual is encompassed within patterns of thought and action that shape the understanding of what is good and what is true. Again, it must be emphasized that such high aims for education are not idealistic and utopian, but realistic and practical. As 'Abdu'l-Bahá explains, "education cannot alter the inner essence of a man, but it doth exert tremendous influence, and with this power it can bring forth from the individual whatever perfections and capacities are deposited within him."[43] Education implies relative progress; while aiming toward sound ideals, a percentage of individuals become incrementally better than before.

Spiritual attraction is another means to foster the positive expression of human agency. It implies love for God, a desire to do that which is pleasing to God, and recognition that service to God is service to humanity. The necessity of treating other human beings as individuals who have rights and deserve respect, honor, and care derives from the understanding that each soul reflects the divine attributes of God. Love for all humanity, attraction to beauty, a commitment to unity, and a desire to seek the truth, all shape the expression of personal action. Prayer, meditation, and study of the Sacred Text are among the disciplines that cultivate this force of attraction.

Yet another factor that helps to constrain and direct initiative is reflection. Each individual is responsible for investigating reality; "each human creature has individual endowment, power and responsibility in the creative plan of God."[44] Through the faculty of the human mind, 'Abdu'l-Bahá explains, individuals are able to master the sciences and the arts, and to discover or create what was previously unknown and bring it into reality. "Through the meditative faculty inventions are made possible, colossal undertakings are carried out; through it governments can run smoothly."[45] Reflection allows one to take account of circumstances, to consider previous experience, to assess the value or strengths of previous action as well as its flaws or weaknesses, and to overcome challenges in order to advance further. So significant is this capacity for reflection, that Bahá'u'lláh makes it a cornerstone of individual moral progress: "Set before thine eyes God's unerring Balance and, as one standing in His Presence, weigh in that Balance thine actions every day, every moment of thy life."[46] Reflection takes a collective form through consultation.

Power and Social Order

Beyond the question of power as exercised by individuals stands the age-old question of power as it pertains to the relationships among the constituents of the social order—individuals, institutions and communities. A full examination of the teachings related to the practice of Bahá'í administration, questions of human governance, and the future evolution of the political order, is beyond the scope of this book. What can be offered here are a few insights into the workings of power in the collective realm.

As with the individual, the primary concern of Bahá'ís in social interaction is the positive expression of human agency. It is not a matter of power-free relations, nor utopian social structures, nor the faultless implementation of universal principles of peace, justice, or unity. Instead, the Bahá'í teachings envision striving and struggle toward a dynamic balance of relations in order to construct a pattern of social advancement that is at the same time incremental and surging, systematic and chaotic, integrated and diverse.

For Bahá'ís, the essential factor that governs human relations is the Covenant, the agreement between God and humanity, "whereby God requires of man certain behavior in return for which He guarantees certain blessings."[47] There is a greater and lesser Covenant. The greater Covenant encompasses the succession of divine Educators that are sent by God over the course of history, including the specific Revelation of the Manifestation suited to the needs of each age that presents the laws and principles that govern individual and collective action in order to inhibit self-interested and destructive behavior and to cultivate that which is conducive to the well-being of humanity. Through the provisions of the lesser Covenant, the center of authority in the Faith to which all must turn is designated and aspects of Bahá'í administration are defined. The meaning of the lesser Covenant, however, is not exhausted by the formal designation of the center of authority of the Faith; it is concerned with the attitudes and behavior that govern the relationships among the believers and between the believers and their institutions. Consider 'Abdu'l-Bahá's statement:

> Today the dynamic power of the world of existence is the power of the Covenant which like unto an artery pulsateth in the body of the contingent world and protecteth Bahá'í unity.
>
> The Bahá'ís are commanded to establish the oneness of mankind; if they cannot unite around one point how will they be able to bring about the unity of mankind?
>
> The purpose of the Blessed Beauty in entering in to this Covenant and Testament was to gather all existent beings around one point so that the thoughtless souls, who in every cycle and generation have been the cause of dissension, may not undermine the Cause.[48]

Bahá'í administration, the "child of the Covenant,"[49] provides a system intended to protect the Faith, to maintain unity, to ensure the integrity of the teachings, and to guide the application of the teachings to ensure that the aims of the Faith are achieved. While adherence to most Bahá'í laws are left to the conscience of individuals, disobedience to some have social implications and may result in the implementation of administrative sanctions that are designed to protect the community and to encourage the individual to rethink his or her actions. In the scheme of Bahá'í administration, however, these instances are very limited and the institutions are urged to be "extremely patient and forbearing in dealing with the friends"[50] and to "exercise care not to pry into the private lives of the believers."[51]

Short of such extreme public acts of violation of Baháʼí law, individuals govern their own thoughts and actions, and the administration is structured to respect and uphold these freedoms. Baháʼís are assured that "at the very root of the Cause lies the principle of the undoubted right of the individual to self-expression, his freedom to declare his conscience and set forth his views"[52] and clear channels are available for this purpose. So, too, with regard to the actions to serve the Faith, neither "the local nor national representatives of the community" are to "decide where the duty of the individual lies;" rather "the individual alone must assess its character, consult his conscience, [and] prayerfully consider all its aspects."[53] The institutions are encouraged to tolerate mistakes, to allow the freedom for a wide range of individual action, and to avoid an atmosphere of criticism that would inhibit initiative.

The purpose of Baháʼí administration is not to restrict but to release, harmonize and canalize the creative powers of individuals to achieve focused, collective action. A positive expression of power is evident, therefore, in Baháʼí social relations. The institutions are to "further the interests, to coordinate the activities, to apply the principles, to embody the ideals and execute the purpose of the Baháʼí Faith."[54] They "should both provide the impulse whereby the dynamic forces latent in the Faith can unfold, crystallize, and shape the lives and conduct of men, and serve as a medium for the interchange of thought and the co-ordination of activities among the divers elements that constitute the Baháʼí community."[55] In this perspective, the locus of power lies with the individual, while authority lies with the Assemblies.

> The authority to direct the affairs of the Faith locally, national-
> ly and internationally, is divinely conferred on elected institutions.
> However, the power to accomplish the tasks of the community
> resides primarily in the mass of the believers. The authority of the
> institutions is an irrevocable necessity for the progress of human-
> ity; its exercise is an art to be mastered. The power of action in the
> believers is unlocked at the level of individual initiative and surges
> at the level of collective volition. In its potential, this mass power,
> this mix of individual potentialities, exists in a malleable form
> susceptible to the multiple reactions of individuals to the sundry
> influences at work in the world. To realize its highest purpose,

this power needs to express itself through orderly avenues of activity. Even though individuals may strive to be guided in their actions by their personal understanding of the Divine Texts, and much can be accomplished thereby, such actions, untempered by the overall direction provided by authorized institutions, are incapable of attaining the thrust necessary for the unencumbered advancement of civilization.[56]

Essential to the relationship between individual and institutions is consultation, which may be considered the heart of Bahá'í ethical-political processes. Consultation is the tool that enables a collective investigation of reality in order to search for truth and achieve a consensus of understanding in order to determine the best practical course of action to follow. The previous chapters explored how consultation serves to assess needs, apply principles, and make judgments in a manner suited to a particular context. Consultation is, therefore, the practical, dialogical means for continually adjusting relationships that govern power, and, thus, to strive for justice and unity.

Bahá'ís do not imagine that individuals participate in a power-free dialogical process; the aim is to direct power as constructively as possible. Consultation is not fragile, it is robust. It can tolerate imperfections. It can be taught from childhood. Consultation requires certain learned personal constraints, but better results are achieved by degree; practice and self-discipline yields improvement. We believe that there must be some context for affirming the goals to which we aspire rather than simply demanding the right to criticize and to withdraw from participation to follow the arbitrary dictates of personal conscience.[57] The application of principles and values in context is itself part of consultation. Although differing opinions enrich the start of the consultative process, continual argumentation is to be avoided because it hides rather than reveals the truth. The expectation that human beings can be shaped by education and experience to achieve more effective and productive approaches to relationships of power is not naïve or idealistic, but is grounded in the practical and constructive experience of history. Over centuries, for example, humanity learned that certain rules of logic and reasoning are essential for rational discussion; if ignored, a writer's arguments are understood to be flawed and ineffectual. Why then, would it not be possible to learn about and adhere to attitudes and conduct required for effective consultation? This is especially true when these necessary conditions are reinforced by a sense of religious obligation. Indeed, we are offering just such an education within our own community comprised of people representing more than 200 countries and territories and of hundreds of ethnic and cultural groups.

Consultation is a vital instrument for social criticism. Because of the importance placed upon unity in Bahá'í teachings, there is a natural tendency to shrink from the idea of any form of criticism. However, critical thought is essential to understanding. Indeed, social criticism is considered to be the *sine qua non* of power and liberal political thought; to suppress criticism is to suppress freedom and to invite oppression. Any society without the capacity for critical thought either stagnates or is reduced to totalitarianism—or both. To state that we obey our Assemblies and do not engage in criticism is an oversimplification that suggests that the power of individuals are suspended or suppressed, and invites a blistering attack or curt dismissal. Such a generalization is a misunderstanding, or at least an incomplete understanding, of the Bahá'í teachings, which distinguish between vicious, destructive criticism that gives free reign to backbiting or fault-finding, imposes personal beliefs, foments discord, or undermines institutions, and the constructive critical thought, properly presented, that is necessary "in order to improve and remedy certain existing conditions" and which is "not only the right, but the vital responsibility of every loyal and intelligent member of the Community to offer fully and frankly."[58]

Collective plans and initiatives are subject to analysis by divergent viewpoints, and these must be heard if there is to be the vibrancy and flexibility that contributes to a diversity of thought and action that fosters learning about human progress and well-being. The Bahá'í teachings uncompromisingly uphold this process. Individuals have freedom of thought, of speech, and of criticism. Institutions must listen.[59] But the teachings do not indulge wallowing in dissent or sedition; the aim is constructive action. It is necessary that a consensus or majority decision be made which all support as it is tested in practice and revised through practical experience. As the Universal House of Justice explains, "vital as it is to the progress of society, criticism is a two-edged sword: it is all too often the harbinger of conflict and contention. The balanced processes of the Administrative Order are meant to prevent this essential activity from degenerating to any form of dissent that breeds opposition and its dreadful schismatic consequences."[60]

One additional consideration in the relations of power between the individual and institutions involves the evolution of Bahá'í administration. The Bahá'í teachings do not offer a fixed set of rules that govern collective affairs or an immutable structure for institutional arrangements. Instead, "the whole machinery of Assemblies, of committees and conventions is to be regarded as a means, and not an end in itself." It is "even as a living organism" that can "expand and adapt itself to the needs and requirements of an ever-changing society." "It should also be borne in mind that the machinery of the Cause has been so fashioned, that whatever is deemed necessary to incorporate into it in order to keep it in the forefront of all progressive movements, can, according to the provisions made by Bahá'u'lláh, be safely embodied therein."[61]

As the Faith expands and its influence spreads, the nature and responsibilities of Bahá'í administrative bodies change. For example, in 1986, formulation of national teaching plans passed from the international level to the Counsellors and National Assemblies. It is also possible that new institutions emerge. Examples are the establishment of the institution of the Counsellors and, more recently, regional counsels and training institutes. Even more radical changes may be anticipated in the distant future with the emergence of a Bahá'í state or a future Bahá'í commonwealth foretold by Shoghi Effendi. However, the conditions for the eventual emergence of these social arrangements require a radical transition in human relations, a transition for which Bahá'ís will not directly be responsible. These conditions are so remote, and the context so obscure, as to make it impossible at this time to realistically define the corresponding relations of power.

As Bahá'í administrative arrangements evolve, mistakes are inevitable. Administrators will not easily learn to live up to the high personal standards expected of them or to the collective responsibilities of the institutions, without making mistakes and sometimes imposing on the rights of the individual. So, too, individuals will inevitably go too far either in pursuing an independent—and occasionally destructive—path, or alternately, being too submissive and inert. This is why the Guardian and the Universal House of Justice have repeatedly appealed to both individuals and institutions to moderate their practice, to have tolerance for excesses born of immaturity, and, for those who possess greater insight or capacity, to do what is right. Mistakes are not aberrations but are inseparable from human action; struggling to overcome them is the mark of human progress. "The advancement of the Cause is an evolutionary process which takes place through trial and error, through reflection on experience and through wholehearted commitment to the teaching Plans and strategies devised by the House of Justice."[62]

Power and Practice

With these insights into the Bahá'í teachings that pertain to the nature of power, it is possible to turn to the question of how the Bahá'í community acts in society at large. As already discussed, it would not be convincing to claim that Bahá'ís exercise no power in any form, for according to contemporary understanding, even to share a thought with the aim of influencing others is to exert a form of power. Questions about the intentions of the Bahá'í community will therefore inevitably arise.

Consider, for example, the Bahá'í vision of humanity's future world order. Do we seek to establish a universal world government or do we stand apart from political processes? In relation to other religions, do we possess the truth which others must accept, or at least, does this truth allow us to "explain" religious reality to others? Or, do we instead believe that Bahá'u'lláh proposes a form of religious relativism, upholding the legitimacy of multiple communities that retain incommensurable claims? Such questions impose dualistic assumptions that distort the deep insights conveyed in the Bahá'í teachings. Yet, if we cannot satisfactorily describe our approach to matters associated with power, others will do it for us, imposing a point of view alien to the nature of the Faith or intentionally portraying it in a negative light.

At issue, then, is not whether Bahá'ís are agents that act in relation to others, but how. If we are not fundamentalists attempting to impose our will on the world, and if we are not relativists engaged in our incommensurable discourse as humanity bobs along on the waves of history, then how do we describe ourselves to those concerned with the exercise of power?

For those who are receptive to Bahá'u'lláh's message, it is the truth of His Cause and the spiritual forces that have been released through the advent of His Revelation that attract humanity to embrace and put into practice His teachings for the realization of His aims for the betterment of the world. "How vast is the tabernacle of the Cause of God!" Bahá'u'lláh proclaims. "It hath overshadowed all the peoples and kindreds of the earth, and will, erelong, gather together the whole of mankind beneath its shelter."[63] "If this Cause be of God," He also states, "no man can prevail against it; and if it be not of God, the divines amongst you, and they that follow their corrupt desires and such as have rebelled against Him will surely suffice to overpower it."[64] Without in any way contradicting this reality, it may also be possible to describe the Faith's influence to some extent in social terms. In so doing, a brief reference to the concept of a community of practice discussed in chapter 4 in the context of science and religion may prove useful.

In his book, *Our Practices, Our Selves,* Todd May observed that from a social perspective, human beings organize themselves into communities of practice, such as scientists, church-goers, or members of the legal profession. To be part of this community "is to be committed to enough of the claims, findings, and theories of that practice—and particularly its 'central' claims, findings, theories, and so on—as to be reasonably seen as being committed to it."[65] In the context of human practices, May argues that power is not only a restraint but also a creative force that enables people to behave in a certain way and produce things that did not exist before. Practices provide dimensions, such as education and tradition, that result in the formation of knowledge, skills, attitudes, and a capacity to do something. When one engages in the practice of tailoring, one learns to create clothing. One engages in the practice of music and is trained to play an instrument. Thus, "our practices go a long way toward making us who we are. . . . And they do so not so much by restraining us, by stopping us from doing things we might otherwise do. Instead they do it by forming us, by creating us to be the kinds of people we are."[66]

According to May, human beings participate in, and are shaped by, a number of different practices simultaneously. Participation in one practice, particularly one that operates at a high level of complexity, influences participation in another. For example, the practice of raising children is sure to be influenced to some degree if a parent is also a doctor or a schoolteacher. So, too, participation in a religious community or political party is certain to influence other practices. Thus the claims and standards of one practice can be used to criticize or influence another resulting in a shift or alteration of the second practice. For example, attitudes held within the practice of one culture—such as the equality of women and men—can stimulate an internal dialogue in another culture to reexamine its tradition and eventually formulate a new standard of behavior. Or a change in society may cause pressures that stimulate evolution of a practice. Ultimately, any change in a practice occurs because its own criteria are invoked or modified, thereby leading to new conclusions.

In this perspective, power is not the possession of a particular person or institution; it is the combined outcome of the relationships that make up a practice. Thus, May states, "as far as practices go, any kind of conspiracy theory about how people become who they are is going to be wildly implausible."[67] It is a practice's complex array of values, behaviors, goals, rules, norms, and so on that contribute to who individuals are or how they act, and not the direct imposition of power or coercion by some institution or group.

Certainly for Bahá'ís May's concept of communities of practice is reductionistic and does not provide an adequate framework for a Bahá'í understanding of human relationships. Nevertheless, it offers a useful insight into how power and influence can be expressed through relationships in a constructive way, without presuming that individuals or communities cannot engage one another, or that every engagement must be coercive or oppressive. This insight can assist in illustrating how agency is exercised within the Bahá'í community and how the community interacts with others to help foster the progress of an ever-advancing civilization without imposing the Bahá'í teachings.

Within the Bahá'í community there are methods, principles, beliefs, knowledge, institutions, behaviors, and processes that are organized and justified according to internal criteria. We are learning to put these various aspects into place according to our best understanding of Bahá'u'lláh's teachings. As a relatively new community, thought and action steadily evolve, resulting in ever more complex and productive patterns of personal behavior, institutional arrangements, community life, and engagement with the wider society. Individuals who are not Bahá'ís are taught and attracted to the Faith, and then enter the community. In this process, there are central ideas that must be accepted if someone is to be considered a member; so, too, there are certain restraints, as found in the laws and the obligations to the Covenant. Yet, as discussed, questions of power cannot be reduced to a matter of restraint. The primary concern is to constructively shape capacity through social and educational processes—such as study of the Word of God, fasting and other spiritual disciplines, and involvement in Bahá'í community life—that influence personal conduct and participation in service to the Faith and in contributing to the betterment of the world. "The Bahá'ís will bring about this improvement and betterment but not through sedition and appeal to physical force—not through warfare, but welfare," 'Abdu'l-Bahá states. And He adds:

> Endeavor to become the cause of the attraction of souls rather than to enforce minds. Manifest true economics to the people. Show what love is, what kindness is, what true severance is and generosity. This is the important thing for you to do. Act in accordance with the teachings of Bahá'u'lláh. All His Books will be translated. Now is the time for you to live in accordance with His words. Let your deeds be the real translation of their meaning. Economic questions will not attract hearts. The love of God alone will attract them. Economic questions are most interesting; but the power which moves, controls and attracts the hearts of men is the love of God.[68]

The Bahá'í community both influences other communities and is influenced by them. Participation in a range of activities associated with culture, the media, the economy, academia, politics and other areas affect Bahá'ís both negatively and positively. Musical talent can enhance devotional life, for example; racial prejudices corrode community relations. The challenge is to make sure such influences bring us nearer to what Bahá'u'lláh intends rather than moving us further from it. What one does and learns as a Bahá'í carries over into all areas of life, such as parenthood, professional life, or citizenship. There is also the conscious effort of the believers or the community to contribute to the internal dialogue and action of other fields of human endeavor by introducing Bahá'í principles, methods, or concepts. A specific example is the dissemination of such documents as *The Promise of World Peace*, *The Prosperity of Humankind*, and the letter of the Universal House of Justice to religious leaders in April 2002. Another is the effort by Bahá'ís who are experts to "transform their various disciplines by bringing to bear upon them the light of the Divine Teachings."[69] Influence is, therefore, consciously sought, but as exercised in this way, power is not imposed. As 'Abdu'l-Bahá explains:

> O ye loved ones of God! In this, the Bahá'í dispensation, God's Cause is spirit unalloyed. His Cause belongeth not to the material world. It cometh neither for strife nor war, nor for acts of mischief or of shame; it is neither for quarrelling with other Faiths, nor for

conflicts with the nations. Its only army is the love of God, its only joy the clear wine of His knowledge, its only battle the expounding of the Truth; its one crusade is against the insistent self, the evil promptings of the human heart. Its victory is to submit and yield, and to be selfless is its everlasting glory. In brief, it is spirit upon spirit. . . .

Let all your striving be for this, to become the source of life and immortality, and peace and comfort and joy, to every human soul, whether one known to you or a stranger, one opposed to you or on your side.[70]

As a result of Bahá'í influence, other individuals and other areas of human endeavor may change, but this is because a responsive chord is struck in their internal criteria for justification. Other disciplines, equally, have the opportunity to exert influence on the Bahá'í community; but this effect is mediated by Bahá'í standards and methods.

The Bahá'í teachings directs us toward an approach to participation in the life of society that represents an alternative to either imposing ideal methods and systems or yielding to constant doubt and criticism. In avoiding one extreme, we do not offer formulaic answers, do not sit in judgment, and do not compel others to accept Bahá'í teachings. This is not to deny that Bahá'u'lláh provides truths that are of benefit for all humanity. But it is an acknowledgement that individuals independently embrace these truths, and that our efforts to mine the gems of the Revelation will take centuries of effort and contributions from a host of constructive human disciplines. In avoiding the other extreme, we do not succumb to a call for constant criticism, do not deny that progress—by degree—is possible, and do not accept that all perspectives are equally valid. Of course humility, tolerance, and an acceptance of ambiguity are necessary for investigating reality and seeking truth; however, constant criticism is a luxury afforded to those who do not have to accomplish anything in the world. A practical approach to the problem of power accepts that the exercise of human agency is more than imposing restraints, that influence is reciprocal, and that learning to find better arrangements of human relations can emerge through experience over time.

Consider, for example, the question of Bahá'í association with other religions. The Bahá'í teachings outline an approach that avoids triumphalism and relativism. Within the Faith, Bahá'ís act on their teachings. There are relationships, values, knowledge, and behaviors that conform to internal standards of justification. People may enter or leave the community based on free choice in accepting or rejecting its essential precepts. Through education, experience, and effort, Bahá'ís are transformed individually and collectively.

In the wider society, the Faith engages other religious communities in a spirit of "friendliness and fellowship."[71] Acknowledging wholeheartedly the divine origin and truths of these communities, it works with them to foster unity, promote understanding, and achieve common goals. Each religious community has its own criteria for the justification of knowledge, beliefs, and behaviors. Through an open engagement with other religions, Bahá'ís have an opportunity to gain a better insight into current understandings of the Faith, to possibly revise and deepen them as necessary, producing a more profound adherence to Bahá'u'lláh's Revelation. There is also the opportunity for Bahá'ís to influence other individuals and religious communities. But any change would be derived from the internal criteria of a particular community; it would be a remembrance or calling forth of that which is already within as a result of an external stimulus.

Individuals from diverse religious backgrounds may, of their own choice, join the Bahá'í community. Because of the Bahá'í belief in the oneness of religion, this is not a rejection of previous beliefs, but a fulfillment.[72] A Christian, for example, upon becoming a Bahá'í does not reject Christ, but finds the spirit and message of Jesus renewed in the teachings of Bahá'u'lláh. The potentialities inherent in such Bahá'í verses that call for "the union of all its peoples in one universal Cause, one common Faith"[73] and which state that "all men will adhere to one religion, will have one common faith, will be blended into one race, and become a single people"[74] can become manifest only through influence and free choice. The power of such influence is the power to cultivate constructive potentialities, not the power to coerce and compel.

This perspective avoids triumphalism, another expression of foundationalism, because Bahá'ís do not assume a position of superiority to judge, criticize, or define the beliefs of others. It also is incompatible with a form of religious relativism,[75] because Bahá'ís do not believe that the diverse religious perspectives are incommensurable, nor do we believe that all contemporary teachings of all religious communities can be accepted at the same time.

Bahá'ís believe that Bahá'u'lláh's teachings are intended for all humanity,[76] but that each person must be free to accept them or not. If people hold to their own beliefs, we are to treat them no differently than a member of the Bahá'í community. To teach the Faith, according to the principles in the Bahá'í Writings is not to impose views because we believe they are correct and others are wrong. Teaching is sharing what one knows about Bahá'u'lláh with others who do not know and are interested to hear. It is necessary for the teacher to respond to questions and help overcome barriers, but only if the person desires it—a "seeker" in the true sense.

Consider another example of the exercise of power through influence, that of Bahá'í involvement in social action. Bahá'ís do not work to directly incorporate Bahá'í teachings into law, as noted above. Nor do they believe that the solutions to humanity's problems can be found merely in attacking, in an isolated fashion, specific ills. Rather, Bahá'í efforts for social change are intended to contribute toward a general transformation of society. As the Universal House of Justice explains:

> We should also remember that most people have no clear concept of the sort of world they wish to build, nor how to go about building it. Even those who are concerned to improve conditions are therefore reduced to combating every apparent evil that takes their attention. Willingness to fight against evils, whether in the form of conditions or embodied in evil men, has thus become for most people the touchstone by which they judge a person's moral worth. Bahá'ís, on the other hand, know the goal they are working towards and know what they must do, step by step, to attain it. Their whole energy is directed towards the building of the good, a good which has such a positive strength that in the face of it the multitude of evils—which are in essence negative—will fade away and be no more. To enter into the quixotic tournament of demolishing one by one the evils in the world is, to a Bahá'í a vain waste of time and effort. His whole life is directed towards proclaiming the Message of Bahá'u'lláh, reviving the spiritual life of his fellow-men, uniting them in a Divinely-created World Order, and then, as that Order grows in strength and influence, he will see the power of that Message transforming the whole of human society and progressively solving the problems and removing the injustice which have so long bedeviled the world.[77]

The aim of establishing a new world order does not mean, however, that Bahá'ís will create this order in isolation and offer it as a completed gift to humanity. The world is in a transitional stage. A social reality whose watchword is the oneness of humanity is the inevitable outcome of the forces at work. Every step in this direction is a balm to human ills. Every step away is a cause of continuing turmoil that draws the peoples of the world deeper into the search for solutions. The Bahá'í community is part of the world and there is a constant interplay between the two; the very nature of this interaction contributes to the ongoing evolution of both the community and society.

Bahá'ís do not seek political power to change the global order to conform to the ideas found in our Sacred Writings; indeed, the Writings indicate that humanity itself will, of necessity, forge the basis of global order and peace.[78] Our part is "the task of breathing life into this unified body—of creating true unity and spirituality."[79] Our efforts to contribute to social progress and justice engage groups and governmental and non-governmental organizations in a manner that avoids patterns of conflict and attempts to build patterns of collaboration. The Bahá'í principle of non-involvement in politics is not non-involvement in social action, but rather non-involvement in a type of partisan political activity that is based upon competition and struggle for power and that seeks the ascendancy of one's views over those of others, who are perceived as adversaries or competitors. Bahá'ís attempt to reach out to other groups and agencies at local, regional, national, and international levels and collaborate in identifying problems, consulting on possible solutions, engaging in practical activities for social well-being, building consensus, and where possible, creating social, legal, or political change. This alternative approach reflects 'Abdu'l-Bahá's expressed hope that the "ancient politics whose foundation is war be discarded" and the "modern politics founded on peace raise the standard of victory."[80]

The profound change that Bahá'u'lláh intends for humanity will not be achieved easily. It can only unfold through a series of stages over centuries in which the conditions of one stage create the possibilities for further change and progress. This is similar to the ecological concept of the succession of communities. In the case of a forest that has been completely destroyed by fire, for example, the mature forest is not immediately restored. Rather, a collection of simple plants appears initially that creates the conditions for another, more complex group of plants to take root. Over time, successive aggregations of plants and wildlife follow, each shaping the environment to facilitate the emergence of a more complex community of organisms, until the mature forest appears. The Bahá'í community, in its own growth and development, has experienced an organic unfoldment of stages as illustrated by the progressive implementation of Bahá'í law, the development of administrative structures, and the advances, from Plan to Plan, of the teaching work. Engagement with the wider society and the evolution of society toward Bahá'u'lláh's intended purpose will likewise advance from stage to stage.[81]

A fundamental feature of ethical and political thought is the attitude of an individual ("the self") toward other people ("the other"). One perspective acknowledges three modes of engagement.[82] First, is when the other is viewed as an object—a subject of research or a victim of oppression that is merely a recipient of the action and judgments of the self. In the second mode, the other is human, but the self claims to know the truth about the other completely, engaging him or her from a distance, offering certainty and authoritative direction; an example is the traditional relationship of a doctor and patient. The third mode is one of reciprocity and mutual recognition; the self influences the other, but when the other speaks, the self must also be prepared to be called into question and, perhaps, to change. The Bahá'í teachings are unequivocal in requiring that a believer see "the other" as a being of equal worth and potentiality, with rights and responsibilities identical to those of "the self." "Beware lest ye prefer yourselves above your neighbors,"[83] Bahá'u'lláh states. "The other" is even given a moral priority: "Blessed is he who preferreth his brother before himself."[84] 'Abdu'l-Bahá makes the following appeal:

> O ye lovers of this wronged one! Cleanse ye your eyes, so that ye behold no man as different from yourselves. See ye no strangers; rather see all men as friends, for love and unity come hard when ye fix your gaze on otherness. And in this new and wondrous age, the Holy Writings say that we must be at one with every people; that we must see neither harshness nor injustice, neither malevolence, nor hostility, nor hate, but rather turn our eyes toward the heaven of ancient glory. For each of the creatures is a sign of God, and it was by the grace of the Lord and His power that each did step into

the world; therefore they are not strangers, but in the family; not aliens, but friends, and to be treated as such.[85]

And again He states:

> O peoples of the world! The Sun of Truth hath risen to illumine the whole earth, and to spiritualize the community of man. Laudable are the results and the fruits thereof, abundant the holy evidences deriving from this grace. This is mercy unalloyed and purest bounty; it is light for the world and all its peoples; it is harmony and fellowship, and love and solidarity; indeed it is compassion and unity, and the end of foreignness; it is the being at one, in complete dignity and freedom, with all on earth. . . .
>
> For this reason must all human beings powerfully sustain one another and seek for everlasting life; and for this reason must the lovers of God in this contingent world become the mercies and the blessings sent forth by that element King of the seen and unseen realms. Let them purify their sight and behold all humankind as leaves and blossoms and fruits of the tree of being. Let them at all times concern themselves with doing a kindly thing for one of their fellows, offering to someone love, consideration, thoughtful help. Let them see no one as their enemy, or as wishing them ill, but think of all humankind as their friends; regarding the alien as an intimate, the stranger as a companion, staying free of prejudice, drawing no lines.[86]

The principle of the oneness of humanity that is the central teaching of Bahá'u'lláh, which fully respects diversity, tolerates no division between "us" and "them". For Bahá'ís there can be no question, then, of dominating or compelling others, even for benevolent ends. "One's beliefs are an internal and personal matter," the Universal House of Justice explains; "no person or institution has the right to exert compulsion in matters of belief."[87] Can Bahá'ís carry out an open dialogue with others, truly allowing what they believe to be influenced by others? Certitude in our acceptance of Bahá'u'lláh and His teachings does not discount genuine open dialogue and a search for truth, since what changes through such discourse is not Bahá'u'lláh's Revelation, but our understanding of Bahá'u'lláh's Revelation. The influence of dialogue with others should assist Bahá'ís to obtain a deeper grasp of what Bahá'u'lláh intends and how the teachings are to be translated into action.[88] In the same way, as described above, Bahá'í influence on others represents a fulfillment of their own beliefs or an acceptance of truths that catalyzes an internal process of personal or group transformation. If, or for Bahá'ís when, the high aims voiced by Bahá'u'lláh are realized—a world commonwealth, the union of all peoples, the Most Great Peace, and a divine civilization—it cannot be the result of a conspiracy, of absolutist tendencies, or of imposed power, but rather, through the impulse of His Revelation in free interaction with others.

In the relationship between the Bahá'í community and the wider society, the burden of the proof of the ideals of Bahá'u'lláh's teachings rests with the Bahá'ís. Humanity has good reason to question whether any such high-minded sentiments are a mask for an imposition of power. It is only through deeds that Bahá'ís can demonstrate the reality of His words, and thereby convince and have the desired influence upon the peoples of the world.

Toward a New Social Reality—a New World Order

For centuries humanity has engaged in a struggle to know reality and to utilize that knowledge to create a productive and sound social order. The tools of this enterprise were reason and science. Confidence in the ultimate success of this enterprise reached its peak early in the twentieth century; by the end of that same century, however, humanity was coming to the understanding that certain knowledge lay beyond its grasp and that efforts to forge a better world depended upon the fragile agreements that shape human relations.

The understanding that social reality is constructed through human agreement rather than grounded upon absolute knowledge of reality need not spell disaster for the world. The people of the world are obliged to take responsibility to use the capacity to know, circumscribed as it may be, in order to collaborate in the creation of a social order that proves its worth through the fruits it produces for the progress, the happiness and the well-being of all. Attention, in the decades that lie ahead, must not be focused on despair, the wanton unraveling of the old social order, or on a self-serving exploitation of the situation, but on learning to use the contemporary insights about knowledge, learning and social reality to invigorate the centuries long process of the forward march of civilization. Yet, none of this can be done in darkness. The light of revelation must shed its illumination on human thought and action.

In the book, *Cosmopolis*, Stephen Toulmin explores the history of modernity and the quest to establish the social order upon a rational foundation. He argues that the attachment to abstract theory and to certainty that was initiated by Descartes and bolstered by Newtonian physics in the Enlightenment was actually a move away from a learning-oriented worldview, born almost a century earlier from Renaissance humanism, which promoted a balance between theory and practice.

Toulmin describes how, over centuries, all of the initial assumptions of the Enlightenment that introduced a mechanistic vision of the universe were gradually revised over time, reaching a climax in the twentieth century debate between modernism and postmodernism. He concludes that humanity stands on the "Far Side of Modernity,"[89] about to begin a "third phase in Modernity," or a "new and distinctive 'post-modern' phase."[90] As we enter a new stage in intellectual history, he states, "we need to balance the hope for certainty and clarity in theory with the impossibility of avoiding uncertainty and ambiguity in practice."[91]

Humanity, uncertain about the future, registers its hopes and concerns under the suggestive term "post" modern. It diagnoses, to some degree, the breakdown of the old world order. But Bahá'u'lláh describes the parameters of a postmodern reality, the far side of modernity. "Heavenly teachings applicable to the advancement in human conditions have been revealed in this merciful age," 'Abdu'l-Bahá explains. "This reformation and renewal of the fundamental reality of religion constitute the true and outworking spirit of modernism, the unmistakable light of the world, the manifest effulgence of the Word of God, the divine remedy for all human ailment and the bounty of eternal life to all mankind."[92]

Bahá'u'lláh Himself testifies that "no sooner had the First Word proceeded, through the potency of Thy will and purpose, out of His mouth, and the First Call gone forth from His lips than the whole creation was revolutionized, and all that are in the heavens and all that are on earth were stirred to the depths. Through that Word the realities of all created things were shaken, were divided, separated, scattered, combined and reunited, disclosing, in both the contingent world and the heavenly kingdom, entities of a new creation, and revealing, in the unseen realms, the signs and tokens of Thy unity and oneness."[93] And He affirms: "By My Self! The day is approaching when We will have rolled up the world and all that is therein, and spread out a new order in its stead."[94]

References

'Abdu'l-Bahá. *'Abdu'l-Bahá on Divine Philosophy*. The Tudor Press, 1918.

_____. *Paris Talks: Addresses Given by 'Abdu'l-Bahá in Paris in 1911*. 11th ed. London: Bahá'í Publishing Trust, 1969.

_____. *The Promulgation of Universal Peace: Talks Delivered by 'Abdu'l-Bahá During His Visit to the United States and Canada in 1912*. 2nd ed. Wilmette, IL: Bahá'í Publishing Trust, 1982.

_____. *The Secret of Divine Civilization*. 3rd ed. Wilmette, IL: Bahá'í Publishing Trust, 1983.

_____. *Selections from the Writings of 'Abdu'l-Bahá*. Haifa: Bahá'í World Centre, 1978.

_____. *Some Answered Questions*. Compiled and translated by Laura Clifford Barney. 5th ed. Wilmette, IL: Bahá'í Publishing Trust, 1982.

_____. *Tablets of 'Abdu'l-Bahá*. Volume 1. New York: Bahá'í Publishing Committee, 1930.

_____. *The Tablets of the Divine Plan*. Revised ed. Wilmette, IL: Bahá'í Publishing Trust, 1977.

_____. *The Will and Testament of 'Abdu'l-Bahá*. Wilmette, IL: Bahá'í Publishing Trust, 1971.

Arbab, Farzam. "Promoting a Discourse on Science, Religion, and Development." *The Lab, the Temple, and the Market: Reflections at the Intersection of Science, Religion, and Development*. Edited by Sharon M. P. Harper. International Development Research Center, Canada. Kumarian Press, 2000.

Arbab, Haleh. Talk presented at the Colloquium on Science, Religion and Development. India International Centre, New Delhi. November 2000.

Bahá'í World Centre. *Century of Light*. Haifa: Bahá'í World Centre, 2001.

_____. *Readings on Social and Economic Development*. Palabra Publications, 2000.

_____. *The Six Year Plan: Summary of Achievements*. Haifa: Bahá'í World Centre, 1993.

Bahá'u'lláh. *Epistle to the Son of the Wolf.* Wilmette, IL: Bahá'í Publishing Trust, 1976.

———. *Gleanings from the Writings of Bahá'u'lláh.* 2nd edition. Wilmette, IL: Bahá'í Publishing Trust, 1976.

———. *The Hidden Words of Bahá'u'lláh.* Wilmette, IL: Bahá'í Publishing Trust, 1939.

———. *The Kitáb-i-Aqdas: The Most Holy Book.* 1st English edition. Haifa: Bahá'í World Centre, 1993.

———. *The Kitáb-i-Íqán.* 2nd edition. Wilmette, IL: Bahá'í Publishing Trust, 1950.

———. *Prayers and Meditations.* Wilmette, IL: Bahá'í Publishing Trust, 1987.

———. *The Summons of the Lord of Hosts.* Haifa: Bahá'í World Centre, 2002.

———. *Tabernacle of Unity.* Haifa: Bahá'í World Centre, 2006.

———. *Tablets of Bahá'u'lláh Revealed after the Kitáb-i-Aqdas.* Haifa: Bahá'í World Centre, 1978.

Bahá'u'lláh and 'Abdu'l-Bahá. *The Importance of Obligatory Prayer and Fasting.* A compilation prepared by the Research Department of the Universal House of Justice, 2000.

Bahá'u'lláh, 'Abdu'l-Bahá, Shoghi Effendi and the Universal House of Justice. *Compilation of Compilations.* Volume 3. Bahá'í Publications Australia, 2000.

Bahá'u'lláh, the Báb, and 'Abdu'l-Bahá. *Bahá'í Prayers.* Wilmette, IL: Bahá'í Publishing Trust, 2002.

Bahá'u'lláh, the Báb, 'Abdu'l-Bahá, Shoghi Effendi and the Universal House of Justice. *Compilation of Compilations.* Volumes 1 and 2. Bahá'í Publications Australia, 1991.

———. *Lights of Guidance: A Bahá'í Reference File.* Compiled by Helen Hornby. 2nd edition. New Delhi, India: Bahá'í Publishing Trust, 1988.

Bernstein, Richard J. *Beyond Objectivism and Relativism: Science, Hermeneutics, and Praxis.* University of Pennsylvania Press, 1983.

Burbules, Nicholas C. "Postmodern Doubt and Philosophy of Education." *The Philosophy of Education,* 1995. Philosophy of Education Society, 1996.

Carvalho, John J. "Overview of the Structure of a Scientific Worldview." *Zygon: Journal of Religion and Science,* vol. 41, no. 1, March 2006.

Fairfield, Paul. *The Ways of Power: Hermeneutics, Ethics, and Social Criticism.* Duquesne University Press, 2002.

Flyvbjerg, Bent. *Making Social Science Matter: Why Social Inquiry Fails and How It Can Succeed Again.* Cambridge University Press, 2001.

Gadamer, Hans-Georg, *Truth and Method.* 2nd revised edition. New York: Continuum, 1998.

Giddens, Anthony. *New Rules of Sociological Method: a Positive Critique of Interpretative Sociologies.* Stanford University Press, second edition, 1993.

International Teaching Centre. *Attaining the Dynamics of Growth: Glimpses from Five Continents.* Bahá'í World Centre, 2008.

―――――. *Reflections on Growth.* Numbers 7 and 8.

May, Dann. "A Preliminary Survey of Hermeneutical Principles Found Within the Bahá'í Writings," *Journal of Bahá'í Studies,* vol. 1, no. 3, 1989.

May, Todd. *Our Practices, Our Selves: Or, What it Means to be Human.* The Pennsylvania State University Press, 2001.

Momen, Moojan. "Fundamentalism and Liberalism: Towards an Understanding of the Dichotomy." *The Bahá'í Studies Review,* vol. 2.1, 1992.

―――――. "Methodology in Bahá'í Studies." *The Bahá'í Studies Review,* vol. 10, 2001/2002.

Office of Social and Economic Development. *For the Betterment of the World.* Bahá'í World Centre, second edition, 2008.

Roosta, Manigeh. "Adult Learning and Community Development: A Case Study of the FUNDAEC's University Center for Rural Well-Being in Risaralda, Colombia." Doctoral thesis, 1999.

The Ruhi Institute, *Learning About Growth,* Palabra Publications, 1991.

―――――. *Walking Together on a Path of Service: Book 7.* Palabra Publications, 2001.

Searle, John R. *The Construction of Social Reality.* New York Free Press, 1995.

Shoghi Effendi. *The Advent of Divine Justice.* Wilmette, IL: Bahá'í Publishing Trust, 1974.

―――――. *Arohanui: Letters from Shoghi Effendi to New Zealand.* Suva, Fiji: Bahá'í Publishing Trust, 1982.

―――――. *Bahá'í Administration.* Wilmette, IL: Bahá'í Publishing Trust, 1974.

―――――. *Citadel of Faith: Messages to America 1947-1957.* Wilmette, IL: Bahá'í Publishing Trust, 1970.

―――――. *Dawn of a New Day: Messages to India 1923-1957.* New Delhi: Bahá'í Publishing Trust, 1970.

―――――. *Directives from the Guardian.* Hawaii: Bahá'í Publishing Trust, 1973.

―――――. *God Passes By.* Wilmette, IL: Bahá'í Publishing Trust, 1974.

―――――. *Messages to America.* Wilmette, IL: Bahá'í Publishing Trust, 1947.

―――――. *Messages to the Bahá'í World: 1950-1957.* Wilmette, IL: Bahá'í Publishing Trust, 1971.

―――――. *The Promised Day is Come.* Rev. ed. Wilmette, IL: Bahá'í Publishing Trust, 1980.

_____. *The World Order of Bahá'u'lláh*. 2nd ed. Wilmette, IL: Bahá'í Publishing Trust, 1974.

Shoghi Effendi and the Universal House of Justice. *A Special Measure of Love: The Importance and Nature of the Teaching Work among the Masses*. Wilmette, IL: Bahá'í Publishing Trust, 1974.

Sosa, Ernest. "The Raft and the Pyramid." *Epistemology: An Anthology*. Blackwell Publishers, 2000.

Toulmin, Stephen. *Cosmopolis: The Hidden Agenda of Modernity*. The University of Chicago Press, 1992.

The Universal House of Justice. *Constitution of the Universal House of Justice*. Haifa: Bahá'í World Centre, 1972.

_____. *Issues Related to the Study of the Bahá'í Faith*. Wilmette, IL: Bahá'í Publishing Trust, 1999.

_____. *Messages from the Universal House of Justice 1963-1986: The Third Epoch of the Formative Age*. Wilmette, IL: Bahá'í Publishing Trust, 1996.

_____. *The Five Year Plan 2001-2006: Messages of the Universal House of Justice*. 2nd edition. Palabra Publications, 2003.

_____. *Rights and Responsibilities: The Complementary Roles of the Individual and Institutions*. Bahá'í Canada Publications, 1997.

_____. *Turning Point: Selected Messages of the Universal House of Justice and Supplementary Materials 1996-2006*. Palabra Publications, 2006.

_____. *A Wider Horizon: Selected Messages of the Universal House of Justice 1983-1992*. Palabra Publications, 1992.

Notes

1   Bahá'u'lláh, *Lawḥ-i-Ḥaqqu'n-Nás*, provisional translation by Kevin Brown.

2   Bahá'u'lláh, *The Tabernacle of Unity*, p. 4.

CHAPTER 1

1   'Abdu'l-Bahá, *'Abdu'l-Bahá on Divine Philosophy*, p. 292. Similarly, a letter written on behalf of Shoghi Effendi states: "The whole purpose of Bahá'u'lláh is that we should become a new kind of people, people who are upright, kind, intelligent, truthful, and honest and who live according to His great laws laid down for this new epoch in man's development. To call ourselves Bahá'ís is not enough, our inmost being must become ennobled and enlightened through living a Bahá'í life." (*Compilation of Compilations*, vol. 2, p. 13.)

2   'Abdu'l-Bahá, *Paris Talks*, p. 17.

3   Bahá'u'lláh, *Tablets of Bahá'u'lláh*, p. 142.

4   Bahá'u'lláh, *Gleanings from the Writings of Bahá'u'lláh*, p. 338.

5   'Abdu'l-Bahá, *The Secret of Divine Civilization*, pp. 1-2.

6   Searle's approach is not relativistic; his thoughts about social reality rest upon an objective physical reality. "The overall picture," Searle explains ". . . proceeds by way of external realism through the correspondence theory [of truth] to the structure of social reality." (John Searle, *The Construction of Social Reality*, pp. 199-200.) Searle's perspective on the "construction of social reality" stands in distinction to the "social construction of reality"—the idea that human reality itself is entirely a social creation. See the critique of social construction by Ian Hacking, in *The Social Construction of What?* The question of knowing reality is explored in more detail in chapters 4 and 5.

7   Searle, *The Construction of Social Reality*, pp. 1-2.

8   ". . . social facts in general, and institutional facts especially, are hierarchically structured. Institutional facts exist, so to speak, on top of brute facts." (Searle, *The Construction of Social Reality*, pp. 34-35.) For Bahá'ís, social reality must rest upon the facts of spiritual as well as physical reality.

9   Searle, *The Construction of Social Reality*, pp. 3-5.

10 Social reality is ontologically subjective and epistemologically objective. (Searle, *The Construction of Social Reality*, pp. 12-13.) Ontology has to do with the nature of being, epistemology with what we know. Subjectivity pertains to what is personal, and objectivity to what is independent of personal opinion. Thus, to say that social reality is ontologically subjective means that the features of social reality do not have an existence outside of the consensus of the human beings that create it. For example, a certain piece of paper is money because of the intent of the social agents that created it, not because of its inherent physical qualities. To say that social reality is epistemologically objective means that what we know about social reality isn't just a matter of the opinion of one individual, but consists of objectively ascertainable facts. Thus, determining whether a particular piece of paper is money is not a matter of the personal opinion of a single individual.

11 Matthew 6:10.

12 'Abdu'l-Bahá, *The Promulgation of Universal Peace*, pp. 101-02.

13 Bahá'u'lláh, *Tablets of Bahá'u'lláh*, p. 166.

14 Bahá'u'lláh, *The Kitáb-i-Íqán*, p. 241. For more concerning the Bahá'í responsibility to translate thought into action, see "Clay into Crystal: How Thought Shapes Structure in the Pursuit of Justice," by Holly Hansen, a talk given at the meeting of the Association for Bahá'í Studies, September 2001, http://bahai-library.org/conferences/clay.crystal.html.

15 Bahá'u'lláh, *Gleanings*, p. 215.

16 Bahá'u'lláh, *Tablets of Bahá'u'lláh*, p. 130.

17 'Abdu'l-Bahá, *The Promulgation of Universal Peace*, p. 57.

18 Shoghi Effendi, *The World Order of Bahá'u'lláh*, p. 170.

19 Shoghi Effendi, *The World Order of Bahá'u'lláh*, pp. 170-71.

20 Shoghi Effendi, *The World Order of Bahá'u'lláh*, p. 42.

21 Shoghi Effendi, *The World Order of Bahá'u'lláh*, pp. 33-34.

22 On behalf of Shoghi Effendi, *Compilation of Compilations*, vol. 2, p. 421.

23 Shoghi Effendi, *The World Order of Bahá'u'lláh*, p. 163.

24 Bahá'u'lláh, in *The Advent of Divine Justice*, p. 31.

25 Bahá'u'lláh, in *Messages from the Universal House of Justice, 1963-1986: The Third Epoch of the Formative Age*, p. 376.

26 Bahá'u'lláh, *Tablets of Bahá'u'lláh*, p. 71.

27 On behalf of Shoghi Effendi, message dated October 23, 1927.

28 Bahá'u'lláh, *Gleanings*, p. 285.

29 Bahá'u'lláh, *Tablets of Bahá'u'lláh*, p. 138.

30   'Abdu'l-Bahá, *Will and Testament of 'Abdu'l-Bahá*, p. 14.

31   'Abdu'l-Bahá, *Selections from the Writings of 'Abdu'l-Bahá*, p. 3.

32   'Abdu'l-Bahá, *The Promulgation of Universal Peace*, p. 190.

33   ". . . the second sort of knowledge, which is the knowledge of being, is intuitive; it is like the cognizance and consciousness that man has of himself.

"For example, the mind and the spirit of man are cognizant of the conditions and states of the members and component parts of the body, and are aware of all the physical sensations; in the same way, they are aware of their power, of their feelings, and of their spiritual conditions. This is the knowledge of being which man realizes and perceives, for the spirit surrounds the body and is aware of its sensations and powers. This knowledge is not the outcome of effort and study. It is an existing thing; it is an absolute gift.

"Since the Sanctified Realities, the supreme Manifestations of God, surround the essence and qualities of the creatures, transcend and contain existing realities and understand all things, therefore, Their knowledge is divine knowledge, and not acquired—that is to say, it is a holy bounty; it is a divine revelation." ('Abdu'l-Bahá, *Some Answered Questions*, pp. 157-58.)

34   Bahá'u'lláh speaks of knowledge that is "unrevealed" which "if we chose to divulge it to mankind, would cause every human being to recognize the Manifestation of God and to acknowledge His omniscience. . . ." (Bahá'u'lláh, *Summons of the Lord of Hosts*, p. 35.) He has also acknowledged that there are truths that words cannot contain. (*Gleanings*, p. 176.) Furthermore, a specific example of knowledge withheld, according to Shoghi Effendi, is the "knowledge which, when applied, will largely, though not wholly, eliminate fear." (*Compilation of Compilations*, vol. 1, p. 249.) This is not to imply, however, that a Revelation may not, in some sense, encompass all knowledge of reality. Bahá'u'lláh has explains that "It is in Our power, should We wish it . . . to infuse into every letter such a force as to empower it to unfold all the knowledge of past and future ages." (In *The World Order of Bahá'u'lláh*, p. 107.) And, there is the Islamic tradition cited by Adib Taherzadeh "that the Qur'án itself is contained in the opening chapter, that this chapter is embodied in the first verse, that the first verse in its entirety is included in the first letter (B), and that all that is within this letter is condensed in the dot beneath it." (Taherzadeh, *The Revelation of Bahá'u'lláh*, vol. 1, p. 34.) Surely, however, it would require the Manifestation Himself to accurately unravel such intricate and subtle meanings.

35   Bahá'u'lláh acknowledges that one station of the Manifestations is that of distinction, which "pertaineth to the world of creation and to the limitations thereof" and therefore each has "a definitely prescribed mission, a predestined Revelation, and specially designated limitations." "Each one of them is known by a different name, is characterized by a special attribute,

fulfils a definite Mission, and is entrusted with a particular Revelation." (*The Kitáb-i-Íqán*, p. 176.)

36 Bahá'u'lláh, in a message dated November 26, 1986 written by the Universal House of Justice.

37 "Know verily that the veil hiding Our countenance hath not been completely lifted. We have revealed Our Self to a degree corresponding to the capacity of the people of Our age. Should the Ancient Beauty be unveiled in the fullness of His glory mortal eyes would be blinded by the dazzling intensity of His revelation." (Bahá'u'lláh, in *The World Order of Bahá'u'lláh*, p. 116.)

38 "Indeed the measure of Divine Revelation, in every age, has been adapted to, and commensurate with, the degree of social progress achieved in that age by a constantly evolving humanity." (Shoghi Effendi, *The Promised Day is Come*, p. 118.)

39 On behalf of the Universal House of Justice, *Messages: 1963-1986*, pp. 547-48.

40 See John R. Searle, *The Construction of Social Reality*, pp. 59-78.

41 See for example *The Kitáb-i-Aqdas*, p. 123, *The Kitáb-i-Íqán*, p. 115 and *The Dawnbreakers*, p. 320.

42 See 'Abdu'l-Bahá, *Some Answered Questions*, pp. 171-74, on the nature of essential infallibility. If human beings do not join in agreement around the Word, there is no hope that the new social reality can be raised. This acceptance, however, is not enslavement, but liberation. It must be freely made and not coerced. As a consequence, the individual is liberated from the afflictions of the old world order and empowered to become an agent in creating a new civilization. Diversity of thought and freedom of individual action are essential elements of the process of civilization building. In this light, it can be seen that true freedom for the individual is found within the boundaries of the Law of God. (See 'Abdu'l-Bahá, *Selections from the Writings of 'Abdu'l-Bahá*, p. 305.)

43 Bahá'u'lláh, *Gleanings*, p. 42.

44 'Abdu'l-Bahá, *Selections from the Writings of 'Abdu'l-Bahá*, p. 12.

45 'Abdu'l-Bahá, *The Secret of Divine Civilization*, p. 73.

46 'Abdu'l-Bahá, *Selections from the Writings of 'Abdu'l-Bahá*, p. 292.

47 'Abdu'l-Bahá, *The Promulgation of Universal Peace*, p. 144.

48 'Abdu'l-Bahá, *Some Answered Questions*, p. 165.

49 'Abdu'l-Bahá, *The Promulgation of Universal Peace*, pp. 314, 318.

50 Bahá'u'lláh, Tablet to Hájí Mírzá Kamálu'd-Dín, provisional translation by Iskandar Hai.

51 Bahá'u'lláh, *The Kitáb-i-Aqdas*, p. 56.

52 'Abdu'l-Bahá, *The Promulgation of Universal Peace*, p. 63.

53 Particularly with regard to how scientific knowledge changes over time. See, for example, *What is this thing called Science?* by A.F. Chalmers and *The Philosophy of Science*, edited by E.D. Klemke, Robert Hollenger, David Wyss Rudge, with A. David Kline.

54 Bahá'u'lláh, *The Kitáb-i-Aqdas*, p. 85.

55 Bahá'u'lláh, *The Kitáb-i-Íqán*, p. 172.

56 'Abdu'l-Bahá, *Compilation of Compilations*, vol. 1, p. 203.

57 On behalf of Shoghi Effendi, *Compilation of Compilations*, vol. 1, p. 219.

58 The Universal House of Justice, *Turning Point: Selected Messages of the Universal House of Justice and Supplementary Materials, 1996-2006*, p. 30.

59 The Universal House of Justice, *Messages: 1963-1986*, p. 88.

60 Bahá'u'lláh, *Compilation of Compilations*, vol. 1, p. 93.

61 'Abdu'l-Bahá, *The Promulgation of Universal Peace*, p. 72.

62 On behalf of Shoghi Effendi, *Compilation of Compilations*, vol. 1, p. 103.

63 Bahá'u'lláh, *Tablets of Bahá'u'lláh*, p. 143; *The Kitáb-i-Íqán*, p. 193.

64 The Universal House of Justice, *Lights of Guidance*, pp. 179-80.

65 Bahá'u'lláh, *Tablets of Bahá'u'lláh*, p. 88.

66 'Abdu'l-Bahá, *Compilation of Compilations*, vol. 1, p. 98.

67 'Abdu'l-Bahá, *Compilation of Compilations*, vol. 1, p. 95.

68 "He who expresses an opinion should not voice it as correct and right but set it forth as a contribution to the consensus of opinion, for the light of reality becomes apparent when two opinions coincide." ('Abdu'l-Bahá, *The Promulgation of Universal Peace*, p. 72.)

69 'Abdu'l-Bahá, in *Bahá'í Administration*, p. 22.

70 The Universal House of Justice, *Rights and Responsibilities*, p. 17.

71 ". . . true consultation is spiritual conference in the attitude and atmosphere of love. Members must love each other in the spirit of fellowship in order that good results may be forthcoming. Love and fellowship are the foundation." ('Abdu'l-Bahá, *Promulgation of Universal Peace*, pp. 72-73.)

72 On behalf of Shoghi Effendi, *Compilation of Compilations*, vol. 1, p. 106.

73 "If they agree upon a subject, even though it be wrong, it is better than to disagree and be in the right, for this difference will produce the demolition of the divine foundation. Though one of the parties may be in the right and they disagree that will be the cause of a thousand wrongs, but if they agree and both parties are in the wrong, as it is in unity the truth will be revealed and the wrong made right." ('Abdu'l-Bahá, *Compilation of Compilations*, vol. 1, p. 96.)

74 The Universal House of Justice, *Rights and Responsibilities*, pp. 45-46.

75 On behalf of Shoghi Effendi, *Lights of Guidance*, p. 82.

76   The Universal House of Justice, *Messages: 1963-1986*, p. 390.

77   Shoghi Effendi, *Bahá'í Administration*, pp. 62-63.

78   Shoghi Effendi, *The World Order of Bahá'u'lláh*, p. 195.

79   On behalf of Shoghi Effendi, *Compilation of Compilations*, vol. 2, p. 59.

80   Shoghi Effendi, *God Passes By*, p. 324.

CHAPTER 2

1   Shoghi Effendi, *The World Order of Bahá'u'lláh*, p. 23.

2   Shoghi Effendi, *The World Order of Bahá'u'lláh*, p. 18.

3   Shoghi Effendi, *The World Order of Bahá'u'lláh*, pp. 18-19.

4   Shoghi Effendi, *The World Order of Bahá'u'lláh*, p. 19.

5   'Abdu'l-Bahá, *Tablets of the Divine Plan*, p. 49.

6   Shoghi Effendi, *Citadel of Faith*, p. 5.

7   "In the Bahá'í Faith there are two authoritative centers appointed to which the believers must turn, for in reality the Interpreter of the Word is an extension of that centre which is the Word itself. The Book is the record of the utterance of Bahá'u'lláh, while the divinely inspired Interpreter is the living Mouth of that Book—it is he and he alone who can authoritatively state what the Book means. Thus one centre is the Book with its Interpreter, and the other is the Universal House of Justice guided by God to decide on whatever is not explicitly revealed in the Book." (The Universal House of Justice, *Messages: 1963-1986*, p. 160.)

8   "Wittengenstein explained that the meaning of a text cannot be inferred from its author's intention, because nobody, not even the author himself, can know what the intention was. The meaning of a text depends, on the contrary, on the linguistic usages current in the community in which the text is being read. This argument became Derrida's famous slogan that 'the author of the text is dead' and readers can, therefore, interpret the text any which way they like. Such interpretation is simply one more text which is again open to the same treatment, and so on, ad infinitum." (Peter Munz, *Beyond Wittgenstein's Poker*, p. 61.)

9   Bahá'u'lláh, *Gleanings*, p. 338.

10   Bahá'u'lláh, *Summons of the Lord of Hosts*, p. 14.

11   "Every human being is ultimately responsible to God for the use which he or she makes of these possibilities; conscience is never to be coerced, whether by other individuals or institutions.

     "Conscience, however, is not an unchangeable absolute. One dictionary definition, although not covering all the usages of the term, presents the common understanding of the word 'conscience' as 'the sense of right and wrong as regards things for which one is responsible; the faculty or principle which pronounces upon the moral quality of one's actions or motives, approving the right and condemning the wrong.'

"The functioning of one's conscience, then, depends upon one's understanding of right and wrong; the conscience of one person may be established upon a disinterested striving after truth and justice, while that of another may rest on an unthinking predisposition to act in accordance with that pattern of standards, principles and prohibitions which is a product of his social environment. Conscience, therefore, can serve either as a bulwark of an upright character or can represent an accumulation of prejudices learned from one's forebears or absorbed from a limited social code.

"A Bahá'í recognizes that one aspect of his spiritual and intellectual growth is to foster the development of his conscience in the light of Divine Revelation—a Revelation which, in addition to providing a wealth of spiritual and ethical principles, exhorts man 'to free himself from idle fancy and imitation, discern with the eye of oneness His glorious handiwork, and look into all things with a searching eye.' This process of development, therefore, involves a clear-sighted examination of the conditions of the world with both heart and mind. A Bahá'í will understand that an upright life is based upon observance of certain principles which stem from Divine Revelation and which he recognizes as essential for the well-being of both the individual and society. In order to uphold such principles, he knows that, in certain cases, the voluntary submission of the promptings of his own personal conscience to the decision of the majority is a conscientious requirement, as in wholeheartedly accepting the majority decision of an Assembly at the outcome of consultation." (On behalf of the Universal House of Justice, *Issues Related to the Study of the Bahá'í Faith*, p. 40.)

12 Bahá'u'lláh, *Tablets of Bahá'u'lláh*, p. 71.

13 Bahá'u'lláh, *The Kitáb-i-Íqán*, p. 86.

14 To more fully understand the concept of interpretation, it is useful to examine more closely the ways in which Shoghi Effendi exercised this capacity. In an insightful presentation at the Bahá'í World Centre in 1984, Ian Semple described seven aspects of the function of Interpreter as exercised by Shoghi Effendi. While these categories were acknowledged to be "a purely arbitrary division," they nevertheless illustrate a range of applications. These seven aspects include defining the meaning of specific texts; explaining the thought conveyed by the texts (expounding their meaning); developing seminal statements in the Sacred Text; refusal to comment further on certain texts or to make statements not covered in the Writings; defining the sphere of authoritative interpretation; illuminating the overall significance of the Revelation; and taking a long and uninterrupted view over a series of generations.

15 On behalf of the Universal House of Justice, *Messages: 1963-1986*, p. 518.

16 On behalf of the Universal House of Justice, *Messages: 1963-1986*, p. 646.

17   ". . . the Interpreter of the Word is an extension of that center which is the Word itself." (The Universal House of Justice, *Messages: 1963-1986*, p. 160.)

18   This point is explained further in the section on hermeneutical principles. The House of Justice states: "Just as the Will and Testament of 'Abdu'l-Bahá does not in any way contradict the Kitáb-i-Aqdas but, in the Guardian's words, 'confirms, supplements, and correlates the provisions of the Aqdas,' so the writings of the Guardian contradict neither the revealed Word nor the interpretations of the Master." (The Universal House of Justice, *Messages: 1963-1986*, p. 156.)

19   The Universal House of Justice, *Messages: 1963-1986*, p. 56.

20   See note #126 in *The Kitáb-i-Aqdas*. The meaning of certain statements in the Revelation and in the authoritative interpretations are intentionally veiled and progressively clarified in order to guide the believers in a gradual manner. "Know of a certainty that in every Dispensation the light of Divine Revelation hath been vouchsafed unto men in direct proportion to their spiritual capacity. Consider the sun. How feeble its rays the moment it appeareth above the horizon. How gradually its warmth and potency increase as it approacheth its zenith, enabling meanwhile all created things to adapt themselves to the growing intensity of its light. How steadily it declineth until it reacheth its setting point. Were it, all of a sudden, to manifest the energies latent within it, it would, no doubt, cause injury to all created things. . . . In like manner, if the Sun of Truth were suddenly to reveal, at the earliest stages of its manifestation, the full measure of the potencies which the providence of the Almighty hath bestowed upon it, the earth of human understanding would waste away and be consumed; for men's hearts would neither sustain the intensity of its revelation, nor be able to mirror forth the radiance of its light. Dismayed and overpowered, they would cease to exist." (Bahá'u'lláh, *Gleanings*, pp. 87-88.)

21   "In fact, he who reads the Aqdas with care and diligence will not find it hard to discover that the Most Holy Book itself anticipates in a number of passages the institutions which 'Abdu'l-Bahá ordains in His Will. By leaving certain matters unspecified and unregulated in His Book of Laws, Bahá'u'lláh seems to have deliberately left a gap in the general scheme of Bahá'í Dispensation, which the unequivocal provisions of the Master's Will have filled." (Shoghi Effendi, *The World Order of Bahá'u'lláh*, p. 4.)

22   Shoghi Effendi, *The World Order of Bahá'u'lláh*, p. 110.

23   'Abdu'l-Bahá, in *The World Order of Bahá'u'lláh*, p. 138.

24   Shoghi Effendi, *The World Order of Bahá'u'lláh*, p. 151.

25   The Universal House of Justice, *Messages: 1963-1986*, p. 160.

26   On behalf of Shoghi Effendi, *Lights of Guidance*, p. 237.

27   On behalf of the Universal House of Justice, message dated March 9, 1987. However, the letter adds, "the manner in which an individual presents his

interpretation is important. For example, he must at no time deny or contend with the authoritative interpretation, but rather offer his idea as a contribution to knowledge, making it clear that his views are merely his own."

28 On behalf of the Universal House of Justice, *Messages: 1963-1986*, p. 518. In the letter, this paragraph is preceded by a more detailed explanation: "You express the fear that the authority conferred upon 'Abdu'l-Bahá, the Guardian and the Universal House of Justice could lead to a progressive reduction in the 'available scope for personal interpretation,' and that 'the actual writings of the Manifestation will have less and less import,' and you instance what has happened in previous Dispensations. The House of Justice suggests that, in thinking about this, you contemplate the way the Covenant of Bahá'u'lláh has actually worked and you will be able to see how very different its processes are from those of, say, the development of the law in Rabbinical Judaism or the functioning of the Papacy in Christianity. The practice in the past in these two religions, and also to a great extent in Islám, has been to assume that the revelation given by the Founder was the final, perfect revelation of God's Will to mankind, and all subsequent elucidation and legislation has been interpretative in the sense that it aimed at applying this basic revelation to the new problems and situations that have arisen. The Bahá'í premises are quite different. Although the revelation of Bahá'u'lláh is accepted as the Word of God and His Law as the Law of God, it is understood from the outset that revelation is progressive, and that the Law, although the Will of God for this Age, will undoubtedly be changed by the next Manifestation of God. Secondly, only the written text of the revelation is regarded as authoritative. There is no Oral Law as in Judaism, no Tradition of the Church as in Christianity, no Hadíth as in Islám. Thirdly, a clear distinction is drawn between Interpretation and Legislation. Authoritative interpretation is the exclusive prerogative of 'Abdu'l-Bahá and the Guardian, while infallible legislation is the function of the Universal House of Justice."

29 On behalf of the Universal House of Justice, message dated March 9, 1987.

30 Shoghi Effendi, *The World Order of Bahá'u'lláh*, p. 100. So too, Bahá'u'lláh states: "No understanding can grasp the nature of His Revelation, nor can any knowledge comprehend the full measure of His Faith." (*The Kitáb-i-Íqán*, p. 243.)

31 *The Kitáb-i-Aqdas*, note 130, p. 221.

32 On behalf of the Universal House of Justice, *Issues Related to the Study of the Bahá'í Faith*, p. 42.

33 Bahá'u'lláh, *The Kitáb-i-Íqán*, p. 192.

34 Bahá'u'lláh, *The Kitáb-i-Íqán*, p. 211.

35 The Universal House of Justice, *Messages: 1963-1986*, p. 39.

36 Shoghi Effendi, *The Advent of Divine Justice*, p. 52.

37   The Universal House of Justice, *Messages: 1963-1986*, p. 88.

38   On behalf of the Universal House of Justice, message dated March 9, 1987.

39   On behalf of the Universal House of Justice, *Messages: 1963-1986*, p. 518.

40   The Universal House of Justice, *Messages: 1963-1986*, p. 88.

41   The Universal House of Justice, *Messages: 1963-1986*, p. 88.

42   On behalf of the Universal House of Justice, *Issues Related to the Study of the Bahá'í Faith*, p. 42.

43   "With regard to the accusation that to make such distinctions borders on restriction of the freedom of speech, one should accept that civil society has long recognized that utterance can metamorphose into behavior, and has taken steps to protect itself and its citizens against such behavior when it becomes socially destructive. Laws against sedition and hate-mongering are examples that come readily to mind." (On behalf of the Universal House of Justice, *Issues Related to the Study of the Bahá'í Faith*, pp. 42-43.)

44   On behalf of the Universal House of Justice, *Issues Related to the Study of the Bahá'í Faith*, p. 38. 'Abdu'l-Bahá repeated warned the Bahá'ís in His talks and writings about individuals who insist upon the correctness of their own views and described the role of the Covenant in protecting against such problems. For example, He states: "As to the most great characteristic of the revelation of Bahá'u'lláh, a specific teaching not given by any of the Prophets of the past: It is the ordination and appointment of the Center of the Covenant. By this appointment and provision He has safeguarded and protected the religion of God against differences and schisms, making it impossible for anyone to create a new sect or faction of belief. To ensure unity and agreement He has entered into a Covenant with all the people of the world, including the interpreter and explainer of His teachings, so that no one may interpret or explain the religion of God according to his own view or opinion and thus create a sect founded upon his individual understanding of the divine Words. The Book of the Covenant or Testament of Bahá'u'lláh is the means of preventing such a possibility, for whosoever shall speak from the authority of himself alone shall be degraded. Be ye informed and cognizant of this. Beware lest anyone shall secretly question or deny this to you. There are some people of self-will and desire who do not communicate their intentions to you in clear language. They envelop their meanings in secret statements and insinuations. For instance, they praise a certain individual, saying he is wise and learned ... conveying this to you in an insidious way or by innuendos. Be ye aware of this! Be awakened and enlightened! ... The purport of my admonition is that certain people will endeavor to influence you in the direction of their own personal views and opinions. Therefore, be upon your guard in order that none may assail the oneness and integrity of Bahá'u'lláh's Cause. Praise be to God! Bahá'u'lláh left nothing unsaid. He explained everything. He left no

room for anything further to be said. Yet there are some who for the sake of personal interest and prestige will attempt to sow the seeds of sedition and disloyalty among you. To protect and safeguard the religion of God from this and all other attack, the Center of the Covenant has been named and appointed by Bahá'u'lláh. Therefore, if anyone should set forth a statement in praise or recognition of another than this appointed Center, you must ask him to produce a written proof of the authority he follows. . . . My purpose is to explain to you that it is your duty to guard the religion of God so that none shall be able to assail it outwardly or inwardly." (*The Promulgation of Universal Peace*, pp. 455-56.)

So too, a message written on behalf of the Universal House of Justice explains: "The Covenant is the 'axis of the oneness of the world of humanity' because it preserves the unity and integrity of the Faith itself and protects it from being disrupted by individuals who are convinced that only their understanding of the Teachings is the right one—a fate that has overcome all past Revelations. The Covenant is, moreover, embedded in the Writings of Bahá'u'lláh Himself. Thus, as you clearly see, to accept Bahá'u'lláh is to accept His Covenant; to reject His Covenant is to reject Him." (*Messages: 1963-1986*, p. 519.)

45 Some of these principles have been discussed in various articles, including "A Preliminary Survey of Hermeneutical Principles Found Within the Bahá'í Writings," by Dann J. May, *Journal of Bahá'í Studies*, 1989, vol. 1, no. 3 and "Some Interpretive Principles in the Bahá'í Writings," by Seena Fazel and Khazeh Fananapazir, *The Bahá'í Studies Review*, 1992, vol. 2 no. 1.

46 Bahá'u'lláh, *Tablets of Bahá'u'lláh*, p. 143.

47 On behalf of Shoghi Effendi, *Compilation of Compilations*, vol. 1, p. 212.

48 Bahá'u'lláh, *Gleanings*, p. 272. Further consideration of this principle can be found in "Seeing with the Eye of God: Relationships Between Theology and Interpretation" by Michael Sours, *Bahá'í Studies Review*, vol. 1, issue 1, 1991.

49 Bahá'u'lláh, *The Kitáb-i-Aqdas*, p. 56.

50 On behalf of Shoghi Effendi, *Lights of Guidance*, p. 476.

51 On behalf of Shoghi Effendi, message dated March 19, 1946.

52 The Universal House of Justice, *Messages: 1963-1986*, p. 156.

53 On behalf of the Universal House of Justice, message dated April 27, 1995.

54 Bahá'u'lláh, *The Kitáb-i-Íqán*, pp. 254-55.

55 "Whoso layeth claim to a Revelation direct from God, ere the expiration of a full thousand years, such a man is assuredly a lying imposter. . . . Whosoever interpreteth this verse otherwise than its obvious meaning is deprived of the Spirit of God and of His mercy which encompasseth all created things." (Bahá'u'lláh, *The Kitáb-i-Aqdas*, p. 32.) "The Dispensation of Bahá'u'lláh will last until the coming of the next Manifestation of God,

Whose advent will not take place before at least 'a full thousand years' will have elapsed. Bahá'u'lláh cautions against ascribing to 'this verse' anything other than its 'obvious meaning,' and in one of His Tablets, He specifies that 'each year' of this thousand year period consists of 'twelve months according to the Qur'án, and of nineteen months of nineteen days each, according to the Bayán.'" (Note #62, *The Kitáb-i-Aqdas*, pp. 195-96.)

56 Bahá'u'lláh, *Tafsír-i-Súriy-i-Va__sh__-__Shams__* (Commentary on the Súrah of the Sun), provisional translation by Mark Hellaby.

57 Bahá'u'lláh, *Gleanings*, p. 175.

58 'Abdu'l-Bahá, *Some Answered Questions*, p. 126.

59 Bahá'u'lláh, *Gleanings*, pp. 175-76.

60 Bahá'u'lláh, *Gleanings*, p. 88. For a further elucidation of this principle, see the introduction to the *Synopsis and Codification of The Kitáb-i-Aqdas*, pp. 3-7.

61 Bahá'u'lláh, *Gleanings*, pp. 176.

62 Bahá'u'lláh states: "God hath prescribed matrimony unto you. Beware that ye take not unto yourselves more wives than two. Who contenteth himself with a single partner from among the maidservants of God, both he and she shall live in tranquillity." (*The Kitáb-i-Aqdas*, p. 41.) Note #89, p. 206 explains: "Bahá'u'lláh, Who was revealing His teachings in the milieu of a Muslim society, introduced the question of monogamy gradually in accordance with the principles of wisdom and the progressive unfoldment of His purpose. The fact that He left His followers with an infallible Interpreter of His Writings enabled Him to outwardly permit two wives in the Kitáb-i-Aqdas but uphold a condition that enabled 'Abdu'l-Bahá to elucidate later that the intention of the law was to enforce monogamy."

63 See the memorandum of the Research Department to the Universal House of Justice dated June 27, 1996 entitled "Monogamy, Sexual Equality, Marital Equality, and the Supreme Tribunal." Any personal interpretation that suggests the authorized Interpreter has failed to grasp the intention of Bahá'u'lláh's Writings, or abrogated Bahá'u'lláh's law, or changed his mind about the meaning of the Text, is not consistent with the principle that authorized interpretation is a statement of truth that cannot be varied.

64 "Know thou that polygamy is not permitted under the law of God, for contentment with one wife hath been clearly stipulated. Taking a second wife is made dependent upon equity and justice being upheld between the two wives, under all conditions. However, observance of justice and equity towards two wives is utterly impossible. The fact that bigamy has been made dependent upon an impossible condition is clear proof of its absolute prohibition. Therefore it is not permissible for a man to have more than one wife." ('Abdu'l-Bahá, Note #89 in *The Kitáb-i-Aqdas*, p. 206.)

65 Shoghi Effendi, *God Passes By*, p. 214.

66 Shoghi Effendi, *The World Order of Bahá'u'lláh*, p. 22.

67 On behalf of the Universal House of Justice, message dated April 27, 1995.

68 The Universal House of Justice, *Messages: 1963-1986*, p. 87.

69 "I say unto you: weigh carefully in the balance of reason and science everything that is presented to you as religion. If it passes this test, then accept it, for it is truth! If, however, it does not so conform, then reject it, for it is ignorance!" ('Abdu'l-Bahá, *Paris Talks*, p. 144.)

70 'Abdu'l-Bahá, *Some Answered Questions*, p. 111.

71 'Abdu'l-Bahá, *The Promulgation of Universal Peace*, p. 181.

72 On behalf of the Universal House of Justice, *Compilation of Compilations*, vol. 3, p. 261.

73 'Abdu'l-Bahá. *Some Answered Questions*, pp. 22-23. See also a letter written on behalf of Shoghi Effendi, *Lights of Guidance*, p. 478. Such statements are religious statements and any implications they hold for truth about the physical world would, of course, never be accepted by science unless justified by its own criteria.

74 On behalf of Shoghi Effendi, *Lights of Guidance*, p. 478.

75 An example is 'Abdu'l-Bahá's statements about ether. "Thus man cannot grasp the Essence of Divinity, but can, by his reasoning power, by observation, by his intuitive faculties and the revealing power of his faith, believe in God, discover the bounties of His Grace. He becometh certain that though the Divine Essence is unseen of the eye, and the existence of the Deity is intangible, yet conclusive spiritual proofs assert the existence of that unseen Reality. The Divine Essence as it is in itself is however beyond all description. For instance, the nature of ether is unknown, but that it existeth is certain by the effects it produceth, heat, light and electricity being the waves thereof. By these waves the existence of ether is thus proven. And as we consider the outpourings of Divine Grace we are assured of the existence of God." (*Tablet to August Forel*, p. 5.) The purpose of this passage is to discuss human understanding of God, not the physical universe. As explained in a message written on behalf of the Universal House of Justice: "With reference to your question about the 'ether,' the various definitions of this word as given in the Oxford English Dictionary all refer to a physical reality, for instance, 'an element,' 'a substance,' 'a medium,' all of which imply a physical and objective reality and, as you say, this was the concept posited by nineteenth century scientists to explain the propagation of light waves. It would have been understood in this sense by the audiences whom 'Abdu'l-Bahá was addressing. However, in Chapter XVI of *Some Answered Questions*, 'Abdu'l-Bahá devotes a whole chapter to explaining the difference between things which are 'perceptible to the senses' which He calls 'objective or sensible,' and realities of the 'intellect' which have 'no outward form and no place,' and are 'not perceptible to the senses.' . . . He states

clearly that 'Even ethereal matter, the forces of which are said in physics to be heat, light, electricity and magnetism, is an intellectual reality, and is not sensible.' In other words, the 'ether' is a concept arrived at intellectually to explain certain phenomena. In due course, when scientists failed to confirm the physical existence of the 'ether' by delicate experiments, they constructed other intellectual concepts to explain the same phenomena." (*Messages: 1963-1986*, p. 546.)

Another example is 'Abdu'l-Bahá's statement, that "just as the bodily diseases like consumption and cancer are contagious, likewise the spiritual diseases are also infectious." (*Lights of Guidance*, p. 183.) His purpose is to illustrate the importance of not associating with Covenant-breakers: "If a consumptive should associate with a thousand safe and healthy persons, the safety and health of these thousand persons would not affect the consumptive and would not cure him of his consumptions. But when this consumptive associates with those thousand souls, in a short time the disease of consumption will infect a number of those healthy persons." In making His point, He refers to cancer as contagious, which was a widely held conception at the time. Only later did the scientific community conclude that cancer was not contagious. (Even a 1930 editorial in the *Canadian Journal of Medicine and Surgery* expressed skepticism about the non-contagious character of cancer; see "Cancer," p. 129-31.) Today, some new lines of inquiry are exploring whether certain kinds of cancer could be or could become contagious. (http://www.harpers.org/archive/2008/04/0081988)

76 "The Tablet to a Physician was addressed to a man who was a student of the old type of healing prevalent in the East and familiar with the terminology used in those days, and He addresses him in terms used by the medical men of those days. These terms are quite different from those used by modern medicine, and one would have to have a deep knowledge of this former school of medicine to understand the questions Bahá'u'lláh was elucidating." (On behalf of Shoghi Effendi, *Lights of Guidance*, p. 281.) Clearly, even if the Manifestation wanted to make a scientifically valid statement about the nature of the physical world, the limitations of language and the constant evolution of scientific thought would make understanding difficult. Would He use the scientific language of His time, concepts pertaining to the understanding of science a century into the future, or concepts pertaining to the science of 500 years into the future? At any point in time, a "true" statement about physical reality in the Revelation may appear to be in conflict with contemporary scientific understanding.

77 On behalf of Shoghi Effendi, *Lights of Guidance*, p. 558.

78 On behalf of the Universal House of Justice, *Issues Related to the Study of the Bahá'í Faith*, p. 33.

79 Shoghi Effendi, *The Promised Day is Come*, p. vi.

80 On behalf of the Universal House of Justice, *Compilation of Compilations,* vol. 3, p. 259. The philosopher Jürgen Habermas, for example, warns of the tendency toward positivism in the humanities and social sciences. "[T]he historical-hermeneutic sciences ... comprise a scientistic consciousness, based on the model of science. ... Much as the cultural sciences may comprehend their facts through understanding and little though they may be concerned with discovering general laws, they nevertheless share with the empirical-analytic sciences the methodological consciousness of describing a structured reality within the horizon of the theoretical attitude. Historicism has become the positivism of the cultural and social sciences." (*Knowledge and Human Interests,* p. 303.) Positivism is a philosophical perspective that rejects metaphysics and emphasizes observation and experience; in the extreme, it is an excessive belief that only certain methods for the investigation of reality yield true or meaningful results.

81 For example, a letter written on his behalf states: "Historians cannot be sure Socrates did not visit the Holy Land. But believing as we do that 'Abdu'l-Bahá had an intuitive knowledge quite different from our own, we accept His authority on this matter. ..." (On behalf of Shoghi Effendi, *Arohanui: Letters to New Zealand,* p. 87.) In another instance, the House of Justice explained: "The Guardian was meticulous about the authenticity of historical fact. One of the friends in Yazd wrote to him stating that the account given by 'Abdu'l-Bahá in one of His Tablets about events related to the martyrdom of some of the believers in that place was in conflict with known facts about these events. Shoghi Effendi replied saying that the friends should investigate the facts carefully and unhesitatingly register them in their historical records, since 'Abdu'l-Bahá Himself had prefaced His recording of the events in His Tablet with a statement that it was based on news received from Yazd." (The Universal House of Justice, message dated July 25, 1974 to an individual.)

82 See *Tablets of 'Abdu'l-Bahá,* p. 539, and *Lights of Guidance,* p. 509.

83 Shoghi Effendi, *The World Order of Bahá'u'lláh,* p. 134.

84 On behalf of Shoghi Effendi, *Arohanui: Letters to New Zealand,* p. 87.

85 On behalf of the Universal House of Justice, message dated January 12, 2006.

86 On behalf of the Universal House of Justice, message dated April 18, 1989.

87 Dann May, "A Preliminary Survey of Hermeneutical Principles Found Within the Bahá'í Writings," *Journal of Bahá'í Studies,* 1989, vol. 1, no. 3, p. 43.

88 Talk given by Peter Khan in Wilmette, Illinois, June 26, 1981.

89 Bahá'u'lláh, *Gleanings,* p. 326.

90 On behalf of the Universal House of Justice, message dated November 26, 1986.

91   On behalf of the Universal House of Justice, *Compilation of Compilations,* vol. 3, p. 259.

92   "God in His Essence and in His own Self hath ever been unseen, inaccessible, and unknowable." (Bahá'u'lláh, *Epistle to the Son of the Wolf*, p. 118.) "The nature of the soul after death can never be described, nor is it meet and permissible to reveal its whole character to the eyes of men." (Bahá'u'lláh, *Gleanings*, p. 156.)

93   On behalf of Shoghi Effendi, *Lights of Guidance*, p. 550.

94   Bahá'u'lláh, *Tablets of Bahá'u'lláh*, p. 27.

95   "There are many ways in which the institutions and activities of the Bahá'í community can develop, but it must be remembered that the Bahá'í Cause is an organic body, and it is for the World Centre of that Cause to determine the methods and steps by which its potentialities and functions will unfold." (On behalf of the Universal House of Justice, message dated April 20, 1997.)

96   Shoghi Effendi, *The World Order of Bahá'u'lláh*, p. 148. These responsibilities are shared with the Guardian.

97   "On the success of this enterprise, unprecedented in its scope, unique in its character and immense in its spiritual potentialities, must depend the initiation, at a later period in the Formative Age of the Faith, of undertakings embracing within their range all National Assemblies functioning throughout the Bahá'í World, undertakings constituting in themselves a prelude to the launching of world-wide enterprises destined to be embarked upon, in future epochs of that same Age, by the Universal House of Justice, that will symbolize the unity and coordinate and unify the activities of these National Assemblies." (Shoghi Effendi, *Compilation of Compilations*, vol. 1, p. 340.)

98   "You have stated that believers have asked, 'Are the decisions of the Universal House of Justice free from error even if incorrect information has been provided to it?' The infallibility of the House of Justice, like that of the Guardian, is 'conferred,' as distinct from the infallibility of the Manifestation of God, which is 'innate.' The House of Justice, like the Guardian, is not omniscient; when called upon to make a decision, it wants to receive information and facts and at times consults experts on the subject. Like him, it may well change its decision when new facts emerge or in light of changed conditions.

"In the Writings of Bahá'u'lláh and 'Abdu'l-Bahá on this matter, there is no reference to the nature and extent of the information to which the House of Justice should have access when making its decisions. 'Abdu'l-Bahá states, 'Let it not be imagined that the House of Justice will take any decision according to its own concepts and opinions. God forbid! The Supreme House of Justice will take decisions and establish laws through the inspiration and confirmation of the Holy Spirit.'

"Again, He says: 'Whatever will be its decision, by majority vote, shall be the real truth, inasmuch as that House is under the protection, unerring guidance, and care of the one true Lord. He shall guard it from error and will protect it under the wing of His sanctity and infallibility.'

"Bahá'ís, of course, may seek the views of the House of Justice about its decisions if they feel they have new information or that conditions have changed but in doing so should avoid the temptation to use this as an excuse to evade their obligation to obey and thus deprive themselves of the bounty of full obedience." (On behalf of the Universal House of Justice, message dated May 20, 2007.)

99 Bahá'u'lláh, *Tablets of Bahá'u'lláh*, p. 27.

100 'Abdu'l-Bahá, *Will and Testament of 'Abdu'l-Bahá*, p. 11.

101 'Abdu'l-Bahá, *Will and Testament of 'Abdu'l-Bahá*, p. 20.

102 'Abdu'l-Bahá, in *Messages: 1963-1986*, pp. 52-53.

103 'Abdu'l-Bahá, *Will and Testament of 'Abdu'l-Bahá*, p. 14.

104 'Abdu'l-Bahá, *Will and Testament of 'Abdu'l-Bahá*, p. 20.

105 The Universal House of Justice, *Messages: 1963-1986*, p. 56.

106 Shoghi Effendi, *Bahá'í Administration*, p. 39.

107 On behalf of the Universal House of Justice, *Lights of Guidance*, p. 311.

108 Shoghi Effendi, *The World Order of Bahá'u'lláh*, p. 20.

109 Shoghi Effendi, *The World Order of Bahá'u'lláh*, p. 150.

110 'Abdu'l-Bahá, in *The World Order of Bahá'u'lláh*, p. 149.

111 Shoghi Effendi, *Bahá'í Administration*, p. 47.

112 "There is a profound difference between the interpretations of the Guardian and the elucidations of the House of Justice in exercise of its function to 'deliberate upon all problems which have caused difference, questions that are obscure and matters that are not expressly recorded in the Book.' The Guardian reveals what the Scripture means; his interpretation is a statement of truth which cannot be varied. Upon the Universal House of Justice, in the words of the Guardian, 'has been conferred the exclusive right of legislating on matters not expressly revealed in the Bahá'í writings.' Its pronouncements, which are susceptible of amendment or abrogation by the House of Justice itself, serve to supplement and apply the Law of God. Although not invested with the function of interpretation, the House of Justice is in a position to do everything necessary to establish the World Order of Bahá'u'lláh on this earth. Unity of doctrine is maintained by the existence of the authentic texts of Scripture and the voluminous interpretations of 'Abdu'l-Bahá and Shoghi Effendi together with the absolute prohibition against anyone propounding 'authoritative' or 'inspired' interpretations or usurping the function of Guardian. Unity of administration is assured by the authority of the Universal House of Justice.

"'Such,' in the words of Shoghi Effendi, 'is the immutability of His revealed Word. Such is the elasticity which characterizes the functions of His appointed ministers. The first preserves the identity of His Faith, and guards the integrity of His law. The second enables it, even as a living organism, to expand and adapt itself to the needs and requirements of an ever-changing society.'" (The Universal House of Justice, in *Messages: 1963-1986*, p. 56.)

113 "Let it not be imagined that the House of Justice will take any decision according to its own concepts and opinions. God forbid! The Supreme House of Justice will take decisions and establish laws through the inspiration and confirmation of the Holy Spirit, because it is in the safekeeping and under the shelter and protection of the Ancient Beauty, and obedience to its decisions is a bounden and essential duty and an absolute obligation, and there is no escape for anyone." ('Abdu'l-Bahá, in *Messages: 1963-1986*, p. 85.)

114 "The elucidations of the Universal House of Justice stem from its legislative function, while the interpretations of the Guardian represent the true intent inherent in the Sacred Texts. The major distinction between the two functions is that legislation with its resultant outcome of elucidation susceptible of amendment by the House of Justice itself, whereas the Guardian's interpretation is a statement of truth which cannot be varied." (On behalf of the Universal House of Justice, *Messages: 1963-1986*, p. 646.) Elucidation and interpretation hold different connotations; to elucidate is to shed light on the meaning of something complex, while to interpret is to reveal underlying meaning that is derived from special insight.

115 For a more detailed discussion of why dissent is so destructive see Wendy Heller, "The Religious Foundations of Civil Society," part 1, *Journal of Bahá'í Studies*, 10.1/2, 2000.

116 'Abdu'l-Bahá, in *The Kitáb-i-Aqdas*, p. 5.

117 "It is natural that the friends would discuss such matters among themselves, as you and your correspondent have been doing on your Internet discussion group; how otherwise are they to deepen their understanding of the Teachings? But they should recognize that the resolution of differences of opinion on such fundamental questions is not to be found by continued discussion, but in referring to the Universal House of Justice itself, as you have done. Prolonged, unresolved, public discussion of these fundamental questions can do nothing but breed confusion and dissension." (On behalf of the Universal House of Justice, *Issues Related to the Study of the Bahá'í Faith*, p. 30.)

Similarly, a letter written on behalf of Shoghi Effendi cautions the believers about the dangers of making judgments about his sphere of authority: "It is not for individual believers to limit the sphere of the Guardian's authority, or to judge when they have to obey the Guardian and when they are free to reject his judgment. Such an attitude would evidently lead to confusion and to schism. The Guardian being the appointed interpreter of the Teachings, it is his responsibility to state what matters which, affecting the interests of the Faith, demand on the part of the believers, complete and unqualified obedience to his instructions." (*Lights of Guidance*, p. 311.)

In relation to this statement written on behalf of Shoghi Effendi, that the believers should not limit the sphere of the Guardian's authority, a letter written on behalf of the House of Justice states: "In regard to the Universal House of Justice, the same understanding applies." (On behalf of the Universal House of Justice, message dated April 7, 2008.) The same letter further states: "The Universal House of Justice does not intend at this time to elaborate further on previous explanations given of its duties and powers. That the House of Justice itself does not find it necessary to do so should alert the friends as to the unwisdom of their attempting to define so precisely its sphere of action. Nevertheless, it should be mentioned that, while there are explicit passages in the authoritative texts that make reference to the infallibility of the House of Justice in the enactment of legislation, the argument that it is free from error only in this respect is untenable." (On behalf of the Universal House of Justice, message dated April 7, 2008.)

118 Without in any way trying to explicitly define the concept of conferred infallibility, consider that the most extreme possible personal interpretations of this concept produce the same practical result: that the believers should abide by the decisions of the Universal House of Justice without giving rise to dissension that will check the progress or destroy the unity of the Faith. For those who hold to an explicit, or even literal, understanding of the passage "whatsoever they decide is of God," such obedience is straightforward. But even the most metaphorical or symbolic interpretation of the concept leads to the same end. Why do the Bahá'í Writings even raise the concept of infallibility in relation to the House of Justice and discuss its decisions in a manner quite distinct from those of Local and National Assemblies? Shoghi Effendi highlights this emphasis: "Only those who come after us will be in a position to realize the value of the surprisingly strong emphasis that has been placed on the institution of the House of Justice and of the Guardianship." (*The World Order of Bahá'u'lláh*, p. 8.) Even if the statements in the Bahá'í Writings about the infallibility of the Universal House of Justice are personally interpreted by an individual to be nothing more than hyperbole, surely the intention must be to emphasize the importance of obedience and the need to avoid criticism and contention and uphold the authority of the Supreme Body as the central point to which all turn. As 'Abdu'l-Bahá states: "The purpose of the Blessed Beauty in entering in to this Covenant and Testament was to gather all existent beings around one point so that the thoughtless souls, who in every cycle and generation have been the cause of dissension, may not undermine the Cause. He hath, therefore, commanded that whatever emanateth from the Centre of the Covenant is right and is under His protection and favor, while all else is error." ('Abdu'l-Bahá, *Selections from the Writings of 'Abdu'l-Bahá*, p. 208.)

Of course, there are other statements addressing the authority of the House of Justice apart from infallibility.

119 A separate but related issue is whether the Universal House of Justice is infallible without having a living Guardian as member. This matter was clarified many years ago by the Universal House of Justice. (See *Messages: 1963-1986*, pp. 50-58, 83-90, and 156-61.) Nevertheless, the erroneous perspective that the House of Justice requires the presence of the Guardian continues to resurface, especially in arguments initiated by Covenant-breakers.

This error is fueled by a misreading of the statement of Shoghi Effendi that the Guardian "cannot override the decision of the majority of his fellow-members, but is bound to insist upon a reconsideration by them of any enactment he conscientiously believes to conflict with the meaning and to depart from the spirit of Bahá'u'lláh's revealed utterances." (*The World Order of Bahá'u'lláh*, p. 150.) It is argued that this clause means that without the Guardian, the House of Justice might make a decision that conflicts with the meaning or departs from the spirit of the Text. Yet, a careful reading of the entire passage makes it obvious that far from implying that the Universal House of Justice may make an error without the Guardian present to direct its deliberations, in fact, the opposite is true. The passage explains that even if the Guardian were to raise a point for reconsideration, nevertheless, the final word is left to the body of the Universal House of Justice. "He [the Guardian] cannot override the decision of the majority of his fellow-members." "He can never, even temporarily, assume the right of exclusive legislation." As 'Abdu'l-Bahá explains: "That which this body, whether unanimously *or by a majority* doth carry, that is verily the Truth and the Purpose of God Himself." (*Will and Testament of 'Abdu'l-Bahá,* p. 19, emphasis added.)

The passage from Shoghi Effendi, embedded in the wider context of a description of the nature of the Guardianship, is presented as a limitation on the powers of the Guardian, not as a check on the powers of the Universal House of Justice, whose authority and infallibility are strongly affirmed. It suggests that even if the Guardian as a member were to raise certain concerns, it is the decision of the majority that is the final and infallible conclusion of that Body. Of course, it is impossible to imagine that the members of the House of Justice would fail to take into account the Guardian's views. Furthermore, the situation envisioned did not arise nor will it ever arise in practice. Nevertheless, the statement is an indication by Shoghi Effendi that the authority and infallibility of the Universal House of Justice in its sphere of action is incontestable even by the Guardian. How then can any believer, no matter how knowledgeable or insightful, raise any challenge?

120 Bahá'u'lláh, *Tablets of Bahá'u'lláh*, p. 68.

121 'Abdu'l-Bahá, *Some Answered Questions*, pp. 172-73. Note that in this statement conferred infallibility is not simply granted to any individual believer who aspires to be a "holy being" but to those "kept and preserved from error" who are "mediators of grace between God and men" for "if God did not protect them from error, their error would cause believing souls to fall into error." Individual Bahá'ís are clearly subject to error, and even if their views or actions are correct in one instance, they can easily be wrong in another, and, therefore, cannot be a standard for other believing souls.

122 'Abdu'l-Bahá, *Will and Testament of 'Abdu'l-Bahá*, pp. 19-20.

123 'Abdu'l-Bahá, in *Messages: 1963-1986*, p. 85.

124 'Abdu'l-Bahá, *Some Answered Questions*, pp. 173-74.

125 This is not to say that 'Abdu'l-Bahá or possibly to some extent, Shoghi Effendi did not have certain insights into reality that were inspired by divine guidance. That is a separate question that is not explored here. It is just that such capacities are something other than what is meant by conferred infallibility.

126 On behalf of the Universal House of Justice, *Lights of Guidance*, p. 311. Consideration of the Bahá'í concept of conferred infallibility must account for why an inerrant grasp of facts is not a necessary condition, rather than attempt to understand infallibility as being limited to a range of action that does not require knowledge about the world.

Perhaps some deeper insight into the Bahá'í concept of infallibility may come from a better understanding of the nature of speech acts. For example, the philosopher John Searle, in describing the way that words are associated with the world around us, contrasts a "word-to-world" and a "world-to-word" fit. (John R. Searle "A Classification of Illocutionary Acts," *Experience and Meaning: Studies in the Theory of Speech Acts*, pp. 1-29.) That is, words can be used to describe the world or, alternatively, words can be used to describe how the world should be. For example, consider a grocery list. With list in hand one goes to the market to purchase the specified items. Later it is discovered that one of the selected items does not match the product named on the list. To make the words match reality, it is only necessary to change the word on the list to match the incorrectly purchased item. But to make the world match the expressed intent, it is necessary to go back to the store and exchange the incorrect item for that one specified on the list.

From this perspective, it may be that the concept of infallibility as used in the Bahá'í teachings in relation to the Universal House of Justice is associated with a world-to-word fit. A statement by the House of Justice does not describe the world as it is, but describes "what should be done" in a manner that is in conformity with, or does not contradict, the will of God and hence it requires that action of the believers in the world correspond to the words. This divine guarantee is associated with spiritual forces and is, of course, a matter of faith and not empirical observation.

Searle's analysis includes a taxonomy of speech acts and is, of course, much more detailed than discussed here. Among the categories he describes are "declarations," which are statements that bring about a change in the status of the subject under consideration. An example of a declaration is the statement "You are fired." Searle explains, "It is only given such institutions as the Church, the law, private property, the state and a special position of the speaker and hearer within these institutions that one can excommunicate, appoint, give and bequeath one's possessions or declare war." The direction of fit in a declaration is both word-to-world and world-to-word because the statement itself brings about the correspondence between content and reality. "Successful performance guarantees that the proposition content corresponds to the world; if I successfully perform the act of appointing you chairman, then you are chairman." (See "A Classification of Illocutionary Acts.") Some statements of the Universal House of Justice, such as "the Faith of Bahá'u'lláh now enters the fifth epoch of its Formative Age" are of this type. (The Universal House of Justice, message dated January 16, 2001.)

127 'Abdu'l-Bahá, *Will and Testament of 'Abdu'l-Bahá*, p. 14.

128 'Abdu'l-Bahá, *Some Answered Questions*, p. 263.

129 On behalf of Shoghi Effendi, *Directives from the Guardian*, pp. 33-34.

130 On behalf of Shoghi Effendi, *Lights of Guidance*, p. 313.

131 Various passages refer to conferred infallibility in diverse contexts: concerning both its decisions and the establishment of laws ('Abdu'l-Bahá, in *Messages of the Universal House of Justice: 1963-1986*, p. 85); protection ('Abdu'l-Bahá, in *Messages: 1963-1986*, pp. 52-53); the enactment of legislation and the conduct of administrative affairs (Shoghi Effendi, *The World Order of Bahá'u'lláh*, p. 153); and in relation to protecting and administering the Cause, solving obscure questions and deciding upon matters that have caused difference. (The Universal House of Justice, *Messages: 1963-1986*, p. 157.)

132 Statements of Bahá'u'lláh and 'Abdu'l-Bahá refer to the House of Justice all matters that are not expressly or outwardly revealed. "It is incumbent upon the Trustees of the House of Justice to take counsel together regarding those things which have not outwardly been revealed in the Book, and to enforce that which is agreeable to them," Bahá'u'lláh states. "God will verily inspire them with whatsoever He willeth, and He, verily, is the Provider, the Omniscient." (*Tablets of Bahá'u'lláh*, p. 68.) "Unto the Most Holy Book every one must turn, and all that is not expressly recorded therein must be referred to the Universal House of Justice." (*Will and Testament of 'Abdu'l-Bahá*, p. 19.) As mentioned, 'Abdu'l-Bahá goes beyond a reference to deliberate on "matters that are not expressly recorded in the Book" to include "all problems which have caused difference" and "questions that are obscure." (*Will and Testament of 'Abdu'l-Bahá*, p. 20.) Finally, 'Abdu'l-Bahá explicitly states that the conclusions of the House of Justice are not mere opinions: "Let

it not be imagined that the House of Justice will take any decision according to its own concepts and opinions." (In *Messages: 1963-1986*, p. 85.)

Therefore, although the House of Justice is bound by the Revelation and the authorized interpretation of 'Abdu'l-Bahá and Shoghi Effendi, there is a kind of inverse relationship between the unity of thought of the community about the meaning of the Text and the need for elucidations of the House of Justice. When the meaning of the Book is obscure rather than evident, when there is a need to determine how to apply the teachings according to the time and circumstances, when differences arise among the believers, the responsibility falls to the House of Justice to clarify or resolve the matter or to explain what must be done. Its conclusions are as binding as the Text itself.

133 On behalf of the Universal House of Justice, *Lights of Guidance*, p. 311.

134 The Universal House of Justice, *Messages: 1963-1986*, p. 157.

135 Shoghi Effendi, *The World Order of Bahá'u'lláh*, p. 153. In another reference to these administrative functions, the Guardian states: "Severed from the no less essential institution of the Universal House of Justice this same System of the Will of 'Abdu'l-Bahá would be paralyzed in its action and would be powerless to fill in those gaps which the Author of the Kitáb-i-Aqdas has deliberately left in the body of His legislative and administrative ordinances." (*The World Order of Bahá'u'lláh*, p. 148.)

136 On behalf of the Universal House of Justice, *Lights of Guidance*, p. 311.

137 On behalf of the Universal House of Justice, message dated April 7, 2008.

138 On behalf of the Universal House of Justice, message dated January 2, 1991.

139 The Universal House of Justice, *Constitution of the Universal House of Justice*, p. 4.

140 Shoghi Effendi, *Bahá'í Administration*, p. 42.

141 'Abdu'l-Bahá, *Will and Testament of 'Abdu'l-Bahá*, p. 11.

142 Shoghi Effendi, *The World Order of Bahá'u'lláh*, p. 89.

143 'Abdu'l-Bahá, *Will and Testament of 'Abdu'l-Bahá*, p. 14.

144 Bahá'u'lláh, *Tablets of Bahá'u'lláh*, p. 68.

145 On behalf of Shoghi Effendi. *Lights of Guidance*, p. 111.

146 Shoghi Effendi, *Bahá'í Administration*, p. 68.

147 On behalf of Shoghi Effendi, *Compilation of Compilations*, vol. 1, p. 84.

148 On behalf of Shoghi Effendi, *Promoting Entry By Troops*, p. 3.

149 'Abdu'l-Bahá, *Selections from the Writings of 'Abdu'l-Bahá*, p. 209.

150 'Abdu'l-Bahá, *Selections from the Writings of 'Abdu'l-Bahá*, p. 34.

151 See chapter 5 for a discussion of the dangers of fundamentalism and liberalism, of foundationalism and relativism.

152 The Universal House of Justice, *Turning Point*, p. 125.

153 The Universal House of Justice, *Turning Point*, p. 144.

154 Hubert and Stuart Dreyfus, in Bent Flyvbjerg, *Making Social Science Matter: Why Social Inquiry Fails and How It Can Succeed Again*, pp.10-20.

155 On behalf of Shoghi Effendi, *Compilation of Compilations*, vol. 1, pp. 230-31.

CHAPTER 3

1 The Universal House of Justice, *Messages: 1963-1986*, p. 301.

2 'Abdu'l-Bahá, *Tablets of the Divine Plan*, pp. 5-6.

3 Shoghi Effendi, *Citadel of Faith*, p. 32. The first national plan, the Seven Year Plan, was initiated by the Bahá'ís of the United States and Canada in 1937. For a summary of the nature and purpose of Plans up to 1993, see *The Spiritual Conquest of the Planet,* by Melanie Smith and Paul Lample.

4 The Bahá'ís engaged in a range of practices, which the Guardian observed and commented upon, until common, well-understood procedures emerged and were universally adopted. See, for example, a letter written by Shoghi Effendi dated May 27, 1927 (*Bahá'í Administration,* p. 136) and a letter written on his behalf dated February 4, 1935 (*Lights of Divine Guidance, vol. 1*, pp. 67-68) concerning the question of nominations, which he gradually eliminated from the practice of the Western believers.

5 Shoghi Effendi, *Messages to America*, pp. 5-6.

6 Shoghi Effendi, *The World Order of Bahá'u'lláh*, p. 9.

7 Shoghi Effendi, *Citadel of Faith*, p. 76.

8 ". . . it has been found over the entire world that the most effective method of teaching the Faith is the fireside meeting in the home. . . . This method is far more effective than advertising in newspapers, public lectures etc. The Guardian is encouraging the believers over the world, including those on the home fronts, to engage in this method of teaching." (On behalf of Shoghi Effendi, *Lights of Guidance*, p. 247.)

9 On behalf of Shoghi Effendi, *Dawn of a New Day*, p. 76.

10 Shoghi Effendi, *Citadel of Faith*, p. 117.

11 "Premonitory signs can already be discerned in far-off regions heralding the approach of the day when troops will flock to its standard, fulfilling the predictions uttered long ago by the Supreme Captain of its forces." (Shoghi Effendi, *Messages to the Bahá'í World*, p. 101.) See also *Messages to the Bahá'í World*, p. 113. The British protectorate, the Gilbert and Ellice Islands, have since divided: the Gilbert Islands became the major part of Kiribati and the Ellice Islands are now Tuvalu.

12   Bahá'í World Centre, *The Six Year Plan 1986-1992: Summary of Achievements*, p. 20.

13   Bahá'í World Centre, *Century of Light*, p. 101.

14   The Universal House of Justice, *Compilation of Compilations*, vol. 3, p. 184.

15   The Universal House of Justice, *Messages: 1963-1986*, p. 301.

16   The Universal House of Justice, message dated March 22, 1973.

17   On behalf of the Universal House of Justice, message dated July 30, 1987.

18   The Universal House of Justice *A Wider Horizon*, p. 27.

19   The Universal House of Justice *A Wider Horizon*, p. 80.

20   The Universal House of Justice, *Turning Point*, p. 50.

21   The Universal House of Justice, *A Wider Horizon*, p. 79.

22   Bahá'í World Centre, *Century of Light*, pp. 108, 110.

23   The Universal House of Justice, *Turning Point*, p. 31. A summary of the guidance conveyed by the Universal House of Justice since 1996 is found in *Turning Point: Selected Messages of the Universal House of Justice and Supplementary Materials, 1996-2006*, by Palabra Publications.

24   The Universal House of Justice, *Compilation of Compilations*, vol. 3, p. 155.

25   The Universal House of Justice, *Turning Point*, p. 27.

26   The Universal House of Justice, *Turning Point*, p. 49.

27   The Universal House of Justice, *Turning Point*, pp. 7-8.

28   The Universal House of Justice, *Turning Point*, pp. 3-18, 21-82.

29   The Universal House of Justice, *Turning Point*, p. 120.

30   On behalf of the Universal House of Justice, *Turning Point*, p. 268.

31   The Universal House of Justice, *Turning Point*, p. 8.

32   The Universal House of Justice, *Turning Point*, p. 8.

33   The International Teaching Centre, *Turning Point*, pp. 350-51.

34   The Universal House of Justice, *Turning Point*, p. 190.

35   The Universal House of Justice, *Turning Point*, pp. 209-11.

36   The Ruhi Institute, *Learning About Growth*, p. 65.

37   The Ruhi Institute, *Learning About Growth*, pp. 9-10.

38   The Ruhi Institute, *Learning About Growth*, pp. 54-55.

39   For a more detailed exploration, see the notes from a series of talks given by Farzam Arbab at the Portals to Growth Conference in Sydney and Perth, Australia, 2004, especially day three. See also *Learning About Growth* by the Ruhi Institute, *Lectures on Bahá'í-inspired Curricula* by Farzam Arbab, and *Exploring a Framework for Moral Education*, by Lori Noguchi, Holly Hansen, and Paul Lample.

40   See *Learning About Growth*, pp. 30-33, for a more detailed discussion.

41   The Ruhi Institute, *Learning About Growth*, p. 53.

42   Bahá'u'lláh, *Gleanings*, p. 141. "It is because of such considerations that the Five Year Plan [1974-1979] calls for the friends to memorize selections from the Writings." (The Universal House of Justice, *Compilation of Compilations*, vol. 2, p. 37.)

43   Bahá'u'lláh, *Tablets of Bahá'u'lláh*, p. 200.

44   Bahá'u'lláh, *Tablets of Bahá'u'lláh*, p. 200.

45   The Ruhi Institute, *Learning About Growth*, pp. 50-51.

46   At an early stage when nascent institutes or inexperienced tutors presented Ruhi courses in an inflexible way, it appeared to some that the materials called for an approach that is overly rigid and literal. Such, however, is not the purpose for which the materials are designed or the procedures in which tutors are to be trained, as is evident in a study of the tutor training course Book 7, *Walking Together on a Path of Service*. Nor will such an improper approach lead to effective results. Institutes taking this approach will have to be guided over time and through experience to revise and improve. This type of rigidity, however, should be considered in light of the structured experience that is an initial requirement of learning any new skill. As discussed in chapter 4 with regard to learning, the initial stage in the acquisition of new skills tends to be rigid or mechanical in nature. The aim, however, is to set the novice on a path to becoming a competent or even expert performer that can apply new knowledge. Without experience in learning about growth, whether its components or the whole process of entry by troops, it is impossible to judge the value of what is being presented about the results of learning from those that have already had some degree of success. This means that the initial stages of applying the guidance in the Four Year, the Twelve Month, or the first Five Year Plan may have been alien to the practice of some national communities. Early stages of implementation may be perceived to be unnecessarily rigid and awkward. Rather than prematurely intervening to adapt or revise action as a result of such comments, or concluding too early that the guidance "does not apply to us," it was necessary to persevere in the early attempts to apply concepts and methods until a sufficient base of experience was accumulated in order to learn how to fit them to local context. It is in this light that the use of Ruhi materials was encouraged to complement initial activities to learn how to pursue a more systematic approach to advancing the process of entry by troops. Calling for the modification of materials or practices too quickly is equally as harmful as mindless and rigid implementation.

47   The Ruhi Institute, *Walking Together on a Path of Service*, Book 7, pp.102-03.

48   The Ruhi Institute, *Learning About Growth*, p. 54.

49   The Universal House of Justice, *Turning Point*, p. 4.

50   The Universal House of Justice, *Turning Point*, p. 142.

51   The Universal House of Justice, *Turning Point*, p. 167.

52   See *Reflections on Growth* #8, from the International Teaching Centre, July 2005

53   The Universal House of Justice, *Turning Point*, pp. 204-05.

54   The International Teaching Centre, message to all Counsellors dated November 28, 2004.

55   See *Reflections on Growth* #7, from the International Teaching Centre, April 2005

56   The Universal House of Justice, *Turning Point*, p. 195.

57   The Universal House of Justice, *Turning Point*, p. 195.

58   The Universal House of Justice, *Turning Point*, p. 196

59   On behalf of the Universal House of Justice, message dated February 17, 2004.

60   The Universal House of Justice, *Turning Point*, p. 260.

61   In 2006, a similar book was prepared entitled *The Five Year Plan: A Summary of Achievements and Learning*.

62   The Universal House of Justice, *The Five Year Plan*, p. 75. These three documents are included in *Turning Point*, pp. 323-96.

63   The Universal House of Justice, *Turning Point*, p. 178.

64   "Reflection meetings at the level of clusters have become a powerful means of unifying thought and action across institutions and localities; they have lent a potent stimulus to institutional and individual initiatives in a mutually supportive spirit." (The Universal House of Justice, *Turning Point*, p. 184.) See issues 3 and 4 of the newsletter *Reflections on Growth* prepared by the International Teaching Centre.

65   The Universal House of Justice, *Turning Point*, p. 205.

66   The Universal House of Justice, *Turning Point*, p. 197.

67   From a report of an individual, December 2006.

68   The Universal House of Justice, *Turning Point*, p. 8.

69   The Universal House of Justice, *Turning Point*, p. 333.

70   The Universal House of Justice, *Turning Point*, pp. 146.

71   The Universal House of Justice, *Turning Point*, p. 172.

72   The Universal House of Justice, *Turning Point*, p. 146.

73   The Universal House of Justice, *Turning Point*, pp. 203-04.

74   The Universal House of Justice, *Turning Point*, p. 204.

75   The Universal House of Justice, *Turning Point*, p. 206.

76   The Universal House of Justice, *Turning Point*, p. 198.

77 The International Teaching Centre, message to all Counsellors dated November 28, 2004.

78 The Universal House of Justice, *Turning Point*, p. 201. The importance of focus was also emphasized by Shoghi Effendi early in his ministry: "Much as I rejoice in witnessing the abundant signs of unfaltering energy that characterize in various fields and distant lands the mission of the valiant warriors of the Cause, I cannot help observing that, driven by their impetuous eagerness to establish the undisputed reign of Bahá'u'lláh on this earth, they may by an undue multiplication of their activities, and the consequent dissipation of their forces, defeat the very purpose which animates them in the pursuit of their glorious task. . . . Nothing short of the spirit of earnest and sustained consultation with those whom we have prayerfully and of our own accord placed in the forefront of those who are the custodians of the priceless heritage bequeathed by Bahá'u'lláh; nothing less than persistent and strenuous warfare against our own instincts and natural inclinations, and heroic self-sacrifice in subordinating our own likings to the imperative requirements of the Cause of God, can insure our undivided loyalty to so sacred a principle—a principle that will for all time safeguard our beloved Cause from the allurements and the trivialities of the world without, and of the pitfalls of the self within. I entreat you, well-beloved brethren, to resolve as you never have resolved before to pledge undying loyalty and sleepless vigilance in upholding so essential a principle in the course of your manifold activities, that yours may be the abiding satisfaction of having done nothing that may tend in the least to impede the flow or obscure the radiance of the rejuvenating spirit of the Faith of Bahá'u'lláh." (*Bahá'í Administration*, pp. 140-41.)

79 The Universal House of Justice, *Turning Point*, p. 120.

80 The Universal House of Justice, *Turning Point*, p. 205.

81 The Universal House of Justice, *Turning Point*, p. 87.

82 The Universal House of Justice, *Turning Point*, p. 146.

83 See "Learning to Administer Growth" (*Turning Point*, pp. 299-310) and "Impact of Growth on Administration Processes" (*Turning Point*, pp. 397-405).

84 "As you continue to labor in your clusters, you will be drawn further and further into the life of the society around you and will be challenged to extend the process of systematic learning in which you are engaged to encompass a growing range of human endeavors. In the approaches you take, the methods you adopt, and the instruments you employ, you will need to achieve the same degree of coherence that characterizes the pattern of growth presently under way." (The Universal House of Justice, Riḍván 2008.)

85 On behalf of the Universal House of Justice, message dated July 9, 2003.

86 The Universal House of Justice, *Turning Point*, pp. 199-200.

87   Shoghi Effendi indicated that it was the "bounden duty" of the individual believer as "the faithful trustee of 'Abdu'l-Bahá's Divine Plan, to initiate, promote, and consolidate, within the limits fixed by the administrative principles of the Faith, any activity he or she deems fit to undertake for the furtherance of the Plan," adding, emphatically, "Let him not wait for any directions, or expect any special encouragement, from the elected representatives of his community. . . ." (*The Advent of Divine Justice*, p. 50.)

88   The Guardian indicated that the "best Assembly is the one that capitalizes the talents of all the members of the group and keeps them busy in some form of active participation in serving the Cause and spreading the Message." (On behalf of Shoghi Effendi, *Lights of Guidance*, p. 37) He also stated that "The members of these Assemblies, on their part, must disregard utterly their own likes and dislikes, their personal interests and inclinations, and concentrate their minds upon those measures that will conduce to the welfare and happiness of the Bahá'í Community and promote the common weal." (*Bahá'í Administration*, p. 41.)

89   While, some believers were concerned about the implications of the changes that took place in institutional structures and responsibilities over the course of the Plans, it is important to recognize that these changes are not a deviation from foundations laid by the Guardian, but a fuller realization of his guidance. "Let us take heed lest in our great concern for the perfection of the administrative machinery of the Cause, we lose sight of the Divine Purpose for which it has been created," Shoghi Effendi warns, which is to serve "as direct instruments for the propagation of the Bahá'í Faith." (*Bahá'í Administration*, p. 103.) Bahá'í administration "is to be regarded as a means, and not an end in itself," and "the whole machinery of assemblies, of committees and conventions" will "rise or fall according to their capacity to further the interests, to coordinate the activities, to apply the principles, to embody the ideals and execute the purpose of the Bahá'í Faith." (*The World Order of Bahá'u'lláh*, p. 9.) The Guardian also explains that "the machinery of the Cause has been so fashioned, that whatever is deemed necessary to incorporate into it in order to keep it in the forefront of all progressive movements, can, according to the provisions made by Bahá'u'lláh, be safely embodied therein," while explicitly associating these modifications to Bahá'í practice with the powers granted by Bahá'u'lláh to the Universal House of Justice: "'God will verily inspire them with whatsoever He willeth, and He, verily, is the Provider, the Omniscient.'" (*The World Order of Bahá'u'lláh*, pp. 22-23.)

90   On behalf of the Universal House of Justice, message dated August 22, 2002.

91   See http://www.news.bahai.org/community-news/regional-conferences/

CHAPTER 4

1   Shoghi Effendi, *The World Order of Bahá'u'lláh*, p. 206.

2   ". . . the task of breathing life into this unified body—of creating true unity and spirituality culminating in the Most Great Peace—is that of the Bahá'ís, who are laboring consciously, with detailed instructions and continuing divine guidance, to erect the fabric of the Kingdom of God on earth, into which they call their fellowmen, thus conferring upon them eternal life." (The Universal House of Justice, *Messages: 1963-1986*, p. 127.)

3   Shoghi Effendi, *The Promised Day is Come*, pp. 411-12.

4   The Universal House of Justice, *Messages: 1963-1986*, p. 126.

5   'Abdu'l-Bahá, *Compilation of Compilations*, vol. 2, p. 164.

6   The Universal House of Justice, *Messages: 1963-1986*, p. 107.

7   'Abdu'l-Bahá, previously untranslated tablet.

8   'Abdu'l-Bahá, *The Secret of Divine Civilization*, p. 3.

9   'Abdu'l-Bahá, *The Secret of Divine Civilization*, p. 39.

10   'Abdu'l-Bahá, *The Promulgation of Universal Peace*, p. 50.

11   'Abdu'l-Bahá, *Paris Talks*, p. 80-81.

12   "If it is not possible, therefore, for a family to educate all the children, preference is to be accorded to daughters since, through educated mothers, the benefits of knowledge can be most effectively and rapidly diffused throughout society." ('Abdu'l-Bahá, in *The Kitáb-i-Aqdas*, p. 200.)

13   Bahá'u'lláh, *Tablets of Bahá'u'lláh*, p. 51.

14   'Abdu'l-Bahá, *Compilation of Compilations*, vol. 1, p. 253.

15   'Abdu'l-Bahá, *Compilation of Compilations*, vol. 1, p. 6.

16   On behalf of Shoghi Effendi, *Compilation of Compilations*, vol. 1, p. 297.

17   Shoghi Effendi, *Compilation of Compilations*, vol. 2, p. 348.

18   The Universal House of Justice, *Messages: 1963-1986*, p. 669.

19   The Universal House of Justice, *Messages: 1963-1986*, p. 94.

20   On behalf of Shoghi Effendi, *Compilation of Compilations*, vol. 1, p. 226.

21   On behalf of the Universal House of Justice, *Messages: 1963-1986*, p. 369.

22   'Abdu'l-Bahá, *The Secret of Divine Civilization*, pp. 107-08.

23   See for example "The Validity and Value of an Historical-Critical Approach to the Revealed Works of Bahá'u'lláh," by John S. Hatcher in *Scripture and Revelation*, Bahá'í Studies Volume III, edited by Moojan Momen and "Historical Methodology and the Development of Bahá'í Scholarship: Toward Dispelling a False Dichotomy," by Sholeh A. Quinn, *Bahá'í Studies Review*, vol. 9, 1999/2000.

24 In this context, it is crucial for Bahá'ís who commit themselves to the study and mastery of any field to keep in mind that a fundamental characteristic of any discipline is that it provides a particular perspective on reality—it does not describe reality itself. The level of abstraction incorporated in a discipline can be forgotten by those experts who are totally immersed within it. This can lead to strange errors when trying to apply the lessons from the discipline back into the real world or when engaging the insights of other disciplines. For a more detailed exploration of this problem, see the discussion of "the fallacy of misplaced concreteness" in *For the Common Good* by Herman Daly and John Cobb, which explores the abstractions made in the field of economics and how the field has structured the thinking of economists and their approaches to the problems of the world, sometime blinding them to obvious truths.

25 John J. Carvalho IV, "Overview of the Structure of a Scientific Worldview," *Zygon: Journal of Religion and Science*, vol. 41, no. 1, March 2006, pp. 117-18.

26 Carvalho, "Overview of the Structure of a Scientific Worldview," *Zygon*, pp. 122-23. A similar perspective on the relationship of science and religion is presented by Mortimer J. Adler in the book *Truth in Religion*: "Mathematics and science are necessarily only part of the whole truth—the truth that we seek to learn about the world, about nature, society, and man. On that assumption, philosophy and religion constitute additional portions or segments of the whole of the truth to be attained. . . . [T]he principle of the unity of truth entails the consequence that the several parts of the one whole of the truth to be attained must coherently fit together. As we have already seen, there cannot be irreconcilable contradictions between the one segment of the whole of truth and another. What is regarded as true in philosophy and religion must not conflict with what is regarded as true in science." (Adler, *Truth in Religion: The Plurality of Religions and the Unity of Truth*, p. 122.)

27 Stephen Toulmin, *Cosmopolis: The Hidden Agenda of Modernity*, p. 144. Similarly, Shoghi Effendi speaks of "the prevailing spirit of modernism, with its emphasis on a purely materialistic philosophy, which, as it diffuses itself, tends increasingly to divorce religion from man's daily life." (*The World Order of Bahá'u'lláh*, p. 183.)

28 The Universal House of Justice, message dated November 26, 2003 to the Followers of Bahá'u'lláh in the Cradle of the Faith.

29 'Abdu'l-Bahá, *The Promulgation of Universal Peace*, p. 107.

30 'Abdu'l-Bahá, *Paris Talks*, pp. 130-31.

31 For a further consideration of the relationship between science and religion from a Bahá'í perspective, see Farzam Arbab, *The Lab, The Temple, and the Market*, pp. 149-51. See also the discussion of the problems of traditional

religious and reductionistic scientific views by Nader Saiedi, in *Gate of the Heart: Understanding the Writings of the Báb*, pp. 3-14.

32   The purpose of this approach is simply to draw out certain insights; it is not intended to suggest that the table truly captures human comprehension and the relationship between science and religion. A number of incorrect implications may be suggested by the table: for example, that there is an exact parallel between the workings of science and religion, or that there is a complete distinction between theoretical and practical knowledge. Level three representing understanding, and level four representing practice could perhaps be more properly presented side by side (as 3a and 3b) rather than hierarchically.

33   There is, of course, not an exact correlation between the universe and the Revelation, or the "book of creation" and the book of Revelation. By the "universe" is meant not just the physical world, but all that pertains to human beings, from the mind to society, that falls within the scope of scientific investigation. While the Revelation comes from outside humanity, the facts and laws of the physical universe, when we know them, are always somehow "discovered" and represented in some form through human understanding, which means there is a blurring of the distinction between levels 2 and 3 in the area of science. Furthermore, while the laws of the universe are fixed, the Revelation is immutable in relation to humanity within the context of a dispensation, when the message is renewed and adjusted in a new Revelation suited to a new age.

34   A question arises as to whether the Revealed Text (R2) makes any true statements about the actual operation of the physical reality (S2) that are not held in the current body of scientific knowledge (S3) or perhaps, which even contradict the currently held facts of physical reality. According to 'Abdu'l-Bahá this is possible. However, such statements would only have implications for religious understanding (R3). They are irrelevant for the purposes of science until such time as the implications of the statements can be encompassed within the body of scientific understanding. For example, the statement from the Qur'án that "The sun moves in a fixed place" is useless to scientists until such time as the knowledge system of science with its appropriate methods for systematic observations and validation of scientific knowledge are applied. Up to that point, a "belief" that the sun is the center of the solar system is scientifically meaningless, as 'Abdu'l-Bahá points out when contrasting the positions of Pythagoras and Plato with that of Copernicus and Galileo. The former "adopted the theory that the annual movement of the sun around the zodiac does not proceed from the sun, but rather from the movement of the earth around the sun" but "this theory had been entirely forgotten." The theory, without scientific evidence does not stand. Yet, as a result of "new observations and important discoveries" made "by the aid of the telescope" the "rotation of the earth, the fixity of the

sun, and also its movement around an axis, were discovered" and "it became evident that the verses of the Qur'án agreed with existing facts, and that the Ptolemaic system was imaginary." (*Some Answered Questions*, pp. 23-24.)

Of course, the Text may serve as an inspiration to scientists who are believers to take actions that lead to scientifically valid discoveries and knowledge; after all, scientists have been inspired by a host of sources. However, until encompassed within the body of scientific understanding (S3) statements within the Revelation (R2) have no scientific validity. We cannot know if our religious interpretation (R3) of that Text as having scientific implications is correct without appropriate scientific inquiry. For while 'Abdu'l-Bahá exhorts us to weigh religious beliefs (R3) in the light of our scientific knowledge (S3) the reverse is not suggested. In fact, the Text (R2) upholds the scientific process (S3 and S4), as indicated by such statements as 'Abdu'l-Bahá's support for Copernicus. Bahá'u'lláh Himself makes this point when, castigating the fanciful beliefs of a certain individual with regard to alchemy and spiritual understanding, He proclaims: "We cherish the hope that either a king or a man of preeminent power may call upon him to translate this science from the realm of fancy to the domain of fact and from the plane of mere pretension to that of actual achievement." (*The Kitáb-i-Íqán*, p. 189.)

35   "If the religious beliefs of mankind are contrary to science and opposed to reason, they are none other than superstitions and without divine authority, for the Lord God has endowed man with the faculty of reason in order that through its exercise he may arrive at the verities of existence. Reason is the discoverer of the realities of things, and that which conflicts with its conclusions is the product of human fancy and imagination." ('Abdu'l-Bahá, *The Promulgation of Universal Peace*, p. 316.)

36   "Weigh not the Book of God with such standards and sciences as are current amongst you, for the Book itself is the unerring Balance established amongst men." (Bahá'u'lláh, *The Kitáb-i-Aqdas*, p. 56.)

37   "Should a man try to fly with the wing of religion alone he would quickly fall into the quagmire of superstition, whilst on the other hand, with the wing of science alone he would also make no progress, but fall into the despairing slough of materialism." ('Abdu'l-Bahá. *Paris Talks*, p. 143.)

38   Todd May, *Our Practices, Our Selves: Or, What It Means to be Human*, p. 8.

39   May, *Our Practices, Our Selves*, pp. 100-01.

40   Moojan Momen, "Methodology in Bahá'í Studies," *The Bahá'í Studies Review*, vol. 10, 2001/2002, p. 80.

41   "In past dispensations many errors arose because the believers in God's Revelation were overanxious to encompass the Divine Message within the framework of their limited understanding, to define doctrines where definition was beyond their power, to explain mysteries which only the wisdom

and experience of a later age would make comprehensible, to argue that something was true because it appeared desirable and necessary. Such compromises with essential truth, such intellectual pride, we must scrupulously avoid." (The Universal House of Justice, *Messages: 1963-1986*, p. 87.)

"With regard to the harmony of science and religion, the Writings of the Central Figures and the commentaries of the Guardian make abundantly clear that the task of humanity, including the Bahá'í community that serves as the 'leaven' within it, is to create a global civilization which embodies both the spiritual and material dimensions of existence. The nature and scope of such a civilization are still beyond anything the present generation can conceive. The prosecution of this vast enterprise will depend on a progressive interaction between the truths and principles of religion and the discoveries and insights of scientific inquiry. This entails living with ambiguities as a natural and inescapable feature of the process of exploring reality." (On behalf of the Universal House of Justice, message dated May 19, 1995 to an individual.)

"Bahá'u'lláh has given certain teachings which Bahá'ís believe to be true; they offer these teachings to the rest of mankind. Whosoever accepts them is a Bahá'í, but everyone is free to reject them. No one is ever compelled to become a Bahá'í, nor is anyone compelled to remain a Bahá'í. If one has accepted the Bahá'í Faith and later concludes that one has made a mistake, one is free to withdraw, and no stigma is attached to such an action. In all such things Bahá'ís uphold Bahá'u'lláh's principle of independent investigation of truth." (The Universal House of Justice, message dated May 1, 1991 to an individual.)

42 A relativistic approach to practices is rejected. (See May, *Our Practices, Our Selves*, pp. 125-35). Searle's argument about truth and correspondence to reality is also relevant. (*The Construction of Social Reality*, pp. 149-76.) Searle affirms that "all true statements about the world can be consistently affirmed together." Thus, he rejects the perspective of conceptual relativism that we can describe the world in different ways that may contradict one another, and yet each of these perspectives is "true" in themselves. This position assumes that the same statement could be true of the world in one conceptual system but false in another. A standard example proposes the different representations of Aristotelian physics vs. Newtonian physics or the Mercator projection of the earth's surface vs. a standard globe. On the Mercator projection, Greenland is larger than Brazil, while on the globe, Greenland is a smaller area than Brazil. This difference is not a result of incommensurable realities, Searle explains, but results from the fact that some models or representations are mistaken or distort reality more than others. While we are "always confronted with the problems of vagueness, indeterminacy, family resemblance, open texture, contextual dependency, the incommensurability of theories, ambiguity, the idealization involved in theory construction, alternative interpretations, the underdetermination of

theory by evidence, and all the rest of it," nevertheless, "these are features of our systems of representation, not of the representation-independent reality." Once statements from different representational systems are reconciled with one another, if they cannot be consistently affirmed together, they cannot all be true.

43   The Universal House of Justice, *Messages: 1963-1986*, p. 602.

44   The Universal House of Justice, *Messages: 1963-1986*, p. 602.

45   A statement approved by the Universal House of Justice, "Bahá'í Social and Economic Development: Prospects for the Future," *Readings on Bahá'í Social and Economic Development*, pp. 12-13.

46   The Universal House of Justice, *Messages: 1963-1986*, p. 602.

47   'Abdu'l-Bahá, *Lights of Guidance*, p. 303.

48   This reference was made in the context of a discussion about "the social, humanitarian, educational and scientific pursuits centering around the Dependencies of the Ma<u>sh</u>riqu'l-A<u>dh</u>kár." (Shoghi Effendi, *Bahá'í Administration*, p. 186.)

49   Bahá'u'lláh, *Gleanings*, p. 93.

50   Shoghi Effendi, *Compilation of Compilations*, vol. 1, pp. 297-98.

51   The Universal House of Justice, *Messages: 1963-1986*, p. 602.

52   Office of Social and Economic Development, *For the Betterment of the World*, p. 3.

53   A statement approved by the Universal House of Justice, "Bahá'í Social and Economic Development: Prospects for the Future," *Readings on Bahá'í Social and Economic Development*, p. 17.

54   See *Readings on Bahá'í Social and Economic Development* for the first three documents.

55   Examples of these projects at all level of complexity can be found in *For the Betterment of the World*, in the *Bahá'í World* volumes, in *One Country* newsletter and Web site www.onecountry.org and at the Bahá'í World Web Site, www.bahai.org.

56   The Universal House of Justice, *Readings on Bahá'í Social and Economic Development*, p. 94.

57   On behalf of the Universal House of Justice, message dated September 24, 1996.

58   On behalf of the Universal House of Justice, in "The Evolution of Institutional Capacity for Social and Economic Development," *Readings on Bahá'í Social and Economic Development*, pp. 26-27.

59   The information on FUNDAEC provided here is drawn largely from a 1999 doctoral thesis by Manigeh Roosta entitled "Adult Learning and Community Development: A Case Study of the FUNDAEC's University

Center for Rural Well-Being in Risaralda, Colombia." Additional information can be found at http://www.fundaec.org/en/ and http://www.bcca.org/services/lists/noble-creation/fundaec1.html.

60 Talk given by Haleh Arbab at the Colloquium on Science, Religion and Development, November 21-24, 2000, India International Centre, New Delhi, pp. 1-2.

61 Haleh Arbab, Colloquium on Science, Religion and Development, pp. 6-7, 8.

62 Haleh Arbab, Colloquium on Science, Religion and Development, pp. 7-8.

63 Farzam Arbab, *The Lab, The Temple, and the Market*, pp. 149-51.

64 The Universal House of Justice, *Readings on Bahá'í Social and Economic Development*, p. 92.

65 Office of Social and Economic Development, *For the Betterment of the World*, p. 34.

66 Bahá'u'lláh, *Tablets of Bahá'u'lláh*, p. 171.

67 Bahá'u'lláh, *Tablets of Bahá'u'lláh*, pp. 96-97.

68 'Abdu'l-Bahá, *Selections from the Writings of 'Abdu'l-Bahá*, p. 97.

69 Shoghi Effendi, *Compilation of Compilations*, vol. 2, p. 348.

70 On behalf of the Universal House of Justice, *Issues Related to the Study of the Bahá'í Faith*, p. 35.

71 On behalf of the Universal House of Justice, *Compilation of Compilations*, vol. 3, p. 241.

72 On behalf of the Universal House of Justice, *Issues Related to the Study of the Bahá'í Faith*, p. 25.

73 Bahá'u'lláh, *The Kitáb-i-Aqdas*, p. 34. He also states: "O ye the dawning-places of knowledge! Beware that ye suffer not yourselves to become changed, for as ye change, most men will, likewise, change. This, verily, is an injustice unto yourselves and unto others. Unto this beareth witness every man of discernment and insight. Ye are even as a spring. If it be changed, so will the streams that branch out from it be changed. Fear God, and be numbered with the godly. In like manner, if the heart of man be corrupted, his limbs will also be corrupted. And similarly, if the root of a tree be corrupted, its branches, and its offshoots, and its leaves, and its fruits, will be corrupted. Thus have We set forth similitudes for your instruction, that perchance ye may not be debarred by the things ye possess from attaining unto that which hath been destined for you by Him Who is the All-Glorious, the Most Bountiful." (*The Summons of the Lord of Hosts*, p. 21.)

74 Bahá'u'lláh, *Compilation of Compilations*, vol. 1, p. 3.

75 'Abdu'l-Bahá, *The Secret of Divine Civilization*, p. 34.

76 'Abdu'l-Bahá, *The Secret of Divine Civilization*, pp. 59-60.

77 'Abdu'l-Bahá, *Risáliy-i-Siyásíyyih*, para. 60, provisional translation.

78 Flyvbjerg, *Making Social Science Matter*, p. 32. That is, according to Flyvbjerg, the social sciences study "self-reflecting humans" not "physical objects" and "must therefore take account of changes in the interpretations of the objects of study."

79 See chapter 5.

80 Of course, the Bahá'í community must in turn, learn to respond to new insights in a moderate way, avoiding extremes that lead either to easy acceptance or hasty rejection. Both extremes can result in chaos and disorder. The first seeks radical shifts in belief or practice based on partially understood concepts that have not been adequately explored in relation to the authoritative Text. The second is born of fanatical rejection of new ideas that gives rise to anti-intellectualism, oppression and stagnation. As a letter written on behalf of the Universal House of Justice has stated: "In past Dispensations the believers have tended to divide into two mutually antagonistic groups: those who held blindly to the letter of the Revelation, and those who questioned and doubted everything. Like all extremes, both of these can lead into error. . . . Bahá'ís are called upon to follow the Faith with intelligence and understanding. Inevitably believers will commit errors as they strive to rise to this degree of maturity, and this calls for forbearance and humility on the part of all concerned, so that such matters do not cause disunity or discord among the friends." (Message dated October 7, 1980.)

Another such letter indicated: "The House of Justice agrees that it is most important for the believers, and especially those who hold positions of responsibility in the Administrative Order, to react calmly and with tolerant and enquiring minds to views which differ from their own, remembering that all Bahá'ís are but students of the Faith, ever striving to understand the Teachings more clearly and to apply them more faithfully, and none can claim to have a perfect understanding of this Revelation." (Message dated July 18, 1979.)

It must also be observed that sometimes problems arise that are not attributable to the original intent of an author. Ideas put forward to pursue an academic line of thought can be misappropriated by others intent on imposing a particular perspective on the wider community.

81 This is not an appeal for the "mission-oriented" scholarship dismissed by Will van der Hoonen ("Unfreezing the Frame: the Promise of Inductive Research in Bahá'í Studies," *The Bahá'í Studies Review*, vol. 10, 2001/2002, p. 113). It is recognition of the fact that the social sciences and humanities can never be objective in the classical sense of the natural sciences. They are bound in a web of interpretation and action, of justification, knowledge and power, and should be practiced in a manner that is constructive in the light of this reality. How to address this problem in a manner satisfactory to both communities of practice is a challenge that must be resolved by learned Bahá'ís.

82   Bahá'u'lláh, *Gleanings*, p. 196.

83   'Abdu'l-Bahá, *Selections from the Writings of 'Abdu'l-Bahá*, pp. 70-72.

CHAPTER 5

1   Nicholas C. Burbules, "Postmodern Doubt and Philosophy of Education," *The Philosophy of Education*, 1995, pp. 40-41.

2   The effort includes, for some, making a new place for the contribution of religion to society. See Hunter Baker, "Competing Orthodoxies in the Public Square: Postmodernism's Effect on Church-State Separation," in *Journal of Law and Religion*, vol. 20, n. 1, 2004-05, pp. 97-121.

3   Summarized from Moojan Momen, "Fundamentalism and Liberalism: Towards an Understanding of the Dichotomy," *The Bahá'í Studies Review*, vol. 2.1, 1992.

4   Shoghi Effendi, *Dawn of a New Day*, p. 61.

5   On behalf of Shoghi Effendi, *Compilation of Compilations*, vol. 2, p. 21. A letter written on behalf of the Universal House of Justice further explains: ". . . the House of Justice has noted your understandable repugnance at an apparent temptation to use misleading and invidious labels like 'traditionalists' and 'liberals', which divide the Bahá'í community. To the extent that this divisive habit of mind may persist in the Bahá'í community, it is obviously a carry-over from non-Bahá'í society and a manifestation of an immature conception of life. If Bahá'ís were to persist in this mode of thinking, it would bring to naught even the most worthwhile intellectual endeavor as has so conspicuously been the case with societies of the past." (*Issues Related to the Study of the Bahá'í Faith*, pp. 17-18.)

6   Bahá'u'lláh, *Tablets of Bahá'u'lláh*, p. 138.

7   'Abdu'l-Bahá, *Bahá'í Prayers*, pp. 300-01.

8   "The most striking feature of contemporary moral utterance is that so much of it is used to express disagreements; and the most striking feature of the debates in which these disagreements are expressed is their interminable character. I do not mean by this just that such debates go on and on and on—although they do—but also that they apparently find no terminus. There seems to be no rational way of securing moral agreement in our culture." (Alasdair MacIntyre, *After Virtue: A Study in Moral Theory*, p. 6.)

9   On behalf of Shoghi Effendi, *Dawn of a New Day*, p. 129.

10   Shoghi Effendi, *Bahá'í Administration*, pp. 63-64.

11   'Abdu'l-Bahá, *The Promulgation of Universal Peace*, p. 144.

12   Richard J. Bernstein, *Beyond Objectivism and Relativism: Science, Hermeneutics, and Praxis*, p. 8.

13   Among these are foundationalism and positivism. For the purposes of this book, foundationalism and objectivism are considered to be the same. Bernstein explains: "Objectivism is closely related to foundationalism and the search for an Archimedean point. The objectivist maintains that unless we can ground philosophy, knowledge, or language in a rigorous manner we cannot avoid radical skepticism." (*Beyond Objectivism and Relativism*, p. 8.)

14   Bernstein, *Beyond Objectivism and Relativism*, pp. 8-9. In light of these definitions, Bernstein notes that the opposite of objectivism is, actually, subjectivism—that all human knowledge is grounded in personal or subjective experience. The opposite of relativism is absolutism—that one can have certain and complete knowledge of the external reality. He observes, however, that both subjectivism and absolutism have been completely discredited. The arguments against these positions, which will not be covered here, imply that the voices of objectivism and relativism must therefore be qualified: a fallibilistic objectivism and a non-subjective relativism. It should also be understood that extreme relativism is self-contradictory: to claim that a relativist position is true, conflicts with the position itself that truth is relative. So relativism itself may be true and false. Indeed, it seems as if relativism is not a true position in itself, but rather the alternative to the effort to vindicate a fixed basis of knowledge; it is, as Bernstein contends, the specter that haunts the failure of objectivism.

15   Bernstein, *Beyond Objectivism and Relativism*, p. 9.

16   Bernstein, *Beyond Objectivism and Relativism*, p. 18. In subsequent writings Bernstein refers to this as the "anxiety of relativism" or the "incommensurability anxiety." See Bernstein, "Can We Justify Universal Moral Norms?" in *Universalism vs. Relativism: Making Moral Judgments in a Changing, Pluralistic, and Threatening World*, p. 5.

17   According to Bernstein, phronēsis is "a form of reasoning that is concerned with choice and involves deliberation. It deals with that which is variable and about which there can be differing opinions. It is a type of reasoning in which there is a mediation between general principles and a concrete particular situation that requires choice and decision. In forming such a judgment there are no determinate technical rules by which a particular can simply be subsumed under that which is general or universal. What is required is an interpretation and specification of universals that are appropriate to this particular situation. . . ." (*Beyond Objectivism and Relativism*, p. 54.)

18   Physicist David Bohm makes a similar point: "Thus, in scientific research, a great deal of our thinking is in terms of theories. The word "theory" derives from the Greek "theoria," which has the same root as the "theatre," in a word meaning "to view" or "to make a spectacle." Thus, it might be said that a theory is primarily a form of insight, i.e. a way of looking at the world, and not a form of knowledge of how the world is. . . .

"The Newtonian form of insight worked very well for several centuries but ultimately (like the ancient Greek insights that came before) it led to unclear results when extended into new domains. In these new domains, new forms of insight were developed (the theory of relativity and the quantum theory). These gave a radically different picture of the world from that of Newton (though the latter was, of course, found to be still valid in a limited domain). If we supposed that theories gave true knowledge, corresponding to 'reality as it is', then we would have to conclude that Newtonian theory was true until around 1900, after which it suddenly became false, while relativity and quantum theory suddenly became the truth. Such an absurd conclusion does not arise, however, if we say that all theories are insights, which are neither true nor false but, rather, clear in certain domains, and unclear when extended beyond these domains. . . .

". . . In this activity, there is evidently no reason to suppose that there is or will be a final form of insight (corresponding to absolute truth) or even a steady series of approximations to this. Rather, in the nature of the case, one may expect the unending development of new forms of insight (which will, however, assimilate certain key features of the older forms as simplifications, in the way that relativity theory does with Newtonian theory). As pointed out earlier, however, this means that our theories are to be regarded primarily as ways of looking at the world as a whole (i.e. world views) rather than 'as absolutely true knowledge of how things are' (or as a steady approach toward the latter)." (David Bohm, *Wholeness and the Implicate Order*, pp. 4-6.)

19   Charles Sanders Peirce, in Bernstein, *Beyond Objectivism and Relativism*, p. 224.

20   There is a range of views that may be considered "nonfoundational." The term "nonfoundationalism" is used with some differences of meaning in philosophy and theology. The introduction of this concept is not intended to equate a Bahá'í perspective on knowledge with any of these particular approaches, but to point to an alternative to foundationalist and relativist views that may have more in common with the Bahá'í teachings. The use of this term is not intended in the sense of "anti-foundationalism" which is synonymous with relativism. It is also, most definitely, not intended to equate a Bahá'í approach to knowledge with a type of theological argument that uses nonfoundationalism to shelter religious beliefs from rational inquiry; in light of the argument presented in this book, such an approach would be considered relativism not nonfoundationalism.

21   Ernest Sosa, "The Raft and the Pyramid," in *Epistemology: An Anthology*, p. 136.

22   Bahá'u'lláh, *The Importance of Obligatory Prayer and Fasting*, p. 6. Bahá'u'lláh makes it clear that one purpose of His Revelation is to eliminate religious fanaticism. "Gird up the loins of your endeavor, O people of Bahá,

that haply the tumult of religious dissension and strife that agitateth the peoples of the earth may be stilled, that every trace of it may be completely obliterated. For the love of God, and them that serve Him, arise to aid this sublime and momentous Revelation. Religious fanaticism and hatred are a world-devouring fire, whose violence none can quench. The Hand of Divine power can, alone, deliver mankind from this desolating affliction." (*Epistle to the Son of the Wolf*, p. 14.)

23 Shoghi Effendi, *Bahá'í Administration*, p. 42.

24 On behalf of Shoghi Effendi, message dated July 5, 1947, cited in "Issues Concerning Community Functioning," a memorandum prepared by the Research Department at the Bahá'í World Centre at the request of the Universal House of Justice, February 1993.

25 'Abdu'l-Bahá, *Some Answered Questions*, p. 220.

26 "Consequently, it has become evident that the four criteria or standards of judgment by which the human mind reaches its conclusions are faulty and inaccurate. All of them are liable to mistake and error in conclusions. But a statement presented to the mind accompanied by proofs which the senses can perceive to be correct, which the faculty of reason can accept, which is in accord with traditional authority and sanctioned by the promptings of the heart, can be adjudged and relied upon as perfectly correct, for it has been proved and tested by all the standards of judgment and found to be complete. When we apply but one test, there are possibilities of mistake. This is self-evident and manifest." ('Abdu'l-Bahá, *The Promulgation of Universal Peace*, p. 255.)

27 Luke 6:48

28 Bahá'u'lláh, *Tablets of Bahá'u'lláh*, p. 168.

29 Bahá'u'lláh, *Gleanings*, pp. 163, 164-165.

30 See, for example, the article by Moojan Momen, "Relativism: A Basis for Bahá'í Metaphysics," *Studies in Honor of the Late Hasan M. Balyuzi: Studies in the Bábí and Bahá'í Religions*, vol. 5, pp. 185-218.

31 Bahá'u'lláh, *The Tabernacle of Unity*, p. 10.

32 Bahá'u'lláh, *Tablets of Bahá'u'lláh*, p. 184.

33 'Abdu'l-Bahá, *Some Answered Questions*, p. 173.

34 'Abdu'l-Bahá, *The Promulgation of Universal Peace*, p. 22.

35 'Abdu'l-Bahá, *Some Answered Questions*, p. 298.

36 On behalf of Shoghi Effendi, *Lights of Guidance*, p. 475.

37 'Abdu'l-Bahá, *Paris Talks*, p. 128.

38 On behalf of Shoghi Effendi, *Lights of Guidance*, p. 565.

39 'Abdu'l-Bahá, *Paris Talks*, p. 129.

40 'Abdu'l-Bahá, *Some Answered Questions*, p. 301.

41   'Abdu'l-Bahá, *Selections from the Writings of 'Abdu'l-Bahá*, p. 88.

42   'Abdu'l-Bahá, *Paris Talks*, p. 53.

43   'Abdu'l-Bahá, *Selections from the Writings of 'Abdu'l-Bahá*, pp. 291.

44   The concept of "tradition" raised here must, of course, be distinguished from 'Abdu'l-Bahá's use of the term to criticize the inert form of religion plagued by dogma, superstition and prejudice which stands as an obstacle to the investigation of truth.

45   Shoghi Effendi, *Citadel of Faith*, p. 117.

46   Shoghi Effendi, *Bahá'í Administration*, p. 90.

47   On behalf of Shoghi Effendi, *A Special Measure of Love*, pp. 20-21.

48   Hans-Georg Gadamer, *Truth and Method*, p. 298.

49   Shoghi Effendi, *Bahá'í Administration*, p. 62.

50   Bahá'u'lláh, *Compilation of Compilations*, vol. 1, p. 93.

51   Bahá'u'lláh, *Compilation of Compilations*, p. 93.

52   Bahá'u'lláh, *Compilation of Compilations*, p. 97. 'Abdu'l-Bahá observes: "The principle of consultation is one of the most fundamental elements of the divine edifice." (*Compilation of Compilations*, vol. 1, p. 97.)

53   The relationship between the Revelation, community, and meaning may be an important reason for the mission of the Báb, which could be understood—at least in part—as raising up a community of people that had a capacity to hear what Bahá'u'lláh had to say.

54   Shoghi Effendi, *God Passes By*, pp. 244-45.

55   On behalf of the Universal House of Justice, message dated October 20, 1977 to an individual believer.

56   Shoghi Effendi, *Citadel of Faith*, p. 21.

57   "The problems of society which affect our community and those problems which naturally arise from within the community itself, whether social, spiritual, economic or administrative, will be solved as our numbers and resources multiply, and as at all levels of the community the friends develop the ability, willingness, courage and determination to obey the laws, apply the principles and administer the affairs of the Faith in accordance with divine precepts." (The Universal House of Justice, Riḍván 1993.)

58   The Universal House of Justice, *Messages: 1963-1986*, p. 160.

CHAPTER 6

1   Bahá'u'lláh, *Gleanings*, p. 288.

2   'Abdu'l-Bahá, *Paris Talks*, p. 179.

3   'Abdu'l-Bahá, *Selections from the Writings of 'Abdu'l-Bahá*, p. 20.

4   Jürgen Habermas, in Flyvbjerg, *Making Social Science Matter*, p. 90.

5   Anthony Giddens, *New Rules of Sociological Method*, pp. 128-29.

6   Michael Foucault, in Flyvbjerg, *Making Social Science Matter*, p. 117.

7   Foucault, in Flyvbjerg, *Making Social Science Matter*, pp. 120-21.

8   "We should admit that power produces knowledge . . . that power and knowledge directly imply one another; that there is no power relation without the correlative constitutions of a field of knowledge, nor any knowledge that does not presuppose and constitute at the same time power relations. . . ." (Foucault, "What is Enlightenment," *The Foucault Reader*, p. 46.)

9   Foucault, in Michael Kelly, *Critique and Power: Recasting the Foucault/ Habermas Debate*, p. 22.

10 See Huston Smith, *Beyond the Postmodern Mind: The Place of Meaning in a Global Civilization*, pp. 11-12. "Instead of 'these are the compelling reasons, grounded in the nature of things, why you should believe in God,' the approach of the Church to the world today tends to be, 'This community of faith invites you to share in its venture of trust and commitment.' The stance is most evident in Protestant and Orthodox Christianity and Judaism, but even Roman Catholic thought, notwithstanding the powerful rationalism it took over from the Greeks, has not remained untouched by the Postmodern perspective. It has become more attentive to the extent to which personal and subjective factors provide the disposition to faith without which theological arguments prove nothing. . . . By including God within a closed system of rational explanation, modernism lost sight of the endless qualitative distinction between God and man. Postmodern theology has reinstated this distinction with great force. If God exists, the fact that our minds cannot begin to comprehend his nature makes it necessary for us to acknowledge that he is Wholly Other."

11 See Kelly, *Critique and Power: Recasting the Foucault/Habermas Debate*, p. 366. See also Richard Rorty, *Contingency, Irony, and Solidarity*, p. 45: "The difference between a search for foundations and an attempt at redescription is emblematic of the difference between the culture of liberalism and older forms of cultural life. For in its ideal form, the culture of liberalism would be one which was enlightened, secular, through and through. It would be one in which no trace of divinity remained, either in the form of a divinized world or a divinized self. Such a culture would have no room for the notion that there are nonhuman forces to which human beings should be responsible. It would drop, or drastically reinterpret, not only the idea of holiness but those of 'devotion to truth and of fulfillment of the deepest needs of the spirit.' The process of de-divinization which I have described . . . would, ideally, culminate in our no longer being able to see any use for the notion that finite, mortal, contingently existing human beings might derive the meanings of their lives from anything except other finite, contingently

existing human beings. In such a culture, warnings of 'relativism,' queries whether social institutions had become increasingly 'rational' in modern times, and doubts about whether the aims of liberal society were 'objective moral values' would seem merely quaint."

12   See Michael Kelly, *Critique and Power: Recasting the Foucault/Habermas Debate.* Also Bent Flyvberg, "Habermas and Foucault: Thinkers for Civil Society?" *British Journal of Sociology*, vol. 49, no. 2, June 1998.

13   "Its teachings revolve around the fundamental principle that religious truth is not absolute but relative, that Divine Revelation is progressive, not final." (Shoghi Effendi, *The World Order of Bahá'u'lláh*, p. 58.) In a philosophical sense, Shoghi Effendi's use of the term "relative" in this context is more closely related to nonfoundationalism than to relativism. Religious truth is relative to time and context across dispensations; it is not relative to the persons or groups holding them (relativistic and incommensurable).

14   'Abdu'l-Bahá, *The Secret of Divine Civilization*, pp. 27-29.

15   Bahá'u'lláh, *The Tabernacle of Unity*, pp. 35-37.

16   Bahá'u'lláh, *Tablets of Bahá'u'lláh*, p. 51. This, as 'Abdu'l-Bahá explains, is a statement of the "Most Great Infallibility." (*Some Answered Questions*, p. 171.) Whatever the Manifestation of God does, is proper and cannot be questioned by humanity; it represents the will and purpose of God.

17   Bahá'u'lláh, *Tablets of Bahá'u'lláh*, p. 108.

18   Bahá'u'lláh, *Tablets of Bahá'u'lláh*, p. 109.

19   Bahá'u'lláh, *Gleanings*, p. 213.

20   Bahá'u'lláh, *Gleanings*, p. 96.

21   Bahá'u'lláh, *The Hidden Words*, p. 19.

22   On behalf of the Universal House of Justice, *Messages: 1963-1986*, p. 518.

23   The Universal House of Justice, *Compilation of Compilations*, vol. 1, p. 47.

24   Bahá'u'lláh, *The Kitáb-i-Aqdas*, p. 21.

25   Shoghi Effendi, *The Advent of Divine Justice*, p. 20.

26   The Universal House of Justice, *Turning Point*, p. 42.

27   Bahá'u'lláh, *The Kitáb-i-Aqdas*, p. 7.

28   On behalf of Shoghi Effendi, *Lights of Guidance*, p. 2.

29   On behalf of the Universal House of Justice, *Issues Related to the Study of the Bahá'í Faith*, p. 27.

30   Shoghi Effendi, *Bahá'í Administration*, p. 64.

31   On behalf of Shoghi Effendi, *Compilation of Compilations*, vol. 1, p. 405.

32   On behalf of Shoghi Effendi, *Lights of Guidance*, p. 70.

33   The Universal House of Justice, message dated July 21, 1968 to a National Assembly

34 'Abdu'l-Bahá, *Selections from the Writings of 'Abdu'l-Bahá*, pp. 268-69.

35 'Abdu'l-Bahá, *Selections from the Writings of 'Abdu'l-Bahá*, p. 279.

36 'Abdu'l-Bahá, *The Secret of Divine Civilization*, pp. 103-104.

37 'Abdu'l-Bahá, *Selections from the Writings of 'Abdu'l-Bahá*, p. 302.

38 'Abdu'l-Bahá, *Selections from the Writings of 'Abdu'l-Bahá*, p. 305.

39 Bahá'u'lláh, *Gleanings*, p. 200.

40 'Abdu'l-Bahá, *Selections from the Writings of 'Abdu'l-Bahá*, p. 136.

41 'Abdu'l-Bahá, *Selections from the Writings of 'Abdu'l-Bahá*, p. 132.

42 'Abdu'l-Bahá, in a message written on behalf of the Universal House of Justice dated February 8, 1998.

43 'Abdu'l-Bahá, *Selections from the Writings of 'Abdu'l-Bahá*, p. 131.

44 'Abdu'l-Bahá, *The Promulgation of Universal Peace*, p. 293.

45 'Abdu'l-Bahá, *Paris Talks*, p. 175.

46 Bahá'u'lláh, *The Summons of the Lord of Hosts*, p. 213.

47 On behalf of the Universal House of Justice, *Compilation of Compilations*, vol. 1, p. 111.

48 'Abdu'l-Bahá, *Selections from the Writings of 'Abdu'l-Bahá*, p. 208.

49 Shoghi Effendi, *God Passes By*, p. 243.

50 On behalf of the Universal House of Justice, message dated February 20, 1977.

51 On behalf of the Universal House of Justice, message dated September 11, 1995. Sanctions, which involve restrictions of the privileges of membership, are to be applied only when "conduct is blatant and flagrant or is harmful to the name of the Faith" and only after "the believer has been given sufficient warning before the imposition of sanctions." (On behalf of the Universal House of Justice, message of February 20, 1977.) Of course, the action by the institutions to sanction individuals in any way is directed toward those individuals who have already professed, in becoming believers, their willingness to embrace the Bahá'í standard, including the laws and principles which they have consciously violated. Any individual is free to leave the Bahá'í community if they do not accept the standards of membership presented in the Bahá'í teachings. So, too, the institutions may not recognize as members, those who consciously reject aspects of the teachings, in keeping with the statement written on behalf of Shoghi Effendi that "allegiance to the Faith cannot be partial and half-hearted." "Either we should accept the Cause without any qualification whatsoever or cease calling ourselves Bahá'ís. The new believers should be made to realize that it is not sufficient for them to accept some aspects of the teachings and reject those which cannot suit their mentality in order to become fully recognized and active followers of the Faith. In this way all sorts of misunderstandings will vanish

and the organic unity of the Cause will be preserved." (On behalf of Shoghi Effendi, *Lights of Guidance*, p. 69.)

52 Shoghi Effendi, *Bahá'í Administration*, p. 63.

53 Shoghi Effendi, *Citadel of Faith*, p. 148.

54 Shoghi Effendi, *The World Order of Bahá'u'lláh*, p. 9.

55 Shoghi Effendi, *Bahá'í Administration*, p. 109.

56 The Universal House of Justice, *Rights and Responsibilities*, p. 41.

57 For example, a letter written on behalf of Shoghi Effendi states: "With reference to the absolute pacifists, or conscientious objectors of war; their attitude, judged from the Bahá'í standpoint, is quite anti-social and due to its exaltation of the individual conscience leads inevitably to disorder and chaos in society. Extreme pacifists are thus very close to the anarchists, in the sense that both of these groups lay an undue emphasis on the rights and merits of the individual. The Bahá'í conception of social life is essentially based on the subordination of the individual will to that of society. It neither suppresses the individual nor does it exalt him to the point of making him an anti-social creature, a menace to society. As in everything, it follows the 'golden mean.' The only way that society can function is for the minority to follow the will of the majority." (*Lights of Guidance*, p. 407.)

58 On behalf of Shoghi Effendi, *Compilation of Compilations*, vol. 1, p. 452.

59 "Among the most outstanding and sacred duties incumbent upon those who have been called upon to initiate, direct and coordinate the affairs of the Cause of God as members of its Spiritual Assemblies are: to win by every means in their power the confidence and affection of those whom it is their privilege to serve; to investigate and acquaint themselves with the considered views, the prevailing sentiments and the personal convictions of those whose welfare it is their solemn obligation to promote; to purge their deliberations and the general conduct of their affairs of self-contained aloofness, the suspicion of secrecy, the stifling atmosphere of dictatorial assertiveness and of every word and deed that may savor of partiality, self-centeredness and prejudice; and while retaining the sacred right of final decision in their hands, to invite discussion, ventilate grievances, welcome advice and foster the sense of interdependence and co-partnership, of understanding and mutual confidence between themselves and all other Bahá'ís." (The Universal House of Justice, *The Constitution of the Universal House of Justice*, Article IV.)

60 The Universal House of Justice, *Rights and Responsibilities*, p. 16. 'Abdu'l-Bahá offers a number of warnings about those who spread dissent in pursuit of their own aims. For example: "Now some of the mischief-makers, with many stratagems, are seeking leadership, and in order to reach this position they instill doubts among the friends that they may cause differences, and that these differences may result in their drawing a party

to themselves. But the friends of God must be awake and must know that the scattering of these doubts hath as its motive personal desires and the achievement of leadership. Do not disrupt Bahá'í unity, and know that this unity cannot be maintained save through faith in the Covenant of God." ('Abdu'l-Bahá, *Selections from the Writings of 'Abdu'l-Bahá*, pp. 214-15.)

61 Shoghi Effendi, *The World Order of Bahá'u'lláh*, pp. 22-23.

62 On behalf of the Universal House of Justice, message dated August 22, 2002.

63 Bahá'u'lláh, *Gleanings*, p. 92.

64 Bahá'u'lláh, *Gleanings*, p. 220.

65 May, *Our Practices, Our Selves*, pp. 100-01.

66 May, *Our Practices, Our Selves*, p. 175.

67 May, *Our Practices, Our Selves*, p. 177.

68 'Abdu'l-Bahá, *The Promulgation of Universal Peace*, pp. 238-39.

69 On behalf of the Universal House of Justice, *Messages: 1963-1986*, p. 369.

70 'Abdu'l-Bahá, *Selections from the Writings of 'Abdu'l-Bahá*, p. 256.

71 Bahá'u'lláh, *Gleanings*, p. 95.

72 "The Revelation, of which Bahá'u'lláh is the source and center, abrogates none of the religions that have preceded it, nor does it attempt, in the slightest degree, to distort their features or to belittle their value. It disclaims any intention of dwarfing any of the Prophets of the past, or of whittling down the eternal verity of their teachings. It can, in no wise, conflict with the spirit that animates their claims, nor does it seek to undermine the basis of any man's allegiance to their cause. Its declared, its primary purpose is to enable every adherent of these Faiths to obtain a fuller understanding of the religion with which he stands identified, and to acquire a clearer apprehension of its purpose." (Shoghi Effendi, *The World Order of Bahá'u'lláh*, p. 57.)

73 Bahá'u'lláh, *Gleanings*, p. 255.

74 'Abdu'l-Bahá, *Some Answered Questions*, p. 65.

75 The concept of religious pluralism can be distinguished from religious relativism. What is argued against here is the idea that different religions exist side by side because their teachings are completely subjective and incomparable, or because they do not make truth claims that can be contrasted and evaluated. Such a perspective may be more accurately described as religious relativism rather than religious pluralism. It is quite a different idea to acknowledge the practical expression of pluralism among religions that results from historical circumstances, tolerance, and the right of individuals to independently investigate truth.

76 Bahá'u'lláh states: "The summons and the message which We gave were never intended to reach or to benefit one land or one people only. Mankind

in its entirety must firmly adhere to whatsoever hath been revealed and vouchsafed unto it." (*Tablets of Bahá'u'lláh*, p. 96.)

And He directly appeals to the members of all religious communities: "O followers of all religions! We behold you wandering distraught in the wilderness of error. Ye are the fish of this Ocean; wherefore do ye withhold yourselves from that which sustaineth you? Lo, it surgeth before your faces. Hasten unto it from every clime." (*The Summons of the Lord of Hosts*, p. 59.)

77   The Universal House of Justice, message dated October 24, 1990.

78   ". . . great Plan of God, tumultuous in its progress, [is] working through mankind as a whole, tearing down barriers to world unity and forging humankind into a unified body in the fires of suffering and experience. This process will produce in God's due time, the Lesser Peace, the political unification of the world." (On behalf of the Universal House of Justice, *Messages: 1963-1986*, p. 333.) "As to the Lesser Peace, Shoghi Effendi has explained that this will initially be a political unity arrived at by decision of the governments of various nations; it will not be established by direct action of the Bahá'í community." (On behalf of the Universal House of Justice, *Messages: 1963-1986*, p. 656.) And a letter written on behalf of the House of Justice explains: "...although Bahá'ís believe that the Teachings and Order of Bahá'u'lláh are the solution to the current problems of mankind, they abstain completely from ever attempting to put them into effect through political action. Only if people voluntarily accept them and submit themselves freely to this Order will it be implemented in the world. Bahá'ís should never attempt to impose their belief on anyone." (Message dated May 1, 1991.)

Bahá'í efforts are instead illustrated by the following statement written on behalf of Shoghi Effendi: "War is really nothing more but the result of existing forces. Should we desire to end that devastating consequence we should go back to the basic causes and remedy those evils. We should eliminate the hatreds, national bigotry, mistrust and self-aggrandizement as well as economic, social and religious differences which now prevail in the world if we desire to establish an abiding peace. And nothing can achieve this save the Teachings of Bahá'u'lláh, for they change the human heart and also prescribe definite precepts that would render our social environment healthy and peaceful." (*Lights of Guidance*, p. 418.)

79   On behalf of the Universal House of Justice, *Messages: 1963-1986*, p. 333.

80   'Abdu'l-Bahá, *Tablets of 'Abdu'l-Bahá*, vol. 1, p. 39. Commenting on this passage in *Making the Crooked Straight*, chapter 6, "Bahá'í Political Thought," Ulrich Gollmer suggests that "When the scripture states that Bahá'ís should not engage in politics, it is this type of political activity that is meant." See also, in this regard, the thoughtful comments of Arash Abizadeh in "Politics Beyond War: Ulrich Gollmer's Contribution to Bahá'í Political Thought," *World Order*, 2004, vol. 35, no. 3, pp. 19-23. Another contribution along

these lines is made by Michael Karlberg, in the book, *Beyond the Contest of Culture,* and in the articles, "Western Liberal Democracy as New World Order?" published in *The Bahá'í World*: 2005-2006, pp. 133-56 and "The Power of Discourse and the Discourse of Power," *International Journal of Peace Studies,* 10:1, 2005.

81 See Roshan Danesh in "The Politics of Delay: Social Meanings and the Historical Treatment of Bahá'í Law," *World Order,* 2004, vol. 35, no. 3, pp. 33-45.

82 Fairfield, *The Ways of Power,* pp. 155-57.

83 Bahá'u'lláh, *Gleanings,* p. 315.

84 Bahá'u'lláh, *Tablets of Bahá'u'lláh,* p. 71.

85 'Abdu'l-Bahá, *Selections from the Writings of 'Abdu'l-Bahá,* p. 24.

86 'Abdu'l-Bahá, *Selections from the Writings of 'Abdu'l-Bahá,* pp. 1-2.

87 The Universal House of Justice, message dated April 4, 2001.

88 If, as Bahá'ís certainly believe, Bahá'u'lláh's Revelation is from God, then the search for truth will only strengthen certitude, it will not weaken it. Understanding Bahá'u'lláh's Revelation and translating the teachings into action is determined by searching for truth, not by avoiding a search for truth. 'Abdu'l-Bahá explains: "In order to find truth we must give up our prejudices, our own small trivial notions; an open receptive mind is essential. If our chalice is full of self, there is no room in it for the water of life. The fact that we imagine ourselves to be right and everybody else wrong is the greatest of all obstacles in the path towards unity, and unity is necessary if we would reach truth, for truth is one. . . . 'Seek the truth, the truth shall make you free.' So shall we see the truth in all religions, for truth is in all and truth is one!" (*Paris Talks,* p. 136.)

89 Toulmin, *Cosmopolis,* p. 139. This is the title of his fourth chapter.

90 Toulmin, *Cosmopolis,* pp. 200-01. Toulmin argues that modernity began with the Renaissance and that the Enlightenment was a reaction to the social chaos that came from the failure of humanist ideals after the assassination of King Henri IV of France (Henry of Navarre). Thus, for Toulmin the first phase of modernity is from the 1500s to the start of the Enlightenment, the second phase stretches from the Enlightenment to the 20th century, and the new "third phase" begins with the questions raised by postmodernism.

91 Toulmin, *Cosmopolis,* p. 175.

92 'Abdu'l-Bahá, *The Promulgation of Universal Peace,* p. 439.

93 Bahá'u'lláh, *Prayers and Meditations,* p. 295.

94 Bahá'u'lláh, *Gleanings,* p. 313.

Index